Racialization, Crime, and Criminal Justice in Canada

RACIALIZATION, CRIME, AND CRIMINAL JUSTICE IN CANADA

WENDY CHAN AND DOROTHY CHUNN

UNIVERSITY OF TORONTO PRESS

Library and Archives Canada Cataloguing in Publication

Chan, Wendy, 1966–   , author
   Racialization, crime and criminal justice in Canada / Wendy Chan and Dorothy Chunn.

Includes bibliographical references and index.

Issued in print and electronic formats.

ISBN 978-1-4426-0820-7 (bound).—ISBN 978-1-4426-0574-9 (pbk.).—ISBN 978-1-4426-0575-6 (pdf).—ISBN 978-1-4426-0576-3 (epub)

   1. Discrimination in criminal justice administration—Canada.   2. Racism in criminology—Canada.   3. Crime and race—Canada.   4. Minorities—Legal status, laws, etc.—Canada.   5. Criminal justice, Administration of—Canada.   I. Chunn, Dorothy E. (Dorothy Ellen), 1943–   , author   II. Title.

HV9960.C2C48 2014   364.089'00971   C2013–906788–4

C2013–906789–2

We welcome comments and suggestions regarding any aspect of our publications—please feel free to contact us at news@utphighereducation.com or visit our Internet site at www.utppublishing.com.

North America
5201 Dufferin Street
North York, Ontario, Canada, M3H 5T8

2250 Military Road
Tonawanda, New York, USA, 14150

ORDERS PHONE: 1–800–565–9523
ORDERS FAX: 1–800–221–9985
ORDERS E-MAIL: utpbooks@utpress.utoronto.ca

UK, Ireland, and continental Europe
NBN International
Estover Road, Plymouth, PL6 7PY, UK
ORDERS PHONE: 44 (0) 1752 202301
ORDERS FAX: 44 (0) 1752 202333
ORDERS E-MAIL:
enquiries@nbninternational.com

Every effort has been made to contact copyright holders; in the event of an error or omission, please notify the publisher.

This book is printed on paper containing 100% post-consumer fibre.

The University of Toronto Press acknowledges the financial support for its publishing activities of the Government of Canada through the Canada Book Fund.

Printed in Canada

CONTENTS

ACKNOWLEDGMENTS

We are grateful to the many people who supported this project from the initial conception of the book to its final stages of publication. Their encouragement along the way has made it possible for us to develop and write this book in a way that reflects our main concerns and perspectives on race and crime in Canada.

We thank the staff at University of Toronto Press, in particular Anne Brackenbury, for believing in this project and for guiding us through the process. We found the comments from the anonymous reviewers helpful in fine-tuning our analysis and we appreciate the time and effort they took to review the manuscript carefully.

Many thanks also goes to Department of Sociology and Anthropology at Simon Fraser University, to our colleagues in the department, and to our friends and family members who remain strong pillars of support for us, and for this project.

INTRODUCTION

As we write this book, news headlines in Canada spotlight the ongoing troubles within Aboriginal communities, the hunger strike by Attawapiskat Chief Theresa Spence, and the uprising of Aboriginal people through the Idle No More movement. This growing movement of resistance to government policies, supported by a diverse range of citizens both inside and outside of Canada, has reinforced, once again, how Aboriginal people in Canada continue to be marginalized and excluded. Decades of institutional mistreatment and a legacy of colonization have resulted in the continued impoverishment of indigenous communities, with the current tendency to blame Aboriginal people for their misfortunes. At the same time, temporary migrant workers, who are coming into Canada at unprecedented rates, face an uphill battle in their search for fair treatment. The Harper government sees this disposable labour force, largely from the Global South, as a means to remain globally competitive, since these workers will provide labour at minimal costs to both the government and employers. The lack of legal protections and options available to migrant workers ensures that any mistreatment or abuse will be difficult to challenge. Finally, the ongoing case of Omar Khadr, a racialized Canadian citizen and child soldier, highlights how fears around terrorism can override the rights of citizenship, resulting in human rights violations, ill-treatment, and torture.[1] The criminalization of Khadr, and the complicity of Harper's government in his mistreatment, is an important reminder of how being Muslim in a post–September 11 context can negate citizenship. Racial prejudices toward Khadr made it possible to assume guilt before innocence, and to bolster the view that he was not entitled to fair, objective, or just treatment from our judicial system.

These examples highlight the current realities for many minority communities in Canada. While some people may argue that these situations have nothing to do with race, we would argue that, on the contrary, they have everything to do with race and racism. Processes of domination and subordination rely on hierarchies of difference to keep racism alive (Miles 2000). The same racism that permits the construction of stereotypes of Aboriginal people as culturally backward or pathological also bolsters the belief that migrant workers in Canada should not be entitled to equal treatment and protection under the law, even though they contribute to the economic growth of the country. Racism is also the reason why Arabs and Muslims are treated as "not one of us," regardless of citizenship status, and, therefore, as not worthy of Canada's protection. As Gilmore states, racism acts "as a limiting force that pushes [the] disproportionate costs of participating in an increasingly monetized and profit-driven world onto those who, due to the frictions of political distance, cannot reach the variable levers of power that might relieve them of those costs" (2002, 16). Indeed, racism continues to shape outcomes for non-white groups in Canada, and as much as we may want to think that race no longer matters, it is still very relevant.

Our starting point for this book is the assertion that race matters, and in the context of crime and criminal justice, that it matters a lot. Race and practices of racism have shaped attitudes about crime and justice, influenced the allocation of resources and the creation of policies and practices, and significantly impacted the identities of racialized people. Racial prejudice has contributed to the over-incarceration of Aboriginal people, the dismissal and/or minimization of criminal victimization involving racialized people, the use of racial profiling by police and other law enforcement agencies, and has perpetuated the view that certain racialized groups in Canada are more prone to crime. Tanovich (2006) argues that the colour of justice in Canada is white. To be non-white in the Canadian justice system is to be more likely viewed as a crime suspect than a crime victim, to experience higher levels of policing and surveillance, to receive harsher penalties if criminally convicted, and most alarmingly, to be at a far greater risk of being shot by the police (Tanovich 2006).

The federal government's enactment in March 2012 of an omnibus crime bill (Bill C-10), which includes the creation of new offences, provisions for new and increased mandatory minimum sentences, and stiffer penalties for youth, will only exacerbate the over-representation of racialized communities in the justice system. Many concerns have been raised about the impact this bill will have on Aboriginal youth (Scoffield 2012), while other critics have labelled Canada the "most regressive western democracy on criminal justice" as a result of this bill (Mallea 2012). Social exclusion and marginalization are just two of the many discriminatory consequences stemming from inequality in the justice system.

Systemic and institutional discrimination by race is a key factor in the differential treatment of racialized people in the Canadian criminal justice system. While being positioned in a location of social disadvantage is also a factor for increased contact with the criminal justice system, this alone cannot adequately explain the over-representation of racialized groups (Millar and Owusu-Bempah 2011). Narratives about Canada, however, are loath to acknowledge the role that institutional policies and practices play in perpetuating racism. Many people see Canada as a diverse, multicultural country, where rights and equality are extended to everyone, and any problems of racial injustice are blamed on racial minorities. Many scholars point out that this notion of Canada as a benevolent and raceless nation reproduces race privilege and the effects of colonization (Razack 1998a). Multicultural narratives of equality and opportunity mask the deep racial disparities in Canadian society, and not all racialized groups support these narratives. For example, studies have found that racialized minorities are, generally, less trusting of receiving fair treatment in the criminal justice system (Wortley and Owusu-Bempah 2009).

Throughout this book, we take as our starting point that how the relationship between race and crime is understood in Canada is deeply problematic. Not only has there been a reluctance to acknowledge problems of racism in Canada, and in particular, within the criminal justice system, but these problems are rarely understood as deeply rooted and structural. Rather, explanations such as individual "bad apples" are offered in cases that arise, and racism itself continues to be denied as something that doesn't happen in Canada. Until we take off our blinders and critically examine the problem, individuals and groups in Canada will not receive the just outcomes they expect from the criminal justice system and the wider society in which they reside.

This book is an effort to do just that. We critically engage with the idea that the unequal treatment of racialized minorities in the criminal justice system is not an aberration or the result of flawed cultural and moral values that lead to higher rates of offending or victimization. We share the view of many other critical scholars who argue that history and context matter, and when the issue of race and crime is properly contextualized it is clear that the legacies of colonization and racial discrimination in Canada have fundamentally shaped contemporary processes of criminal justice. Differential relations of power between white and non-white groups over time have resulted in a racial hierarchy where privilege and superiority are conferred to white groups, while disadvantage and discrimination are more prevalent in non-white groups. Laws and policies reflect the subjectivity of the powerful—the white, affluent adult male. It is his behaviour that forms the basis of proscriptions and remedies, and he is who those in power imagine as they construct the law (Hudson 2006).

Countless examples of the maleness and whiteness of criminal justice have been provided by feminist and race scholars—from the lack of protection from criminal victimization to the punitive treatment of racialized offenders. Racial injustices in the criminal justice system are a reflection of the wider society, and until these injustices, which include the mistreatment of Aboriginal people, are taken seriously by all members of society the potential for remedies will be limited. Like the Idle No More movement and other efforts toward resistance and change, this book is our contribution to reinforcing the message that the harms and injustices stemming from a racially biased criminal justice system are damaging to all members of society.

THE RACIALIZATION OF CRIME

Within criminology, reference to race as a socio-demographic variable in describing victims and offenders in empirical research is routine. Typically, the focus is on comparing different social groups in terms of crime statistics, and examining the extent to which different racial groups are represented as victims and offenders. There is a rich body of work by American and British criminologists who explore a variety of criminological topics, offering a wide range of ideas about race and ethnicity in relation to crime and criminal justice. In Canada, however, this line of inquiry has been significantly limited by a lack of data available on the racial and ethnic backgrounds of offenders and victims. Since the late 1980s, the Canadian government and related law enforcement agencies ceased to systemically collect data about the racial or ethnic backgrounds of individuals within the criminal justice system, whether as offenders, victims, or individuals working in the system. Despite increasing pressure from academics and community organizations, such as the African Canadian Legal Clinic, there is no indication from the current government that the status quo will change.[2] The only official race-related justice statistics made readily available to researchers in Canada are on Aboriginal people in the federal correctional system.

While we do not wish to revisit this debate here, suffice it to say that the lack of data has constrained the ability of researchers to fully assess allegations of racial disparities and discrimination in the Canadian criminal justice system. As a result, the body of scholarly literature on issues of race and racism in the criminal justice system in Canada is much smaller overall when compared to other Western states. There are also significant gaps in some research areas (e.g., crime and mental health), a paucity of research in other areas (e.g., race and criminal victimization), and a lack of statistical data available on a regular basis in general. These challenges highlight not only the need for Canadian researchers to employ more creative approaches in conducting research and providing discussions about this topic, but also that more attention to this area of research is warranted if we are to fully understand the role of race in criminal justice issues.

The task of critically analyzing how racism impacts the criminal justice system and minority groups in Canada has been taken up primarily by critical scholars. For the most part, while mainstream criminology engages with race issues it does so almost entirely with a focus on the race/criminality question, such as finding out the differences between black and white criminals. Furthermore, since mainstream criminology uncritically accepts the validity of official justice statistics as accurate representations of crime, and is less concerned with the social processes that produce official information about crime, explanations produced about criminal behaviour are at the individual and cultural levels of analysis, but not at the structural level (Reiner 1992). Consequently, the task of understanding racism and critiquing the role of the state in perpetuating racial bias in the criminal justice system has been left to feminist criminologists, critical criminologists, critical race scholars, and activists.

A critical engagement with race and crime involves recognizing that crime, and state reactions to crime, can only be understood within a sociological framework that acknowledges material and social relationships in capitalist society. How crime is defined does not occur in a vacuum, but within specific social, political, and economic circumstances. For example, when unemployment rates rise compliance with social rules declines, and state repression typically follows. The increasing criminalization of poverty, which has a disproportionate impact on racialized people, is a clear example of how the state deploys ideological constructs, such as the labelling of poor people as dangerous, to legitimize punitive sanctions. Poor, racialized people are not only stigmatized by these policies, they are also branded as the "enemy" for failing to rise above their predicament.

State restructuring of social policies in the last several decades has contributed significantly to current practices within the criminal justice system. Neo-liberal economic and social policies based on principles of free markets, deregulation, and privatization give primacy to the individual over community. The idealized subject is now a citizen-consumer who is responsibilized into making prudent choices both economically and socially. In the context of law and order, the citizen-consumer contributes to community policing by reporting signs of danger while also agreeing to be policed (Hyatt 2011). Crime policies problematize and emphasize individual behaviours, such as being homeless or squeegeeing, rather than broader social and economic policies that give rise to these social problems.

At the same time, the demands of racial minority groups are redefined as threatening and violent, and they are blamed for causing social unrest and crime. For example, the treatment of several groups of asylum seekers who arrived in Canada by sea demonstrates how migration resulting from the effects of global economic inequality was redefined by the state and mainstream media as a threat to national sovereignty, and subsequently criminalized. The migrants were jailed as soon as they arrived, and were deported shortly thereafter. Their only "crime" was their desperation for economic opportunities, yet as they became objects of public fear and anxiety state responses to this threat took the form of increased control and regulation. A number of activists and scholars have argued that the fact that these migrants were from some of the poorest, non-white countries globally facilitated their criminalization and their construction as a threat to national security. The question many posed was, "whose national security?"

Highlighting how the state scapegoats people of colour by suggesting that they are the cause of social ills and a threat to social stability is a key theme in the work of critical scholarship on race and crime. This involves examining the many different sites where people of colour have been marginalized and excluded through policies that have their roots in the fear of crisis in crime and disorder. Ideologies of race have played a powerful role in the treatment of racialized people, often to detrimental ends. Exposing the racial biases of the justice system, along with how processes of criminalization have influenced policies and attitudes in other social institutions as a mode of governance of racial groups, is a central aim of this book.

In developing our claim that the differential treatment of racialized minorities by the police and other agents of the criminal justice system is related to racial discrimination, we draw on national and international scholarship to advance our analysis. Despite the lack of race-related justice statistics in Canada, there remains a wealth of evidence pointing to the presence of racial bias and stereotyping (Wortley and Owusu-Bempah 2012). A core theme in our argument throughout this book is that crime is racially constructed insofar as the discourse of crime and justice is heavily influenced by certain modes of race-thinking.[3] The racialization of crime refers to the idea that racial traits are believed to be a contributing factor to understanding criminal behaviour and crime rates. The perception that racialized minorities are innately "criminal" is not new, and over time it has given rise to episodes of moral panics—the construction of racialized groups as a "problem" in need of regulation and control, and elevated levels of public fear and anxiety about crime. Typically, young, black men are regarded as the classic figure of the "criminal other" in the public imagination.

In emphasizing the entrenched patterns of racial disparities in the justice system, however, we are not suggesting that racism operates without conscious intent. Rather, we seek to give primacy to the role of institutional dynamics, while also recognizing that a broad range of behavioural and systemic practices, both conscious and unconscious, are implicated in reproducing racial inequities in the criminal justice system. Practices of racial profiling, for example, highlight the importance of examining the relationship between the institution and culture of policing and the work of individual police officers in understanding the role of racial profiling for police work.

We share Omi and Winant's (1994) view that the state is inherently racial in that it does not stand above racial conflicts, but is thoroughly immersed in racial contests. They note that "the racial order is equilibrated by the state—encoded in law, organized through policy-making, and enforced by a repressive apparatus" (1994, 84).

Racial politics in Canada have contributed to the expansion of crime control policies, where we are now seeing the deployment of criminal justice strategies and practices in areas of social welfare, immigration, and national security. Practices of criminal justice govern how particular populations are constructed and configured by the state as a category of concern, and current conceptions of crime and disorder are characterized by a racialized fear of crime as well as a racialized contempt for the poor. One consequence of this approach, as Simon (2007) observes, is that it creates a more racially polarized society, such that a culture of fear and control, rather than trust, dominates decision making in all spheres of life. Throughout this book, we examine the various criminal justice practices that reinforce hierarchies of humanity, perpetuate race-based narratives about crime, and legitimize punitive legislation that disproportionately impacts and targets racialized groups.

STRUCTURE OF THE BOOK

This book is comprised of 10 chapters divided into four main parts that address a broad range of theoretical and substantive issues on race, racialization, and criminal justice. Each section covers different aspects of the criminal justice system and its influence on related social and economic institutions. Some of these topics have received significant attention from other criminologists, as in the discussions on policing and corrections, while others, like the criminalization of racial groups, have not been as widely discussed in the criminological literature. Our aim is to provide a critical analysis of more conventional topics on race and crime while also focusing on the neglected areas of discussion. By offering a wider discussion, we hope to demonstrate that the relationship between race and crime is far from simple. Processes of racialization and criminalization are shaped by the interplay of individual agency and intent on the one hand, and institutional structures and constraints on the other. The outcomes of these processes occur within the parameters of specific histories, contexts, and circumstances. Our analysis of race and crime is thus predicated on a multi-dimensional, sociological approach that seeks to illustrate how the lives of racialized Canadians have been affected by criminal justice policies and practices.

In Part 1, Chapter 1, we outline our understanding of the concepts of race, racism, and racialization, and how these intersect with crime and the criminal justice system. Following Omi and Winant (1994), we consider "race" to be a socially constructed category that is fluid and unstable, where meanings are constantly being contested and transformed through political struggle. Categories of race are located within a field of racial discourse, where different modes of race-thinking inform and shape racial distinctions, practices, and outcomes. For example, race and ethnicity draw boundaries around zones of belonging and non-belonging, and as such, they are subjective elements of identity construction as well as responses to labels of identity and difference (Rattansi 2007, 89). Canada's history of indigenous colonization, racialized immigration policies, and white settlement offers an interesting context in which to understand issues of race and racism. National mythologies of Canada as a white nation, and the erasure of racialized exploitation of First Nations and people of colour, persist even as larger urban centres are increasingly moving toward a majority–minority population. Since September 11, the importance attached to racial markers of difference has magnified the socially constructed nature of race, while also reminding us that racialized differences are one of the most powerful signifiers of exclusion.

We are also mindful that race intersects with other social characteristics, such as gender, class, sexual orientation, immigration status, and disability, to produce racialized positions. In Part 2, our examination of how the criminal justice system produces and reinforces socially structured inequalities involves adopting an intersectional and interlocking approach[4] that takes into account the multiple locations of racialized Canadians. This offers a deeper understanding of the complexity of the lives of racialized minority groups, and recognizes that privilege does not exist without domination (Razack 1998a). For example, in the context of domestic labour, the lives of poor, racialized women are intimately tied to the lives of wealthy white women, such that one does not exist without the other. The intersectional and interlocking nature of this relationship emerges out of contexts of colonization, racism, and systems of oppression. Using this approach heightens our awareness of how the construction of racialized communities by the dominant society also impacts the gender and class dynamics within racialized communities (Jiwani 2006). It allows us to consider the distinct and varied experiences of marginalization produced by the criminal justice system, the substantive inequalities present within the justice system, and the potential solutions and remedies for claims of injustice and discrimination.

We outline what this approach entails in the context of race and the justice system in Chapter 2. Following this, Chapter 3 explores how an intersectional approach can help us think about the treatment of racialized and criminalized persons with mental illness. This is a group who has not received significant attention in Canadian society, and consequently, their issues and concerns are not well known. We highlight how deep inequalities in the treatment of racialized people in both the mental health system and the criminal justice system have persisted as a result of racial biases. The increasing numbers of racialized people with mental health problems caught up in the criminal justice system points to a precarious situation where continued racial discrimination as well as mistreatment have proven to be a deadly combination. Changing this reality will be an uphill battle. The last chapter of this section, Chapter 4, examines the role of mainstream media in perpetuating and reinforcing racial stereotypes about crime and criminals. Coverage of law and order issues dominates our attention in the media landscape, and the impact it has on our understanding of crime and the development of criminal justice policies and practices has been profound. Racialized groups are over-represented in negative news coverage about crime, and our perceptions about crime and criminals remain distorted. In this chapter, we draw on several high profile cases, such as the case of Reena Virk, to demonstrate how race and racism are deeply embedded in media representations of crime.

The institutions of criminal justice have routinely been criticized for the differential treatment of racialized minorities. From policing to court and correctional processes, many critical scholars have pointed to the over-representation of young, black, or Aboriginal men in all areas of the criminal justice system. In some countries, like the US, the situation is so dire that scholars claim the criminal justice system—in coordination with other social systems, such as welfare and mental health institutions—works to keep racialized people subordinate and fixed within a racial caste system (Roberts 2007).

The chapters in Part 3 examine the impact of policing practices (Chapter 5), sentencing outcomes, rates of imprisonment (Chapter 6), and the treatment of crime victims in racialized communities (Chapter 7). We note that despite the inconsistent and patchwork nature of scholarly research available, there remains strong evidence that racism is a significant problem in all areas of Canada's criminal justice system. We explore which racialized groups are most heavily targeted for punitive treatment or lack of treatment in the case of criminal victimization, and we highlight how other intersecting differences, such as gender, class, or sexual orientation, shape criminal justice outcomes along with race. We share David Tanovich's (2008) argument that more "race talk" as well as critical race standards are needed in the criminal justice system, because adopting the stance that race doesn't matter, or that formal equality is enough, continues to disproportionately disadvantage racialized groups in Canada.

In the final section of our book, Part 4, we explore how processes of criminalization have impacted racialized individuals and groups in Canada outside the criminal justice system. In his book, *Governing through Crime*, Jonathan Simon (2007) argues that American society has shifted from a welfare state to a penal state as a result of mass imprisonment, the war on terror, an obsession with security, and a deep-rooted fear of strangers and their difference. Crime control, he states, has become a central value in how we govern; and predictably, the most marginalized groups in our society bear the brunt of increasingly authoritarian, repressive policies (Simon 2007). We would argue that the situation in Canada is not significantly different, despite lower rates of imprisonment. In examining the criminalization of Muslim and Arab people post–September 11 (Chapter 8), the treatment of immigrants and refugees (Chapter 9), and the criminalization of poor people (Chapter 10), we highlight how successive Canadian governments have adopted a pattern of governing through crime, and how the impact on racialized and poor Canadians has undermined the values of equality, due process, and justice. The ease with which we can now criminalize, marginalize, and exclude racialized groups for non-criminal behaviours, because they allegedly threaten "our way of life," highlights the transformation of state–society relations, where our fears and insecurities have granted more coercive powers to the state in the name of protection. Yet, with no certainty that we are better protected, and given the dire consequences for those at the receiving end of state practices, putting a brake on processes of criminalization seems prudent and overdue.

In this book, we don't claim to be exhaustive in our approach. We have selectively identified topics which we regard to be current and relevant in developing our analysis, and appreciate that some of the topics and issues chosen are broad and complex, and would benefit from much further investigation. Our hope is that this book acts as a springboard for students and scholars to continue probing and challenging our understanding of the relationship between race, racialization, and criminal justice.

NOTES

1 A detailed discussion of this case is provided in Chapter 8.
2 An entire issue of the Canadian Journal of Criminology was devoted to this debate in 1994.
3 We use the term race-thinking to refer to racial ontologies that are premised on the belief that humans can be categorized according to particular racial types or groups, and that these classification systems are natural and therefore inevitable. The term was originally coined by Hannah Arendt (1944).
4 While more detailed discussion of intersectionality is provided in Chapters 1 and 2, for the purposes of clarification here, an intersectional approach recognizes how subordinate groups are located at the intersections of different systems of oppression (e.g., race, class, gender, sexual orientation, immigrant status) (Crenshaw 1991). An interlocking analysis complements an intersectional approach by examining how these systems of oppression operate simultaneously and over time to produce hierarchical relationships (Jiwani 2006).

PART ONE

CONCEPTS, THEORIES, APPROACHES

CHAPTER ONE

CONCEPTS AND THEORIES ABOUT RACE, RACIALIZATION, AND CRIMINAL JUSTICE

In this chapter we explore some of the key concepts and ideas about race and racism, and their relationship to crime and criminal justice, to show how these notions have shaped contemporary discussions and arguments. Our aim is to provide clarification of key concepts as well as a foundation for the discussions that follow in subsequent chapters. We begin with an overview of race and racism, and explore the different debates and issues taken up by race scholars. Section two of this chapter examines the concept of racialization, and the ways in which crime and particular social groups in Canada are racialized. We unpack how this process unfolds in the criminal justice system and offer several explanations for why it occurs, and the impact it has for those affected. The final section of this chapter examines the concept of criminalization. We look at what this concept means, which individuals or groups are more likely to be criminalized in Canada, the social and political context giving rise to practices of criminalization, and the consequences of criminalization.

CONCEPTUALIZING RACE, RACISM, AND RACIAL DIFFERENCE

A wide range of definitions and theories have been developed around how to best understand the concepts of race, racial difference, and racism in Canada (Satzewich 2010; Hier and Bolaria 2007). Although race is part of our everyday language, we often don't think about the different ways it is used or understood locally and globally. Since it is regarded as a problematic concept by many, it is not unusual to see the term referenced in quotation marks as a way of highlighting the complex, political, and contested nature of its usage (Mason 2000). Opinions and debates persist over how the concept of race should be used in the social sciences, with some researchers opting for the term ethnicity instead of race (Li 1999, 6). We believe, however, that the concept of race still has important analytical relevance, and therefore, in our discussions, we use race as an analytical term rather than a descriptive one to describe the power relationships that have significantly impacted social relations in contemporary Canadian society. Although we will not be placing the term race in quotation marks throughout this text, it should be acknowledged that we recognize its contested and problematic status.

Social science research typically regards the category of race as a social construct, although what the social construction of race implies can vary. We share the explanation provided by Robert Miles (2000, 192), who states that "race is an idea created by human beings in certain historical and material conditions and is used to represent the world in certain ways, under certain historical conditions and for certain political interests." For example, sociologists have noted how the construction of race in many societies adopts a framework which Andrea Smith (2006) refers to as the "three pillars of white supremacy." In this framework, one pillar is represented by Slavery/Capitalism, where black people are historically regarded as nothing more than property and seen as inherently "slavable." A racial hierarchy within the capitalist system uses the logic of slavery to locate black people at the bottom of the hierarchy, and to remind everyone else that they should be grateful to not be at the bottom (Smith 2006, 67). The second pillar, Genocide/Capitalism, erases indigenous peoples through the logic of genocide (Smith 2006, 68). Their disappearance, both figuratively and literally, makes it possible for non-native peoples to claim indigenous lands and resources as their own (Smith 2006, 68). The third and last pillar, Orientalism/War, positions non-white people as inferior foreigners and as constant threats to the nation (Smith 2006, 68). During times of war, these perceived threats of internal and external racialized people allow the state to adopt harsh measures to protect itself (Smith 2006, 68). Thus, the social meanings created around race, and other markers of social identity such as gender and sexuality, emerge through power relationships in society, in which being white is equated with privilege and superiority, while being racialized is equated with disadvantage and inferiority (Patel and Tyrer 2011, 4). The dominant group has the power to define subordinate groups through physical and cultural traits, combined with intellectual, moral, and/or behavioural characteristics (Bolaria and Li 1988). These ideas are maintained through political, legal, and religious claims that legitimate the prevailing social order.

Throughout the history of Canada, we have seen the differential treatment of racial groups as a result of definitions imposed by the dominant group. For example, in the context of Canadian immigration in the early part of the twentieth century, northern Europeans were considered much more desirable immigrants by the Canadian government than southern or eastern Europeans, or Asians (Li 1999, 57). Some immigrant groups, such as the Ukrainians, were even stigmatized as "dangerous" because they were seen as communist sympathizers (Avery 1979). Similarly, distinctions were historically made between status Indians and non-status Indians and Metis for legal and bureaucratic reasons tied to colonialism, even though these distinctions had very little to do with any significant cultural or national differences. Thus, the social construction of race emphasizes the many different meanings associated with race as well as the many different social relations that are produced out of these meanings (Miles 1989).

How race is understood and used depends on the specific historical contexts in which it operates. The social construction of race and racism also highlights the need to be mindful of not essentializing ideas about race—to not assume that they are natural, inherent categories that have always existed, that will always exist, and that don't change. How racial groups are defined and understood is always in flux. Today, for example, many southern and eastern European groups have been redefined as part of the white majority, rather than the "peripheral" Europeans they were designated to be in the earlier part of the last century (Satzewich 2000).

In contrast, supporters of the scientific, biologically based notion of race categorized people according to ascribed characteristics, and have historically grouped a wide range of people according to geography, religion, class, or skin colour (Barkan 1992). Although the idea of race predates scientific involvement, science helped in casting divisions between people as natural, fixed, and absolute, and variations in appearance as indicative of deeper, essential differences (Skinner 2006). Gobineau, considered the "grandfather of modern academic racism," divided humanity hierarchically into whites, yellows, and blacks (Gould 1996). He argued that the white race would maintain their superior position only if they remained racially pure and did not dilute their stock by breeding with inferior yellow or brown races.

Gobineau's scheme was widely embraced by ideological racists, influencing the eugenics movement in the twentieth century, and a broad range of scholarly activity, including criminology. For example, Lombroso, a criminological anthropologist working in the late nineteenth century, developed these ideas in his study of human skulls, arguing that criminals, even if white, were part of inferior races that were evolutionary throwbacks to an earlier stage of human development (Bierne and Messerschmidt 1995). Lombroso (1876) claimed the following:

> Many of the characteristics found in savages, and among the coloured races, are also to be found in habitual delinquents. They have in common, for example, thinning hair, lack of strength and weight, low cranial capacity, receding foreheads, highly developed frontal sinuses, darker skin, thicker, curly hair....

Lombroso's findings were favourably received and became a dominant framework for understanding criminality, even though it was challenged by lawyers and other anthropologists at the time (Bierne and Messerschmidt 1995, 351). As Skinner (2006) points out, classifying people according to physical characteristics was intimately connected to political concerns, and the relationship between science, policy, and discourses of race was and is complex and varied.

The development and application of racial classification schemes was more than just an academic exercise. Painter (2010) observes that the creation of classificatory schemes was never done in a disinterested attempt to depict human diversity. Rather, the project was designed to advance the claim that racial hierarchies are valid, and this classification scheme allowed for the adjudication of racial superiority and inferiority based on intelligence and moral character. The work of historians studying the relationship between race and colonialism is an example of how racial classifications became a useful tool for political purposes. From this, justifications for the oppression and exploitation of racial groups were given legitimacy by political leaders. The subjugation of Aboriginal peoples in Canada by European colonizers is one stark example of this way of thinking.

According to Barkan (1992), it was not until the interwar years (1919–38) that the biological validity of race as a concept began to erode within scientific circles, and the use of race typology to explain cultural phenomena was largely rejected. This position developed in direct opposition to the ideological application of scientific racism employed by Nazi Germany at the time. The legitimacy of race was questioned within scientific communities because the notion of racial classification could not withstand the inconsistencies and contradictions being raised in studies on the subject. As a result, scientists came to believe that limiting racial differentiation to physical characteristics would produce a more accurate formulation, and engaging in discriminatory behaviour based on racial difference came to be viewed as racism (Barkan 1992, 3). Yet despite widespread criticism and rejection by scientists of the validity of innate, biologically based differences between races, the ideas derived from racial classification continue to persist in contemporary academic writing (Benedict 1983). For example, Herrnstein and Murray (1994) sought to demonstrate the links between intelligence and race through their study of IQ results.

Despite their controversial claims, Herrnstein and Murray's work had significant influence in the fields of criminal justice and social policy. More recent studies in genomics, which involve DNA mapping, continue to rely on the ideology of racial difference to develop scientific knowledge that can lead to further racial disparities. In health databases, where information is used to develop knowledge about medical conditions and human health, there is an overwhelming amount of DNA information from people of European descent, but very little information available from the non-white population (Chow-White and Duster 2011, 1). On the other hand, in forensic DNA databases, the opposite is true. Non-white groups are over-represented in national DNA forensic databases, and this raises questions about policing practices and issues of privacy (Chow-White and Duster 2011, 2).

The role that the biological concept of race has played throughout the last century has fundamentally shaped how Canadian society has evolved over time. Beliefs that racial characteristics are biologically determined and immutable over time, with some groups deemed more civilized or superior than others, have not only resulted in deeply entrenched racial hierarchies globally but also led to many destructive practices, including the genocide of Jewish people in World War II. A recent news story about a rural high school in the southern US state of Georgia demonstrates how the colour of one's skin can result in entrenched attitudes about racial difference with lasting consequences. In this case, the high school marked its first racially integrated prom in 2013,[1] after historically holding black proms and white proms separately. Similarly, news stories about people in China wearing masks at the beach during the summer, to avoid having their faces tanned, highlights the ongoing perception that fair skin is more desirable in our society (Levin 2012). As a social category, notions of race continue to have an appeal and are widely invoked. Therefore, even though the scientific conception of race has lost much of its currency, attitudes about race persist.

Racism is the product of racial attitudes and beliefs that endure through social life. Like race, racism is a socially constructed phenomenon that, according to Henry and Tator, "is based on the false assumption that physical differences such as skin colour, facial features, and hair colour and texture are related to intellectual, moral or cultural superiority" (2002, 11). Racism can occur at all levels of social interaction—from individuals being spontaneously singled out for discriminatory treatment to the exclusion or exploitation of whole groups in a structured and systemic pattern. It is persistent, complex, changing, and subtle (Solomos and Black 1996). This position is reiterated by Goldberg (1997), who claims that

> racist expressions ... are various—in kind, in disposition, in emo-
> tive affect, in intention, and in outcome. Moreover, racisms are
> not unusual or abnormal. To the contrary, racist expressions are
> normal to our culture, manifest not only in extreme epithets, but
> in insinuations and suggestions, in reasoning and representations,
> in short in the micro expressions of daily life. (20)

Racism is most difficult to challenge when it is structural, unconscious, indirect, and covert. Depending on the context, it can include being denied access to housing, employment, education, and social services, to name a few. The many different manifestations of racism in Canada and elsewhere have led Stuart Hall to observe that since race intersects with many other social phenomena, it is more appropriate to speak about specific "racisms" than it is about a single historical racism, since "one cannot explain racism in abstraction from other social relations" (1980, 337).

Recent expressions of racism give greater emphasis to cultural difference, with culture superseding biology as a key marker of differentiation and exclusion. Cultural racism, or the "new racism," is the inability or unwillingness to tolerate cultural difference (Wieviorka 2002). It involves prejudice for reasons of social customs, manners and behaviour, religious beliefs and practices, and language, with the underlying belief that these cultural (often non-Westernized) characteristics are flawed in some way and should be abandoned in favour of the majority, (Western) culture. Cultural racism is another way of inferiorizing individuals and groups, and excluding them from mainstream society. In Canada, many non-European immigrant groups were historically deemed culturally inferior because they behaved in a way that was regarded as inconsistent with Canadian values and culture. Some scholars argue that these beliefs continue to persist into the twenty-first century, especially when we examine the treatment of Muslim and Arab communities post–September 11, or the current treatment of migrants and refugees (Arat-Koc 2005; Razack 2005). One example of cultural racism can be seen in the recent controversy sparked by the Quebec soccer federation's ban of the turban, and other religious headwear, on the soccer pitch, despite opposition by national and international soccer federations. Their policy was widely seen as racist, since there was no evidence that wearing a turban was a safety problem, and many critics contend that the real aim was to exclude people who wear turbans from being able to play the game.[2] While racism is not always explicitly articulated against these groups, it is clear that an ideology of (Western) superiority undergirds the discriminatory treatment directed at them.

Efforts to understand the complexity of race and racism have led some scholars to examine the role of whiteness. Although many people believe that race should no longer matter, since science has debunked the idea of racial categories and we live in a multicultural, merit-based society, race indeed still matters. Who or what gets defined as normal continues to depend on the invisible and unspoken assumption that "whiteness" is the norm from which access to privilege and power is determined. As Thobani (2002) points out, whiteness reinforces the darkening of the Other and in the process constitutes racial difference as something outside of and subordinate to what is normative. Peake and Ray (2001) argue that whiteness in Canada is conveyed in several ways—through immigration policies that exclude non-white immigrants, through the forced assimilation of Aboriginal people, and in the use of violent subjugation and segregation tactics. It is also apparent in less forceful ways, as in the use of terms such as "ghetto" or "ethnic enclave" to describe non-white neighbourhoods, when these same descriptors are seemingly never attached to predominantly white neighbourhoods (Peake and Ray 2001, 180). Interrogating whiteness forces us to examine how events that are deracialized and normalized are, in fact, part of a racial landscape that defines identities and shapes narratives of belonging. In examining the relationship between race, crime, and culture it is as important to interrogate how whiteness is constructed as it is to understand the construction of minority identities.

Finally, focusing on how race intersects with other social inequalities related to gender, class, sexual orientation, or immigration is an important aspect in our analysis of race and racism in the criminal justice system. An intersectional analysis examines multiple and interlocking experiences of marginalization, recognizing that social categories such as race, class, and gender are not separate and discrete, but heterogeneous and interdependent within and across these categories. In this sense, race is "gendered," and gender is "racialized" (Glenn 2002). There is also an emphasis on recognizing the simultaneity of oppression (Hill Collins 2000; Crenshaw 1991) and the ways in which responses to criminal victimization or criminal events cannot be divorced from the larger context of the realities of multiple forms of social injustice that permeate society (Tifft, Maruna, and Elliott 2006). For criminologists, this includes examining how the criminal justice system responds to victims and offenders based on their social locations.

One of the key advantages of this approach is that it recognizes the simultaneity of discrimination and privilege (Burgess-Proctor 2006). As we discuss in Chapter 2, people are not simply "pure victims" or "pure oppressors" (Hill-Collins 2004). Rather, they experience both discrimination and privilege at various times and places in their lives. The phenomenon of driving while black is an example of how a wealthy, black man may experience the advantages of class privilege (driving an expensive vehicle), while simultaneously experiencing discrimination and disadvantage based on being black and male (being racially profiled). As Madame Justice L'Heureux-Dube, writing the minority decision in *Canada (A.G.) v. Mossop* [1993], acknowledges,

> ... categories of discrimination may overlap, and ... individuals may suffer historical exclusion on the basis of both race and gender, age, and physical handicap, or some other combination. The situation of individuals who confront multiple grounds of disadvantage is particularly complex. Categorizing such discrimination as primarily racially oriented, or primarily gender-oriented, misconceives the reality of discrimination as it is experienced by individuals.

Thus, the benefit of an intersectional approach is that it is able to capture how multiple dimensions of social disadvantage as well as privilege are inter-related and interactive (Daly 1993).

THE RACIALIZATION OF CRIME AND CRIMINAL JUSTICE IN CANADA

Robert Miles (1989) wrote that race as a concept should be abandoned because it signifies nothing and is "analytically useless." The ideology of racism, as opposed to race, is more important in understanding the effects of racism in society (Miles 1989, 72). Hence, racialization as a concept can better explain how racist ideology is embedded in the process of racial cate-gorization. Miles states:

> I therefore employ the concept of racialization to refer to those instances where social relations between people have been struc-tured by the signification of human biological characteristics in such a way as to define and construct differentiated social collec-tivities. The concept therefore refers to a process of categoriza-tion, a representational process of defining an Other (usually, but not exclusively) somatically. (1989, 75)

Other sociologists concur, citing how the concept of race is an intellectual error (Banton 1998) or empty signifier that is dangerous because of its emptiness (Rustin 1991). The Ontario Human Rights Commission claims that race is a myth because "it is impossible to sort humanity into distinct racial groups using any scientific standard" (1995, 74). Racial categories are socially constructed and do not explain the skills, talents, personalities, or behaviours of individuals or groups (Ontario Human Rights Commission 1995). Yet, since race remains a part of the lived experience of many people, finding a way to speak about people's experiences of race has led to a focus on the concept of racialization.

Racialization is about the process by which people are selected, sorted, given attributes, and assigned particular actions (Ontario Human Rights Commission 1995). Social policies and practices maintain and enforce racial boundaries, power relations, and structurally embedded meanings (Omi and Winant 1994; Wacquant 1997). These policies and practices, which exacer-bate and perpetuate the racial hierarchy, can be intentional or unintentional. The concept of race is sustained through these processes, and is thus a product of racialization. The fact that societies continue to make racialized judgments in all areas of social life highlights its powerful effect.

In the context of crime and criminal justice, racialization refers to the ways in which criminal justice processes and situations use the idea of race to define and give meaning to particular populations, as well as their characteristics and actions. Hence, crime is racialized when criminal behaviour is viewed as a trait belonging to the wider racial or ethnic community, such that all "phenotypically similar individuals are rendered pre-criminal and morally suspect" (Covington 1995, 547). In their classic criminological study—*Policing the Crisis*—Hall et al. (1978) demonstrate how moral panics about youth and crime during the late 1970s in the UK were racially charged, where poverty and youth became a crisis for social authority. Social fears about race, crime, and youth coalesced around concerns about mugging (robbing), which was redefined by authority figures as a problem of "unruly youth" and black street crime (Hall et al. 1978). The effect was an overreaction by the state, which included the scapegoating of racialized youth and an increased law-and-order agenda that saw excessive penalties meted out to racialized young offenders (Hall et al. 1978).

As Wacquant explains, the conflation of dangerousness and criminality with blackness has a long legacy in many countries, and it is therefore not surprising that the combination of being young, black, and male is routinely equated with "probable cause" (2005b, 128). Interrogating the racialization of crime involves examining which groups are more likely to receive greater police attention, become targets of searches and arrests, receive fair trials, or be over-represented in the correctional system. In doing so, racial hierarchies and the racialization of a particular nation are exposed, demonstrating how racial difference continues to have significant consequences for racialized individuals and groups (Goldberg 2002; Welch and Schuster 2005a).

Within Canada, there are many examples, both historical and contemporary, of how criminal justice policies and practices are racialized. Mosher's (1996) historical research on the treatment of black offenders in Ontario between 1892 and 1930 found that there was disproportionate police attention on black public-order offenders, and that racialized minority offenders were more likely to experience higher rates of conviction, with lengthier sentences for these crimes. Similarly, Barrington Walker's (2010) historical study of black defendants in Ontario's criminal courts demonstrates how racial difference and crime resulted in discriminatory treatment that was legally supported. At the time, blacks were more likely to be hanged for their crimes, and the experiences of black Canadians in the criminal courts reflected the unequal power relations that emerged out of colonialism (Walker 2010, 11). Black Canadians were not alone in suffering the effects of racial stereotyping and colonial power. Aboriginal groups were also subjected to mistreatment by colonial authorities in the justice system. For example, the over-policing of Aboriginal communities in Canada can be traced back over a century (Backhouse 1999; Hylton 2002). Finally, non-white immigrants were also targeted historically, and the myth that there is a causal link between immigration and crime emerges out of racialized beliefs based on a general distrust of immigrants (Sayad 2004).

Scholars have argued that for many of these racialized groups not much has changed over time. For example, Aboriginal peoples continue to be over-represented at all levels of the criminal justice system, so much so that the Supreme Court of Canada has referred to this as "a crisis in the Canadian justice system," while the Royal Commission on Aboriginal Peoples has described it as "injustice personified" (Rudin 1995). Aboriginal people are more likely than non-Aboriginal people to be incarcerated for minor offences such as failure to pay a fine, to be seen as guilty by a jury, and to be detained upon arrest (Rudin 1995). LaPrairie (1997) argues that several factors help explain the phenomenon of Aboriginal over-representation and why Aboriginal people are so disproportionately involved in, and vulnerable to, the policies and practices of the criminal justice system. These include issues such as racial discrimination in criminal justice processing, higher rates of offending and the commission of offences more likely to result in carceral sentences, and the differential impact of criminal justice policies and practices on Aboriginal offenders due to their socio-economic conditions (LaPrairie 1997, 40–41). Yet, despite all the commissions and inquiries, the mistreatment of Aboriginal people by criminal justice authorities continues to be extensive, with some of the most egregious practices involving Aboriginal offenders dying in police custody (Cheema 2009; BC Civil Liberties Association 2012), Aboriginal people being driven to the outskirts of the city in the winter and forced to walk home and sober up (Chartrand 2005; Comack 2012), and the high rates of victimization of Aboriginal women due to the under-policing of domestic violence in Aboriginal communities (Goel 2000).

Other racialized groups have also reported ongoing discriminatory treatment in the criminal justice system. Thornhill (2008) argues that black people in Canada today remain intensely distrustful of the law and legal system because the legal system has aided and abetted racism and racial discrimination consistently throughout history. Even the presence of the Charter of Rights has not been able to adequately counter the racial injustice experienced in the criminal justice system by marginalized groups (Tanovich 2008). Systemic racism in the criminal justice system, which has resulted in over-incarceration and constant surveillance, has also produced the collateral effects of physical and severe psychological harm, isolation, alienation and mistrust, behavioural changes, breakdowns of or damage to family and social networks, and labour market exclusions (Ontario Human Rights Commission 2003). Efforts to understand the differential treatment of racialized groups has led some scholars to conclude that the continued racialization of criminal justice practices is "part of a historically uninterrupted series of legal and political machinations designed to enforce white supremacy with its economic and social benefits both in and with the law" (Brewer and Heitzeg 2008, 625). As Bonilla-Silva (2001, 103) observes, "all domination is, in the last instance, maintained through social control strategies."

The process of racializing crime and criminal justice involves many different strategies. Two of the most common practices are the over-emphasizing of crimes committed by people of colour, and the use of specific terms and categories in conversations about racialized groups and crime. As we document in more detail in Chapter 4, the media's tendency to over-report on crimes committed by people of colour cannot be understated. Evidence from Canada, the US, and the UK demonstrates how media institutions have consistently presented a biased picture of crime. For example, black suspects are more likely to be represented as superpredators, while black victims are not considered as newsworthy as white victims (Bjornstrom et al. 2010). As Henry and Tator (2002) argue, mainstream media has been pivotal in providing representations of racialized individuals and groups that are primarily negative and stereotypical. They cite the overzealous reporting of the Toronto "Just Desserts" case in 1994 as a case in point. What followed after the incident was not only the over-policing of Jamaican Canadians in the Toronto region, but also the proliferation of stereotypes about the criminality of black people, reinforced by media messages that linked Jamaicans in Canada with violent, drug- and gang-related crime (Henry and Tator 2002). Similarly, Jiwani's (2011) analysis of headlines in the *Globe and Mail* over a one-year period supports the claim that media representations of racialized and immigrant groups reinforce the links between representation and crime. She found that news stories about racialized groups focused predominantly on crime, and, furthermore, were more likely to depict racialized individuals as perpetrators, rather than victims, of crime (Jiwani 2011, 47).

A related strategy of representation in the racialization of crime is the use of encoded terms, which, on the surface, appear neutral, but when examined more closely refer to specific racial groups. Li claims that using such terms allows for the discussion of race in the political arena without suggesting that race is socially significant (2007, 44). He points to debates around immigration in Canada, where government reports use coded terms such as "non-traditional" in referring to "non-white" source countries and the potential "problems" immigrants from those countries pose (Li 2007, 44). Similarly, there has been increasing controversy over the use of the phrase "illegal immigrant," particularly in the US, with activists and scholars contending that the term is not only inaccurate, since irregular immigration is not a criminal offence but a civil one, but that it also serves to dehumanize and marginalize the people it seeks to describe (Hesson 2012). The phrase is often deployed in reference to non-white immigrants and to refugees who immigrate through irregular channels, framing these individuals as criminal, foreign, and other. The term "gang" is another example of a word used primarily to refer to racialized communities. While the term is applicable to all racial groups, Symons (2002) found that police officers consistently referred to gangs that were composed of racialized youth by describing their countries of origin, but when referring to white supremacist gangs, officers described the practices engaged in.

Finally, since September 11, xenophobia toward people of Muslim or Arab origins has resulted in the idea that a "terrorist" is someone who is brown-skinned, and that even if they are Canadian citizens, they are not "Canadian" like the rest of us (Burman 2010). "Canadian-born brown" residents have become the focus of suspicion and fear, prompting the implementation of coercive policies and practices in the name of "national security," and in the process, it is driving a deep wedge between communities in Canada (Burman 2010). As the above examples demonstrate, language becomes an important means by which people of colour and immigrants are branded and racialized (Romero 2008).

The racialization of crime in Canada has led to racialized individuals and groups experiencing a range of injustices as criminal identities become fused with racial identities. Critics of the justice system point out that the law and its practices reflect racist and sexist attitudes, such that criminal justice is "white man's justice" (Hudson 2006, 30). Just as the law treats women in the same way that mainstream society treats them—negating the harms they experience—members of racialized groups find that their harms are not taken seriously (Smart 1989). Differential treatment in the criminal justice system is a result of structural racism—the systematic perpetuation of group disadvantage—rather than a product of individual racist beliefs and actions (Williams 2008). Hudson argues that in order for racial and ethnic minorities to receive the same kind of legal treatment they must prove that, at the very least, they are the "same as" white men or women (2006, 31). Yet, equal treatment has proven to be just as problematic, since it cannot account for the inequities that stem from historical, social, political, and economic differences and which construct peoples' places in the world. The inadequate police protection available to crime victims in racialized communities, and the widespread use of racial profiling by state authorities, highlights the entrenched whiteness within criminal law, and the lack of power that racialized communities have in challenging and contesting constructions of their criminality.

THE CRIMINALIZATION OF RACIAL GROUPS

Despite the increased awareness by scholars and anti-racist activists that racialized communities receive more criminal justice attention as a result of racist assumptions and biased agendas, the legacy of discriminatory treatment and racial disparities in the criminal justice system continues in Canada and other developed nations. Black, male youths continue to assume the role of the "folk devil" (Cohen 1973), and remain the focus of heightened police attention (Brown 2004). Aboriginal people are still vastly over-represented in the criminal justice system (LaPrairie 2002), refugees and migrants have recently been recast as "illegals" and as threats (Dauvergne 2008) while Arabs and Muslims have become the targets of suspicion and concern in issues of national security (Bhabha 2005). In the meantime, the status of racialized groups as victims of crime, or as innocent bystanders, continues to be overlooked and largely ignored by a fearful society that is ready to embrace punitive crime policies.

In this context, it is not surprising to find that despite falling crime rates (Makin 2012), the Canadian government continues to pursue a crime agenda that includes more numerous and lengthy prison terms, mandatory minimum sentences, and tougher penalties for drug and sex offences (CBC News 2011c). The Canadian Centre for Policy Alternatives argues that Aboriginal people will be hardest-hit by the new legislation (Mallea 2010). Conditional sentencing is a vital component in being able to keep Aboriginal people out of prisons and jails, and the concern is that mandatory minimum sentences may sharply curtail how many Aboriginal people will be diverted from incarceration (Mallea 2010, 16). Furthermore, mandatory minimum sentences contravene the sentencing principles established in *R. v. Gladue* (1999) S.C.J. No. 19 (QL) where the Supreme Court of Canada directed judges to consider alternatives to jail for Aboriginal offenders, noting that this was a necessary approach to managing the problem of Aboriginal over-representation in the justice system. Whether intentional or not, the recent legislative changes (particularly, the *Safe Streets and Communities Act*) will now exacerbate Aboriginal over-representation, clearly highlighting how the presence of a racial hierarchy that places whiteness in a position of power and authority conveniently furthers state interests. Many critics of the legislation expect heightened racial inequalities to emerge, particularly in poorer communities where racialized people are at greater risk of criminalization (Scoffield 2012).

The corollary to the racialization of crime is the criminalization and control of racial groups. Similar to racialization, criminalization refers to "the institutionalized process through which certain acts and behaviours are selected and labelled as 'crimes' and through which particular individuals and groups are subsequently selectively identified and differentially policed and disciplined" (Fergusson and Muncie 2008, 103). Examining the concept of criminalization helps in thinking about what crime is—how we understand it, and how we respond to it. A focus on processes of criminalization has become increasingly commonplace in neo-liberal democracies like Canada, where efforts to manage the "crime problem" have assumed greater political priority. David Garland (2001) claims that the social unrest of the 1960s and 1970s, including civil disorder and high crime rates, was a key factor in undermining the legitimacy of the political order. New strategies were needed to address the fact that policies of rehabilitation were not working as they were meant to. Out of this emerged the criminal justice policies of the 1980s, which emphasized populist punitiveness and the risk management of dangerous populations (Garland 2001).

Tony Bottoms has coined the phrase "populist punitiveness" to refer to situations where "politicians encourage punitive laws and sentences and thereby improve their chances of re-election by making such responses to indicators of the public mood or sentiment" (1995, 40). This new approach in crime policy and practice stressed personal responsibility over collective risk spreading, it offered minimal protections against economic harm, it was highly moralistic, and it was harshly enforced (Garland 2001). The ideological assumption held by many governments is that crime is real, and that people need to be protected from crime, especially since we now live in a dangerous world. Criminologists argue that the general public's fear of crime, combined with the politicization of crime, has resulted in punitive "law and order" policies as well as a significant expansion of the criminal law in virtually all industrialized countries (Garland 2001; Simon 2007). This is evident in the sheer number of criminal offences, and the scope of conduct they cover. Governments have responded to citizens' demands (to limit their vulnerability to criminal victimization and threats to their security) through increased criminalization.

In Canada, this response has taken the form of harsher treatment toward groups identified as threats (e.g., migrants, terrorists, refugees, homeless people, youth, people with mental illnesses, etc.), of increased surveillance in all areas of social life, of the rise of private security, and of a massive prison expansion program, to name a few. Many scholars believe that this shift, from the rehabilitative model to the punitive model, was not inevitable, and that it was enabled by economic forces, a rise of conservative agendas, and a public open to conservative change (Garland 2001; Wacquant 2001).

These trends do not affect everyone equally. Racialized ideas of deviancy and victimhood play a central role in criminal justice developments. For example, fear of the racialized "other" could no longer be separated from fear of crime. Patel and Tyrer point out that this is because criminalization does not occur in a vacuum, but is "influenced by contemporary politics, economic conditions and dominant ideologies and is contextualized by variables of social class, gender, sexuality, age, race, religion and ethnicity" (2011, 19). Thus, after September 11, the Muslim and Arab population across the globe faced a form of exclusion in which they were seen, first and foremost, as terrorists or extremists. Similarly, mass incarceration, particularly of racialized groups, was a key strategy for the state to demonstrate its strength and control over crime, despite falling crime rates (Wacquant 2001). Finally, rather than defending their discriminatory approaches, governments invoked notions of "ethnic difference" to explain criminal acts perpetrated against the state and state responses to these events, as in the "war on terror" or the pursuit of "national security" (Bosworth, Bowling, and Lee 2008). These examples suggest that the racial other has significant political purchase, and remains a recurring theme in criminal justice discourse and practice, regardless of the actual relationship between race and crime.

One of the most enduring myths to emerge from discussions of crime control is the belief that black people (particularly young, black men) are more criminogenic than other racial groups, and require greater state control. Anxieties and concerns about "black criminality" can be found across many developed countries (Warde 2012). As mentioned in the previous section, official anxiety in the UK about the criminality of the black population escalated into a moral panic about rising crime rates in the latter half of the twentieth century (Hall et al. 1978). Black communities were criminalized through an increased use of stop and search practices by the police, given harsher sentences by the courts, and portrayed as deviant, fragmented, and unable to properly socialize their children (Smith 2008).

A similar phenomenon occurred in Canada in the early 1990s, following a series of violent conflicts involving the police and the black community in Toronto. Jackson (1994) documents how black organizations challenged policing practices, as well as perceptions that their communities were inherently criminogenic, in their submissions to a task force set up in 1989 to examine the relationship between race, crime, and policing. Despite significant opposition to how black people were represented, the public continued to believe that black communities committed more crimes than other racial groups (Henry, Hastings, and Freer 1996).

However, while in Southern Ontario and various parts of the Atlantic provinces (notably Nova Scotia), the iconic image of criminality is strongly associated with black communities, members of other racialized groups have been depicted as the cause of crime and disorder in other parts of Canada. Comack's (2012) study of policing in the Prairies found that Aboriginal people there had a long and troubled relationship with the police, and were more likely to be over-policed and improperly treated. In the west, people from South Asian and Vietnamese backgrounds are routinely linked to the problem of drug crimes and related offences. Therefore, unlike the US and the UK, although the figure of "the criminal" is racialized, there is no one single racialized group in Canada that occupies this category. Rather, geographical location has strongly shaped which racialized individuals or groups become the target of stereotyping and over-representation in the justice system.

A recent study examining the views of criminal justice professionals on race and justice in Canada highlights the minimal progress achieved in the last two decades (Denny, Ellis, and Barn 2006). Despite the presence of anti-discrimination initiatives, many criminal justice professionals continue to rely on cultural differences for understanding why racialized communities are over-represented in the justice system, rather than emphasizing the unbalanced power relations stemming from socio-economic disadvantage (Denny, Ellis, and Barn 2006, 11). For example, stereotypes about Aboriginal people have contributed significantly to their over-representation, yet the legacy of colonialism is rarely entertained. Webster (2008) claims that regardless of whether one sees the problem as one of "bad people," "bad decisions," or something more complex, the disproportionate representation of racialized people (primarily black and Aboriginal) in the Canadian criminal justice system reinforces and increases the fear of crime for the white majority, who are then more likely to implement criminal justice reforms that continue to disadvantage racialized groups.

A concurrent trend to black and Aboriginal men being over-criminalized in the Canadian criminal justice system is that racialized women are less likely to be taken seriously as victims of crime. Critical scholars contend that the image of a legitimate crime victim is typically white and middle class (Welsh et al. 2006). The harms experienced by poor, racialized women are often downplayed or minimized, accompanied by the suggestion that these women are impervious to trauma (Savarese 2010). Legal responses to sexual assault and domestic violence have been heavily criticized by feminist scholars for misrepresenting the harms that women victims endure, and the ways in which gendered racial violence situates racialized women victims in opposition to racialized male offenders. For example, the use of restorative justice practices in sentencing Aboriginal male offenders has been highly controversial (Cameron 2006; Balfour 2008). Efforts by judges to be more culturally aware have arguably relied on an impoverished notion of culture that exists in a "timeless and unchangeable vacuum outside of patriarchy, racism, imperialism and colonialism," resulting in the re-victimization of women (Razack 1998b, 58). Aboriginal women have pointed out how current models of restorative justice, or Aboriginal justice, are male centred and culturally inappropriate, and therefore, do not correspond to the values and justice practices of the communities to which they are being applied (Cameron 2006, 54). The need to recognize how race, gender, and other structured inequalities shape criminal justice outcomes for racialized women is important for understanding their involvement in criminal activity (Richie 1996) and the power relations that shape processes of resistance (Weber 2001).

Past and present images of racialized people as deviant, lawless, violent, fraudulent, threatening, or dangerous have been perpetuated not only by politicians and the criminal justice system in their pursuit of "law and order" policies, but also by mainstream media, which, as we mentioned earlier, has relied heavily on racial stereotypes of crime and deviance in news reporting. Thus, mainstream media not only racializes crime, but also simultaneously criminalizes racialized communities through the reproduction of dominant cultural values and norms, and by suggesting that racialized communities do not share these values. Murdocca, in an analysis of how the issue of racial profiling was represented in the *Toronto Star* newspaper, found that public knowledge produced through news stories "maintains mainstream fascination with race and crime and guarantees the exclusion of racialized bodies from becoming lawful national/citizen/subject participants" (2004, 165). The presentation of racial bias in news stories is difficult for powerless minority groups to challenge or resist, thereby weakening their ability to participate in and be accepted as a part of mainstream society (Henry and Tator 2002, 225).

Furthermore, patterns of discrimination in the mainstream media have escalated since September 11, particularly toward Arab and Muslim people. Anti-Muslim bias in the media has created an environment that is accepting of the demonizing of Muslim people as evil, warlike, savage, deceitful, and prone to violence (Stockton 1994). As these images become normalized, white subjects seek to distance themselves from the racialized Other, legitimating ideologies and images that mark the Other as inferior, irresponsible, immoral, and non-human (Poynting and Perry 2007, 157). In doing so, the media helps perpetuate a mentality of "us vs. them," which serves to marginalize and criminalize these communities. Thus, racialized communities cannot overcome their marginalization and oppression with the occasional positive news story, as it does little to challenge the complex process of attitudinal formation and confirmation of racialized belief systems (Henry and Tator 2002, 236).

The media's complicity in bolstering political agendas that consistently frame racialized people as outsiders to the Canadian polity stands in stark contrast to the omnipresent rhetoric of inclusiveness and multiculturalism. Smolash (2009) points out that until recently, multicultural civility provided a thin veneer over the racist notions of the nation-state. However, as anxieties and fears heighten around crime and security, the celebration of "ethnic difference" is replaced by a tribal, inward desire for homogeneity, accompanied by the violent expulsion of those who simply "do not belong." The reporting in Canadian newspapers about the "Toronto 18," an alleged terrorist cell, highlights how media racialization and criminalization lends legitimacy to state violence (Smolash 2009, 746). Thus, far from being innocuous, as we discuss further in Chapter 4, media institutions occupy an important role in the criminalization of racialized groups and in the racialization of crimes reported. Their representations of crime and criminals reinforce for the general public the "potential threat" that minority groups represent, thereby allowing their exclusion from mainstream society.

Various explanations have been put forward for understanding the criminalization of racialized individuals and groups. Barlow (2005) contends that as globalization destabilizes communities by sharpening social and economic inequality, it is racialized communities that suffer the most. The criminalization of racialized communities, often through the use of repressive force, is necessary in an era of globalization. Poor, racialized people are distinctly disadvantaged in a global marketplace where they are less able to access privileges that can provide a buffer against social, economic, and political pressures. For example, poverty and homelessness are cited as key factors in many Aboriginal women becoming involved in the criminal justice system (Koostachin 2012). Employment and unemployment rates for racialized and non-racialized Canadians highlight how the labour market is "colour coded," where racialized women experience the highest rates of unemployment and are more likely to be paid less when they are employed (Block and Galabuzi 2011). Racialized people's exclusion from access to the labour market, education, housing, and social services necessitates the use of state force to maintain order in racialized communities (Duster 1997; Mirchandani and Chan 2007). It should come as no surprise, therefore, that prisons and jails are composed disproportionately of non-white populations. Imprisonment is the default solution for capitalism's expendable, surplus, and predominantly racialized population (Wacquant 2001).

A complementary analysis is offered by critical criminologists examining the political economy of crime. They argue that governments declaring a "war on crime" or imposing "law and order" agendas are deflecting society's focus away from the economy and the state, which affects the way people understand where the real source of criminal victimization resides (Reiman 2007; Chambliss 1995). Governments are increasingly unable to manage or regulate the effects of the marketplace for white, middle-class people, and as a result, their overall standard of living has declined. The breakdown of society requires a new approach to governing, since citizens are no longer integrated through full employment and shared welfare rights, and criminal justice is unable to rehabilitate and reintegrate the identifiable minority of criminal offenders (Garland 2001). Crime, therefore, becomes "normalized" as part of the everyday risks whose harmful consequences need to be minimized (Garland 2001).

By creating a culture of fear about criminal victimization and suggesting that racialized people are to blame, politicians are able to capitalize on middle-class anxieties. This approach has also been effective in masking how exploitative the economic system has been toward both working- and middle-class white people. Murakawa (2005) points to the situation in the United States, where crime policy developed in a context where parties and legislators had incentives to put forward racial framings of the crime problem, and because the costs of the policies are "racially concentrated," there are few checks and balances on the "punitive bidding wars" that result. In this way, crime policy is both instrumental and deeply symbolic. The hyper-criminalization of racialized people is borne out of the racially inflected motivations of governments and elites appearing to "do something" about social unrest, economic chaos, and the insecurities of mostly white, middle-class people.

Nowhere is this more clearly displayed than in the current treatment of migrants and asylum seekers around the globe. The criminalization of migrants and refugees in Europe, Australia, and North America demonstrates the ways in which advanced democracies have reconstituted immigration and migration as a "crime problem," complete with systems of surveillance, technologies, and methods of governance that remarkably resemble the institution of criminal justice. In Canada, the intertwining of crime control and immigration control is evident in the arming of border guards, the use of high-tech surveillance technologies in policing the borders, the prompt removal of non-citizens convicted of a crime, and the automatic detention of migrants who arrive through irregular channels. Stumpf (2006) observes that these two systems are united by a similar social function of "acting as gatekeepers of membership" and defining the terms of social inclusion and exclusion. Richmond goes further in claiming that efforts to limit the flow of people escaping economic deprivation or political persecution are effectively "a form of global apartheid" (Richmond 2002, 709).

Anxieties and hostilities toward racialized migrants and refugees are borne out of a belief that "foreignness" is equated with dangerousness as well as a concern that "foreigners" would not be able to assimilate easily (Barmaki 2009). One of the central modes for articulating the transformations of contemporary societies is the representation of immigrants as deviant and threatening, along with linking immigration to crime (Melossi 2003). As a result, the mode of governance for many Western governments is one which abandons democratic, liberal values, and emphasizes a politics of fear of crime and security (Crawford 2002).

The combination of risk avoidance, institutionalized racism, and heightened criminalization has proven to be toxic for racialized communities. Fear of racialized groups is based less on their actual criminality and more on the general perception that they are potentially likely to engage in criminal activities, or other forms of deviant and anti-social behaviour. In response, the state manages these communities of the socially excluded not by increasing efforts to integrate them into the mainstream, or by restoring rights, but instead by constructing them as risks that need to be managed either through incapacitation or until they are able to self-regulate and reintegrate into the community (Fitzgibbon 2004). Whether it is the "war on crime," the "war on drugs," or the "war on terror," targeted racialized groups bear the brunt of the policies implemented by states in the name of public safety. Race has become *the* key risk factor in determining dangerousness and liability to criminalization in late modern society. In some cases, the commission of a criminal act is no longer necessary to demonstrate guilt. Mere membership in a group regarded to have a high probability of offending is sufficient for a pre-emptive strike by the state. Thus, being a Jamaican person in Toronto (D'Arcy 2007), an asylum seeker on a ship (Watson 2009), or an Arab or Muslim person crossing a border in Canada (Bhabha 2005) can lead to an assault on civil liberties, as due process takes a backseat to the many strategies of risk management invoked by the state in the name of safety and security.

The widespread use of racial profiling by various state enforcement agencies across most Western societies is testimony to the pervasive criminalization that racialized communities are experiencing. Although institutional discrimination is present in many different social systems, the impact of racial discrimination in the criminal justice system is particularly harmful and lasting (Tanovich 2008). While the rhetoric of safety legitimates the criminalization of racial groups, in practice, these processes reveal, more than anything, the powerlessness of these groups to challenge their treatment by the state.

CONCLUSION

This chapter highlighted the key concepts of race and racialization, and their connections to the concept of criminalization. It has tried to explain how race and racism in the Canadian criminal justice system are full of complexities and ambiguities insofar as the processes of racialization and criminalization work in tandem, often blurring the categories of offender and victim, and challenging us to rethink what constitutes criminal or deviant behaviour. Expressions of racism have become more complex as patterns of discrimination and inter-group conflict no longer adhere to a simple black/white dichotomy. Heightened concerns about immigration demonstrate the new patterns of hostility and conflict, where, for example, white Canadians have constructed themselves as victims of refugees and "illegal" immigrants (Campbell 2000).

Processes of racialization and criminalization are interconnected in the policies and practices of the justice system, and they intersect with other social institutions (e.g., media) in the perpetuation of racist attitudes and assumptions. The persistent othering of racialized groups is based on perceived and essentialized physical and cultural differences that mark them as objects in need of state control and surveillance. This is directly related to the invisibility and privileges of "whiteness" in discourses about race and crime. The struggle for racial equality in the criminal justice system necessarily entails overcoming racial stereotypes and prejudice, which cause undue harm to racialized communities. In the chapters to follow, we revisit some of these themes and issues through a closer examination of how different social groups are shaped by these processes, and how criminal justice institutions and practices continue to shape our ideas of crime and criminality.

NOTES

1 See Huffington Post, "Integrated prom in Wilcox County in Georgia deemed a success," April 29, 2013, http://www.huffingtonpost.com/2013/04/29/integrated-prom-wilcox-county-georgia_n_3178005.html (Accessed November 11, 2013).
2 See "Quebec soccer federation explains turban ban," Sportsnet.ca, June 3, 2013, http://www.sportsnet.ca/soccer/quebec-soccer-federation-explains-turban-ban/ (Accessed November 11, 2013).

DISCUSSION QUESTIONS

Can you recall any events reported in the news media involving racialized people and crime?

How might we begin a critical conversation about race and crime?

If racial difference is socially constructed, how can we change the way we think about race and crime?

Is the fear of racialized people a reasonable justification for their criminalization?

Provide examples of institutionalized racism in the context of education. How do you think these examples can be linked to crime rates?

What role, if any, should human rights play in the conversation on race and crime?

FURTHER READING

Covington, J. 1995. "Racial classification in criminology: The reproduction of racialized crime." *Sociological Forum* 10 (4): 547–668.

Crenshaw, K. 2011. "Twenty years of critical race theory: Looking back to move forward." *Connecticut Law Review* 43 (5): 1253–354.

Gould, S. 1996. *The Mismeasure of Man.* New York: Norton.

Hall, S., C. Critcher, T. Jefferson, J. Clarke, and B. Roberts. 1978. *Policing the Crisis*. London: MacMillan.
Satewich, V. 2000. "Whiteness limited: Racialization and the social construction of 'peripheral Europeans'." *Social History* 66: 271–90.

WEBSITES OF INTEREST

African Canadian Legal Clinic—http://www.aclc.net/
Anti-Racist Canada—http://anti-racistcanada.blogspot.ca/
Black History Canada—http://blackhistorycanada.ca/index.php?lang=en
Canadian Race Relations Foundation—http://www.crr.ca/
Colours of Resistance Archive—http://www.coloursofresistance.org/
Cultural Survival—http://www.culturalsurvival.org/
Get Diversity—http://www.getdiversity.com/
Native Law Centre—http://www.usask.ca/nativelaw/
Students Exploring Inequality in Canada—http://inequalitygaps.org/
The First Perspective—http://www.firstperspective.ca/

PART TWO

CONSTRUCTING CRIMINAL JUSTICE

The three chapters in this section focus on several key areas of contemporary discussion and debate related to race, crime, and criminal justice. Chapter 2 examines the role of intersectional analysis in demonstrating how race is intertwined and operates concurrently with other social relations such as gender, class, and sexuality, which collectively play an important part in shaping our understanding of crime and criminal justice outcomes and processes. Chapter 3 explores the relationship between competing and often contradictory identities or statuses—for example, "mentally ill" or "criminal"—and how they play out in the criminal justice system. Chapter 4 concerns the widely acknowledged and pivotal impact of mainstream media in shaping public perceptions of these issues. Through several case studies, we analyze how media representations of race and crime occupy a central role in criminal cases and in our understanding of these cases.

Throughout these next three chapters, we attempt to demonstrate the applicability of an intersectional approach to the analysis of race as it is intertwined with other social relations of power in all of our institutions. An intersectional lens makes visible the similarities and the differences among and between categories of marginalized people. It reveals the systemic tilt that is built into the criminal justice system, and the structured inequalities that are maintained through the policing and containment of "troublesome" people. In short, intersectionality illuminates the hegemonic but unstated and taken-for-granted ideas about who is a "real" criminal or victim and how race continues to matter in a neo-liberal world that tells us that we're all equal now.

CHAPTER TWO

INTERSECTIONALITY, CRIME, AND CRIMINAL JUSTICE

As we discussed in Chapter 1, the concept of intersectionality has been invaluable in revealing the interconnectedness of different forms of oppression and in demonstrating "that oppression cannot be reduced to one fundamental type" (Hill Collins 2000, 18). Intersectional perspectives challenge the essentialism of inter-gender and inter-racial analyses that render differences *among* women and *among* men, as well as the commonalities *between* them, invisible (Crenshaw 1989; Hill Collins 1990, 2000; Jhappan 1996). This is a crucial point to bear in mind, since most people who commit "street" crime,[1] as well as the victims of such crime, are marginalized in multiple ways. Consequently, some people are more likely to be viewed as "real" criminals, and others are more likely to be perceived as "legitimate" victims of crime.

INTERSECTIONALITY AND FEMINIST CRIMINOLOGIES

Historically, women lawbreakers were either invisible in analyses of crime and criminal justice because they were "too few to count" (Adelberg and Currie 1987, 1993) or they were depicted in unflattering ways as the product of bio- or psycho-genetic deficits (Lombroso and Ferrero 1895; Pollak 1961). For instance, they were deemed to lack a maternal instinct which would keep them in line, or they were considered to be at the mercy of bodily processes and cycles (e.g., lactation, menstruation, or menopause), which drove them to commit crimes. Feminist scholars and researchers were among the first to recognize the importance of analyzing women's lawbreaking and official responses to it from a gendered perspective. Since the late 1960s, they have contributed to an explosion of research and writing about criminalized women in Canada and other liberal states that has created the foundations of feminist criminologies.[2]

Nonetheless, the picture of the criminalized woman that emerges from the spate of feminist literature in recent decades is by no means a uniform or homogeneous one. While feminist scholars have challenged and rejected traditional conceptions of "the female offender," they themselves hold divergent views on how to interpret women's lawbreaking, and what to do about it. Moreover, feminist perspectives have by no means displaced the conventional bio- and psycho-genetic perspectives on women, crime, and justice that have historically shaped explanations of, and reactions to, women in conflict with the law.

Overall, however, feminists have produced path-breaking work that highlights the interconnectedness of class and gender, and more recently race and sexuality, in the constructions of and responses to women (and men) who commit crime and/or are victims of crime. Even a cursory look at crime statistics shows us that gender is central to the analysis of crime and justice. Historically, men have committed most offences recorded in Canada and other liberal states, and they continue to do so (Adelberg and Currie 1987; Smart 1976). Despite predictions made during the late twentieth century that "liberated" women were fast reaching equality with men in the criminal realm (Adler 1975), Canadian crime statistics show that men continue to comprise the vast majority of individuals who are criminally charged each year, and, in particular, that men commit a disproportionate amount of serious violent crime relative to women (Balfour and Comack 2006). In 2011, for instance, men accounted for 4 out of 5 adults charged, and 80 per cent of people accused of violent crime (Brennan 2012, 20).[3]

WHO IS AN (IN)CREDIBLE LAWBREAKER OR VICTIM OF CRIME?

If we apply an intersectional lens to the categories of "men" and "women," we discover important intra-category differences. Race matters. Generally speaking, racialized men and women who commit or are victims of crime have been treated differently from their white counterparts, other things being equal, and intersectional analysis helps us to highlight those differences (Chan and Mirchandani 2002; see also Thompson 2010). Despite what white and racialized people often have in common (e.g., a marginal social class position), racialized men and women are widely perceived as being more criminogenic and thus as more credible perpetrators of crime than are white men and women overall.

As we will discuss further in Chapter 6 the infamous case of Donald Marshall, a member of the Mi'kmaq First Nation in Nova Scotia who was wrongfully convicted of the murder of a young, black male acquaintance despite the admission of the white man who actually committed the killing, is a graphic illustration of how readily criminal justice agents and the general public presume guilt when a suspect is a racialized individual. Although he admitted committing the crime to others, Roy Ebsary lied to the police, and they then zeroed in on Marshall who was "known" to them because of previous minor incidents (Hickman 1989). The same tunnel vision functions to exclude white suspects from investigation. Many of the most infamous white, male serial rapists and murderers in Canada have escaped official scrutiny for prolonged periods of time because they did not fit the image of "the criminal." Paul Bernardo, Russell Williams, and most notably Robert Pickton all escaped detection for much longer than they should have (Oppal 2012).

In contrast, when racialized women and men report being criminally victimized, police and other legal agents are less likely to view them as "real" victims compared with their white counterparts (Comack 2012). Consider, for example, the disparate ways that authorities and the public responded to the following situations: reaction to the Montreal Massacre, in which 14 white, middle-class women engineering students were murdered in December 1989, and the ongoing crisis of hundreds of missing and murdered women across Canada, a disproportionate number of whom are racialized women. In the aftermath of the Montreal killings, officials at all levels immediately expressed horror and denounced the murders; the 14 women lay in state and members of the public were able to view their caskets and sign condolence books; legal and policy reforms, including the implementation of a federal gun registry, were enacted; and annual events on December 6 have been organized over the years to remind us that the Montreal Massacre is symbolic of the need to eliminate all violence against women (National Film Board of Canada 1990; Yeo 1991; Rosenberg 2003).[4]

In contrast, family members and friends of missing women in different jurisdictions across Canada fought for years with little success to persuade police to investigate the ongoing disappearances. In British Columbia, for example, women began "disappearing" from Vancouver's Downtown Eastside (DTES) during the late 1970s, but both the Vancouver Police Department (VPD) and the RCMP ignored early pleas to investigate missing women stories, rejecting the possibility that there was a pattern to the disappearances. Viewed retrospectively, we can pinpoint three main reasons for the police reluctance. The first is the belief that the women were not "ideal" victims (Lowman 2000; Razack 2000; Jiwani and Young 2006; Comack 2012). Most of the missing women were Aboriginal, survival sex workers, with histories of drug addiction, who had difficult and turbulent lives, though many were clearly still connected to the friends and family who reported them missing. From a police perspective, however, the disappearances of such women were a predictable consequence of the "high risk" lifestyle they had chosen.

The second cause of police inaction was the lack of sustained pressure from sources other than the women's friends, family members, and advocates. This absence of pressure was linked to a third important reason for the VPD's failure to investigate the increasing number of missing women in the DTES—the discourse of disposal that characterized public discussion and media coverage of the ongoing attempts by politicians, police, and residents' groups to move street prostitution out of residential areas (Lowman 2000, 1003–4). The dominant focus on getting rid of street prostitution arguably contributed to a sharp increase in the murders of sex workers on the streets of British Columbia from the 1980s onward (Lowman 2000, 1003–4). By the time police finally acknowledged that a serial killer might be at work, many more women had been murdered, something which could have been avoided if police had acted on the initial reports (Culhane 2003; Hugill 2010; Oppal 2012). Following the release of the Oppal report (2012), the VPD made a public apology to the families of the victims for not investigating much sooner the many reports of missing women (CBC News 2012b).

NORMATIVE EXPECTATIONS AND CRIMINAL JUSTICE

The question, then, is why Aboriginal, black, and other racialized women and men are consistently perceived as more credible perpetrators, and less credible victims, than white people. Considerable research by feminists and other critical scholars demonstrates that, historically, both lawbreakers and victims of crime have been categorized on the basis of their adherence, or lack of adherence, to normative standards of masculinity and femininity; that is, deeply entrenched beliefs enshrined in law and policy about how all women and all men ought to live their lives (Eaton 1986; Daly 1989; Hill Collins 1990; Roberts 1993; Kline 1993; Diduck 1998). These common-sense ideas about good and bad women and men, good and bad mothers and fathers, and good and bad wives and husbands have been naturalized, taken for granted, and unquestioned. They are also the basis for differentiating those who embrace "normality" from those who are either unwilling or unable to do so.

Moreover, racialized women and men are disproportionately more likely to fall into the "bad" categories than are their white counterparts (Kline 1993; Diduck 1998; Roberts 1993; Robson 2004). Intersectional analyses suggest that the perception of many racialized accused and racialized victims as "failures" is based on the belief that they are less likely than white people to observe the norms associated with the traditional nuclear family, organized around heterosexual marriage and a sexual division of labour. This reflects the impact of negative and intersecting assumptions about race, gender, class, and sexuality (Gavigan 1993; Kline 1994). With regard to sexuality, for example, (young) white men have been, and still are encouraged to sow their wild oats before they marry and settle down into monogamy. Likewise, some of the (young) white women who have "fallen" into sexual deviance have always been perceived as salvageable candidates for "sexual rehabilitation" and nuclear family life.

In contrast, racialized men and women have been viewed as inherently promiscuous and as such naturally propelled toward sexual deviance, making them unlikely prospects for monogamous marriage and life in a nuclear family. In the United States, and to a lesser extent in Canada, the images of the black man as a sexually animalistic rapist of white women (Davis 1981), of the black or Aboriginal woman as prostitute (Hill Collins 1990; Razack 2000), and of both as vectors of disease (especially sexually transmitted diseases such as HIV) are deeply rooted within public culture. As we discuss in Chapter 4, ever since the criminalization of the failure to disclose that one has AIDS to a (potential) sexual partner, in Canada and elsewhere, media coverage of prosecutions tends to focus primarily on racialized men (Dej and Kilty 2012; Miller 2005; Persson and Newman 2008).

It is important to bear in mind that, historically, normative standards of masculinity and femininity—how "normal" men and women should think and behave—have been depicted in absolute, universal terms. These essentialized conceptions of masculinity and femininity rest on the assumption that once properly developed, "normal" masculinity and femininity are the same and unchanging for all men and all women (Connell 2009; Comack 2008). As a result, the belief that there is only one acceptable form of masculinity or femininity has become hegemonic, and has been incorporated in law and policy, thereby "disqualifying" and marginalizing other conceptions of masculinity and femininity that exist in society at any given time. The reality, however, is that the reigning standards governing masculine and feminine behaviour have been most closely related to the lived experiences of white, middle-class, heterosexual men and women (Coontz 1992; Kline 1993).

This disjuncture raises the question of why normative expectations that only one segment of the population could consistently meet have continued to prevail in Canada and other liberal states. An important part of the answer seems to be that while a minority of the population in liberal states has always rejected and/or deliberately flouted the normative expectations governing masculinity and femininity, many others have accepted and aspired to live up to them, even though they were often unable to do so. This is not a matter of individual and psychological motivation and choice. Rather, as feminists and other critical scholars have demonstrated, the status quo in liberal democracies is reproduced most easily and effectively when the majority of people adopt the ideas of the ruling elites and believe that these are their own ideas. As long as those who are governed "consent" to the status quo, the use of coercive means to impose the ideas of the powerful on the population is unnecessary (Hall et al. 1978; Gavigan 1988; Kline 1993).

THE "BUT FOR" PHENOMENON

Historically, then, racialized people are less likely to meet the normative expectations embodied in dominant conceptions of masculinity and femininity, and thus are more readily seen as perpetrators of crime, and are less likely to be viewed as victims of crime than are white people. A second, perhaps more important, question is whether these longstanding ideas about femininity and masculinity continue to influence Canadians generally, and criminal justice decision makers specifically, now that neo-liberals have proclaimed the arrival of the age of equality. Some research suggests that they do, although not in exactly the same way as they did historically. Among other things, this research has revealed what might be called the "but for" phenomenon—men and women who meet all the historical criteria of masculinity and femininity associated with being white, middle class and heterosexual, except for one, and who are treated by members of elites and non-elites alike as if they *do* meet all the normative expectations. Barack Obama's presidential victory in 2008 is a prime example of the "but for" phenomenon. Except for race, Barack and Michelle Obama are like any white, upper-middle-class, heterosexual, married couple with two children and a dog. In this scenario, race inferiority becomes race neutrality. As Kimberle Crenshaw points out, however, while Obama's election in 2008 was a historic win, it was also accompanied by "a longstanding conservative project of associating colorblindness with racial enlightenment and racial justice advocacy with grievance politics" (2011, 1315).

Tim Wise (2009, 2010) makes a similar argument. He maintains that Barack Obama became the president of the United States in large part because he is simultaneously constructed as and performs as an exception to Black America. The Obama-as-exceptional construct serves to reinforce the stereotypical ideas that associate "blackness" with being criminal, poor, culturally and morally inferior, and so on. Others have argued that gender and sexuality are central to Obama's acceptance and electability. He is masculine enough to not be seen as queer, yet feminine enough to avoid being seen as the threatening black male. These ideas about the politics of recognition and inclusion in the US context are important to the analysis of how race operates in Canada through, often symbolic, inclusion of assimilated racialized minorities who legitimate white settler national progress.

The "but for" phenomenon has several implications with respect to understanding the contemporary administration of criminal justice. First, not all racialized groups, or all members of racialized groups, are equally oppressed or at risk of criminalization at any given historical moment (Mosher 1998). Members of a racialized group that is reviled at one point in time may achieve "but for" status at another point in time, and vice versa. Second, and relatedly, we need to bear in mind that "whiteness" per se is not an automatic guarantee of lenient treatment in the criminal justice system. In Canada, "white" ethnic minorities (e.g., Irish, Italian, Portuguese, "Slavic") have been targeted historically similar to the Chinese, Japanese, and other racialized groups (Adamoski et al. 2002; McLaren 2002, 2005). Likewise, in the contemporary United States, lesbians sentenced to death, many of whom are white, are significantly over-represented on death row (Farr 2000; Robson 1998).

Finally, as the case of O.J. Simpson illustrates, the "but for" status is always a tenuous one. For many years, Simpson was a football hero, a Hollywood star and celebrity who lived the American Dream as if he were a white man (Johnson and Roediger 1997). He divorced his first wife, an African American, married a conventionally beautiful white woman, had children with her, and lived in luxury. When his marriage broke down, at least in part because of ongoing wife abuse and infidelity, his dream life began to disintegrate, and he was ultimately arrested and tried on charges of murdering his ex-wife, Nicole Brown Simpson, and her friend, Ron Goldman. Although he was acquitted of the charges, Simpson's "but for" status among white Americans was essentially rescinded, as his blackness, and the association between race, predatory sexuality, and criminality, took centre stage (Morrison and Lacour 1997).

RETHINKING THE "CRIMINAL–VICTIM" DICHOTOMY

A third issue of concern to contemporary scholars who conduct intersectional analyses of crime and justice is the traditional divide between "criminal" and "victim," which suggests that an individual or group can have only one identity. Since the 1990s, feminists have produced a growing body of research that challenges this dualism, by demonstrating how the criminal histories of women and men are frequently intertwined in various ways with their own, often horrific, histories of victimization. This research focuses primarily on women's "pathways" into the criminal justice and penal systems, and their social location on a victimization–criminalization continuum (Comack 1996; Balfour and Comack 2006; Balfour 2008).

Some feminists acknowledge the contribution of "blurred boundaries" research to the field of criminology, but worry that "[a] seamless web of victimization and criminalization tends to produce accounts which focus on victimization and leave little agency, responsibility, or meaning to women's lawbreaking" (Daly 1998, 149–50). Others do not talk about a continuum but rather about the multiple statuses that each individual or group embodies at a given time, and the ways in which they are connected or disconnected at a given moment (Bonnycastle 2012). Thus, it is possible to be simultaneously threatening and threatened. It is also possible to be dangerous at one point in time and endangered at another (Donzelot 1980; Kilty and Frigon 2006). For example, Kevin Bonnycastle (2012) conducted life-history interviews with 14 men, most Aboriginal, who had committed one of the most reviled crimes—stranger rape that sometimes led to the death of the woman who was sexually assaulted. She found that the majority of the men had also experienced and/or witnessed serious physical and/or sexual abuse in their own lives. This finding led her to conclude that using the criminal–victim dichotomy to explain these men served to dehumanize them because they were only visible as criminals, whereas recognizing their multiple identities had the opposite effect, by contextualizing, but not condoning or excusing, their violence against women. Deconstructing the criminal–victim dichotomy thus helps us understand why some people are more likely to be viewed solely as criminal monsters and less likely to be seen as victims.

It is important to note, however, that even middle-class, white, heterosexual women can find themselves in the "undeserving" category of offender if they seriously breach the norms of femininity and propriety. In the Canadian context, for instance, Karla Homolka has achieved iconic status as the epitome of the "monstrous feminine" for her participation in the killings of several women, including her younger sister (Kilty and Frigon, 2006).[5] Initially, she was constructed within the legal system and in the media as a fairy-tale princess who thought she had married a prince, but he turned out to be an abusive husband who coerced her to commit acts of sexual sadism and murder.

Ultimately, this construction of Homolka as a victim was erased and replaced by the enduring image of Homolka as an evil witch who manipulated criminal justice officials into granting her an undeserved plea agreement (Kilty and Frigon 2006). In exchange for testifying against her former husband, she was allowed to enter a guilty plea to manslaughter charges and was released from prison after serving a 12-year sentence, whereas Paul Bernardo was convicted of first-degree murder, declared a dangerous offender, and sentenced to life imprisonment. Many Canadians were outraged at what they perceived as an appalling leniency extended to Karla Homolka by the criminal justice authorities (Pearson 1997). Arguably, however, if she is viewed as *both* endangered and dangerous, she should receive a lesser sentence than Paul Bernardo; to give her an identical sentence would be to punish her more severely than him (Kilty and Frigon 2006).

Spatial location is also relevant to the issue of who is considered a "real" victim. For instance, we can see the disqualification of victims in "spaces of racialized poverty" (Comack 2012, 151) such as Vancouver's Downtown Eastside, where (as discussed previously) a "discourse of disposal" (Lowman 2000, 1003–4) dehumanizes (racialized) women and men. Because many of the women in these inner-city spaces are sex workers, they are reluctant to actually report victimization to the police, especially assaults which occurred when they were engaged in criminalized activities, and if they do report, their complaints are not taken seriously. We saw this with the missing women in Vancouver's DTES, who were not deemed to be legitimate victims until police were forced to act (Culhane 2003; Oppal 2012). Police tend to assume that a woman who sells sex enters into a contract with her clients in which she "consents" to the subsequent treatment she receives (Lowman 2000; Razack 2000). This means that men, especially white men, can routinely enter "spaces of racialized poverty," buy sex and drugs, and return to the (white) suburbs where they live. Moreover, they can act with relative impunity while they are in that racialized space. As Sherene Razack puts it, "The contract cancels the violence ..." (2000, 107; see also Lowman 2000).

Moreover, the failure of police to investigate reports of missing women in the DTES was not an aberration. The disqualification of racialized victims is systemic throughout the criminal justice system, as the case of Pamela George illustrates so poignantly (Razack 2000). Like most people, Pamela George had multiple identities. She was a woman of the Saulteaux (Ojibway) nation, the common-law wife of a white man, Lenny Hall, the mother of two young children, and, from time to time, a sex worker in Regina's inner city. On Easter weekend, 1995, one of those occasions when she was working on the inner-city "Stroll" ended with her murder. Her killers, Steven Kummerfield and Alex Ternowetsky, were two 19-year-old white, middle-class, university athletes, who, as it turned out, moved comfortably back and forth between the "degenerate," racialized spaces of the inner city, and the "respectable" white spaces of suburbia and the university. On April 17, 1995, the two men drank heavily, picked up Pamela George on the Regina Stroll, drove to an isolated area on the edge of the city, forced her under threat of death to perform oral sex, and then savagely beat her, leaving her face-down in the mud to die (Razack 2000, 91–92).

A month later, the RCMP arrested and charged Kummerfield and Ternowetsky with the murder of Pamela George.[6] Not surprisingly, "[t]he arrest of two young, white, middle-class men for the murder of an Aboriginal woman working as a prostitute sent shock waves through the white population of this small prairie city" (Razack 2000, 92). Ultimately, the two accused were convicted on the lesser charge of manslaughter and sentenced to six and a half years in prison, a sentence that took into account "the time of twenty months already served" (Razack 2000, 129). While the accused were found guilty and received penitentiary sentences, what makes the administration of criminal justice in the Pamela George case so instructive is the way in which all of the legal actors viewed her identity as a "prostitute" as her "master sta- tus," thereby linking her to criminality and diminishing or even disqualifying her status as a "real" victim. It took the police a month to charge the two white men, because they initially assumed that since George was a "prostitute," the killer must be one of the "usual suspects"—either an Aboriginal man, or George's "racially tainted by association" spouse, Lenny Hall. At trial, both the Crown and the defence insisted on the relevance of George's status as a "prostitute" to the trial's outcome, and the judge "sparked a public furor" after he instructed the jury to factor George's identity as a "prostitute" into their deliberations (Razack 2000, 92). In short, as Razack (2000) argues,

> Ultimately, it was Pamela George's status as a prostitute, hence not as a human being, and her belonging to spaces beyond universal justice that limited the extent to which the violence done to her body could be recognized and the accused made accountable for it. (123)

INTERSECTIONALITY AND EQUALITY

Notwithstanding the argument of feminists and other critical scholars that "old" ideas about masculinity and femininity remain highly influential in the contemporary neo-liberal context, many people in Canada believe that a focus on intersectionality is passé. They assume that under the Charter of Rights and Freedoms all Canadians have achieved equality of opportunity, and are now on an equal playing field. Current law and policy are neutral, which renders historical markers of difference and discrimination, such as race, class, and gen- der, irrelevant in our post-feminist, post-racial society. In other words, we all determine our lives through the choices we make, and must all be held equally accountable if we make "bad" choices, such as committing crimes. These are pervasive beliefs despite considerable evidence that structured inequalities not only continue to exist, but are also widening in Canada and elsewhere.

What explains this contradiction? Some researchers argue that although ideas about equality are dominant in public culture, law, and policy, "old" ideas about difference continue to circulate as well. One major consequence is that the official emphasis on the (formal) equality of all people makes it virtually impossible for marginalized people and their advocates to make the case that their marginality is linked to structured inequalities (racial, sexual, class), rather than their own failings. As Crenshaw puts it,

> Barack Obama's shattering of the political glass ceiling can be anal- ogized to the 'White Only' signs that came down in the 1960s and

1970s. With the collapse of [racial] segregation came the confidence in some quarters that formal equality alone constituted the ultimate realization of racial justice. Yet, this faith in formal equality's triumph over white supremacy was unwarranted, formal equality did little to disrupt ongoing patterns of institutional power and the reproduction of differential privileges and burdens across race (2011, 1312).

Another consequence of equating equality with *formal* equality is that once formal equality is achieved, the focus becomes sameness and the identical treatment of everyone. But if inequalities related to gender, race, class, and sexuality remain, insisting that everyone must receive identical treatment actually entrenches and exacerbates the existing inequalities. For instance, black men who drive expensive cars in white, middle-class neighbourhoods will be stopped routinely by police simply because they fit the image of "the criminal." Why would a black man be in a white residential area unless he is up to no good? In contrast, white men who enjoy historical privilege because of their "whiteness" can be constructed as victims of reverse discrimination if they drive expensive cars in poor, racialized areas in search of drugs or sex and are stopped by police (Glover 2007, 243; Razack 2000).

A different conception of equality—one that links equality to equal life-chances for all, for example—would highlight the reality that we do not yet live in a society that is race (or gender, class, and sexuality) neutral. Arguably, then, there is a continuing need for intersectional analyses of social issues in Canada and other Western states. In addition, it is crucial to examine how intersectionality plays out not only in the criminal justice system but also simultaneously in other institutional sites. With that in mind, we turn to consider the relationship between the mental health and criminal justice systems.

NOTES

1 "Street" crime generally refers to what is defined as crime in the Canadian Criminal Code (RSC 1985, c. 46).

2 See, for example, Burgess-Proctor (2006); Comack (1996); Comack and Brickey (2007); Daly (1994); Daly and Chesney-Lind (1988); Daly and Maher (1998); Gavigan (1983; 1988); Heidensohn (1985); Naffine (1987; 1996); Roberts (1993); Smart (1976); Rafter and Heidensohn (1995); Snider (1994).

3 A moral panic about what was perceived to be a dramatic increase in serious violent crime (i.e., homicide) being committed by female youth through the 1990s was not borne out; however, the adoption of zero tolerance policies in schools, as well as changes in police charging practices, has produced a noticeable increase in the number of female youth being charged with common assault (Barron and Lacombe 2005).

4 We are not suggesting that the official reaction to the Montreal Massacre was in any way unwarranted or inappropriate. Rather, we want to highlight the very different official responses to two cases involving mass violence against women.

5 The young women were Leslie Mahaffy, Kristen French, and Tammy Homolka.
6 The Canadian Criminal Code sets out four categories of culpable homicide: first-degree murder, second-degree murder, manslaughter, and infanticide. See RSC 1985, c. 46, s.229–38.

DISCUSSION QUESTIONS

If you went to bed as a white, middle-class man with no disabilities and woke up the next day as a black, lower-class woman with mental health issues, how, if at all, would your life change?

Do you agree with the argument that "old" ideas about who is a "real" criminal or "real" victim continue to influence the present-day administration of criminal justice?

Can you think of any Canadian examples of racialized individuals or groups who have "but for" status?

Should "whiteness" be part of the conversation about "race" and the criminal justice system?

FURTHER READING

Hill Collins, P. 2000. *Black Feminist Thought: Knowledge, Consciousness, and the Politics of Empowerment*. 2nd ed. New York: Routledge.

Hill Collins, P. 2004. *Black Sexual Politics: African Americans, Gender and the New Racism*. New York: Routledge.

MacDonald, G., R.L. Osborne, and C.C. Smith, eds. 2005. *Feminism, Law, Inclusion: Intersectionality in Action*. Toronto: Sumach Press.

McCall, L. 2009. "The complexity of intersectionality." In *Intersectionality and Beyond: Law, Power and the Politics of Location* ed. E Grabham et al. London: Routledge.

Taylor, Y., S. Hines, and M.E. Casey, eds. 2011. *Theorizing Intersectionality and Sexuality*. New York: Palgrave Macmillan.

WEBSITES OF INTEREST

Gender-Based Analysis Plus—http://www.swc-cfc.gc.ca/gba-acs/index-eng.html
Gender Focus—A Canadian Feminist Blog—http://www.gender-focus.com/
Native Women's Association of Canada—http://www.nwac.ca/
Ontario Women's Justice Network—http://owjn.org/owjn_2009/
Status of Women Canada—http://www.swc-cfc.gc.ca/index-eng.html
The Everyday Sexism project—http://www.everydaysexism.com/
West Coast Leaf—http://www.westcoastleaf.org/

CHAPTER THREE

RACE, CRIME, AND MENTAL HEALTH

Patricia Hill Collins argued that we not only have to analyze "intersecting oppressions," we also need to examine what she calls the "matrix of domination" or "how these intersecting oppressions are actually organized" (2000, 18). Of relevance to our discussion of crime and criminal justice is the "psy complex"—the vast network of psychiatric facilities and attendant professionals and experts that was created during the first half of the twentieth century in most liberal states, and then transformed from the 1970s onwards through an emphasis on the deinstitutionalization and return of the "mentally ill" to the community.

ANTI-PSYCHIATRY AND CRITIQUES OF THE PSY COMPLEX

Until the late twentieth century, we find critiques of the psy complex, but virtually no literature that illuminates how intersecting oppressions (gender, race, class, sexuality) were organized within it. Anti-psychiatry movements, which flowered during the 1960s and early 1970s in Canada and other Western democracies, generated a plethora of critical analyses of "total institutions" like psychiatric hospitals and prisons (Goffman 1962; Laing 1965; Szasz 1970). These scholars and activists presented a generalized critique that focused on the ways in which marginalized people were routinely labelled and often stigmatized for life by authoritative officials, particularly psychiatrists and psychologists. Psychiatric labelling was regarded by many critics as pseudoscientific—it medicalized people unnecessarily and failed to consider the social causes of madness while giving greater control to the role of professionals (Pilgrim 2007). Critics challenged the psy experts who had successfully carved out professional monopolies based on their claimed knowledge of madness, and the expertise to respond to it, as encapsulated in the Diagnostic and Statistical Manual of Mental Disorders (DSM) (Ericson 1976; Rosenhan 1973; Steadman 1972; Ennis and Litwack 1974).[1] While critics don't deny the existence of states of suffering, many questioned how psychiatry interprets such states. These critical analyses continue in the present day, with scholars challenging "the association of mental health service users with 'dangerousness' and the constant coupling of cruel and murderous activities with 'mental illness,' as though 'bad' is tantamount to mad" in debates about the future direction of mental health practice (Beresford 2002).

Although the anti-psychiatry literature was an important antidote to dominant conceptions of mental health, it contained virtually no discussion of the gendered, racialized, and/or sexualized dimensions of madness. It was not until the emergence of new critiques of psychiatry in the late 1980s and onwards that greater attention was placed on anti-racism, feminism and user-centredness (Fernando 1988; Ussher 1991; LeFrancois, Menzies, and Reaume 2013). Critics alleged that mental health services were contaminated by institutional racism, sexism, and the marginalization of service users' own views on their distress. As with the analysis of crime and criminal justice, feminists were among the first scholars and activists to address the gendered nature of definitions and responses to "mental illness" (Ehrenreich and English 1978; Showalter 1985; Busfield 1996). Gender comparisons revealed both similarities and differences; for instance, women and men with mental health problems often had social and economic marginality in common, but received very different psy diagnoses, which feminists attributed to the operation of the same normative expectations about masculinity and femininity that we discussed in Chapter 2 (Chan, Chunn, and Menzies 2005; Ussher 2011). That is, women and men who transgressed the boundaries of appropriate gender norms were more likely to receive a psychiatric diagnosis than those who did not. For example, crimes committed by women were often regarded as signs of madness, whereas for men, their crimes were typically not viewed as a sign of mental illness, since the use of violence was considered "normal."

Feminists have also been instrumental in demonstrating how efforts to domesticate and confine women in the private sphere were made possible through sexist notions that women were prone to hysteria, or were not fit for the labour market (Bankey 2001). Finally, women who did seek out mental health services from psychiatrists and other professionals would confront a system that pathologized women's behaviour and over-medicated their problems (Kitzinger and Perkins 1993; Penfold and Walker 1984). These contributions have been important in highlighting the sexism of mental health definitions, models, and practices, yet they are at risk of producing other exclusions by failing to account for the specificity of women's lives.

Feminists have produced much less work on how race, class, and sexuality influence psy decision making, and most of the literature that does exist has been produced outside of Canada. Yet, historical work, both feminist and non-feminist, consistently points to a racial/ethnic, as well as a gender, bias in Western psychology. In the United States, for instance, blacks have been viewed "as less evolved psychologically than whites, and like women, 'prone' to developing mental illness" (Cermele, Daniels, and Anderson 2001, 232). Clearly, racism, along with class or sexuality, is an important factor in the incidence of mental health, and these intersecting social relations also shape how mental health service providers respond to different groups.

RACIAL DISCRIMINATION, RACIAL DISPARITIES, AND MENTAL HEALTH

The literature on race and the mental health system suggests that racial discrimination plays a role in the development of mental illness, particularly for racialized women, while racism and racial disparities in the mental health system affect the level of services that racialized people receive. Noh et al.'s (1999) study of over 600 Southeast Asian refugees in Canada found that refugees who had experienced racial discrimination experienced higher levels of depression than refugees who did not report such experiences. Furthermore, immigrants and refugees are at greater risk of developing mental health problems when their migration experience also includes a decline in socio-economic status, inability to speak the host country's language, stress and trauma from pre-migration conditions, separation from family, and feelings of isolation (Naidoo 1992, 172). Having their self-esteem severely undermined by these factors creates debilitating effects, and for immigrant and refugee women, their emotional burden is compounded by increased isolation because they are more likely to be at home, in the private sphere, for longer periods of time and they bear the major burden of ensuring the psychological well-being of the family (Naidoo 1992).

These findings are consistent with other studies examining the psychological cost of being a target of discrimination, and point to a link between racial discrimination and psychological distress (Rollock and Gordon 2000; Hyman 2009). Racism is implicated in higher levels of anxiety, substance abuse, self-harm, and negative coping strategies (Hyman 2009). At a community level, racism takes away from the capacity of the community to promote the development of its residents, and affects the overall levels of mental health functioning within the community (Rollock and Gordon 2000). A recent report by the Ontario Human Rights Commission (2012) indicates that racial discrimination and barriers to integration for immigrants remain pressing mental health issues.

In many cultures, there is a significant stigma associated with disclosing mental health issues, and the experiences of both public stigma and self-stigma only aggravate the challenges immigrants and racialized people already face. Stigma is a common problem for many people with mental health problems, as then-Chief Justice Lamer acknowledged in *R. v. Swain* when he remarked that "for centuries, persons with a mental disability have been systematically isolated, segregated from the mainstream of society, devalued, ridiculed, and excluded from participation in ordinary social and political processes" (*R. v. Swain*, 973–74). However, for racialized people, different cultural traditions can result in more severe stigma. For example, strong family connections within Asian cultures locate the person with a mental illness as a member of a larger group, and the stigma of illness therefore is attached not just to the individual, but to the entire collective unit (Ng 1997). Yang (2007) states that feelings of shame along with discrimination against individuals with mental illness and their families are common, and can cause delays in seeking help, underutilization of services, and non-compliance with mental health treatment.

Differential treatment on the basis of race in the mental health system also significantly impacts the general mental health of a racialized community. Many scholars point out that concepts like "mental disorder," "coping," and "normal" are normatively defined by service providers, based on Western notions of mental health and illness that emphasize individual autonomy, efficiency, and self-esteem (Fernando 2012). Wong and Tsang (2004) concur that these are extremely value-laden notions that characterize North American culture, but may not be cross-culturally transferable. Non-Western traditions of mental health tend to emphasize "balance, harmony and stability of the outer world of relationships"—beliefs that are deemed a poor fit with Western approaches to the development of good mental health (Fernando 2012, 114). In addition, racist theories about the psychological development of non-white groups—which have deep, historical roots that, for example, saw Asians as incapable of suffering from depression because they were psychologically underdeveloped and non-Europeans as mentally degenerate because they lacked "culture"—continue to shape psychiatric and therapeutic attitudes about the mental health of racialized groups (Fernando 2012, 115). In a survey conducted with racialized Canadians, respondents noted how symptoms of depression can result in being labelled an "angry black woman," or how doctors assume that it is acceptable to treat immigrant women in a patronizing and condescending manner (Ontario Human Rights Commission 2012). Similarly, the indigenous psychologist Roland Chrisjohn has documented how Aboriginal people, particularly residential school survivors, are more likely to be pathologized as sick individuals than normalized as survivors of institutionally generated trauma (Chrisjohn and Young 2006).

Various scholars argue that psychiatry, as a social institution and a set of practices, perpetuates racist assumptions in its methods of evaluation, observation, research, and treatment (Knowles 1996; Hicks 2004). Fernando (1988, 54) argues that what is considered "normal" is the "white" point of view, which is used as the standard to measure everyone else, but research based on racial groups, on the contrary, applies to those groups alone. A good example of this is evident in close readings of the DSM, which reveal the extent to which race, ethnicity, and sexuality receive specific mention. For instance, researchers who conducted an analysis of how gender and race/ethnicity are constructed in the case studies in the DSM-IV casebook, which is used for clinical training, found that the ostensibly neutral case studies were actually suffused with racial and gender markers (Cermele, Daniels, and Anderson 2001). As a result, racialized people appeared to be pathological relative to the "cultural construction of 'whiteness' as the normative point of reference," and images of men and women with mental illness were "consistent with our cultural constructions of men as subject and woman as object" (ibid., 244). These racialized and gendered perceptions not only exacerbate popular misconceptions, inaccuracies, and stereotypes, but they can also lead to the misdiagnosis of patients (Williams and Williams-Morris 2000). Studies in the United States have demonstrated that paranoid schizophrenia is over-diagnosed in African Americans while affective disorders are under-diagnosed, and that misdiagnoses are common even when formal diagnostic criteria are applied (Loring and Powell 1988; Neighbors et al. 1989). The opposite is true for white people, who are more likely to be diagnosed with a mood disorder but less likely to be diagnosed with schizophrenia (Neighbors et al. 2003).

The lack of equity in mental health service delivery is a well-documented phenomenon in many Western countries. The needs of racialized people are not adequately met, and despite various reforms to policies and practices, the issue of inequalities in care persists. Racialized health disparities, or the "biological expressions of race relations," have their roots in structural discrimination, racism, and white privilege (Krieger 2006; Patychuk 2011). Many scholars have thus highlighted the need to understand how race relations, and processes of racialization, shape health outcomes for different groups to promote equity in health. Yet research with medical practitioners in Canada points to a medical culture that denies the existence of bias, prejudice, and discrimination. In Beagan and Kumas-Tan's (2009) study with family physicians, differences of race, class, and sexuality were not considered to cause any tensions in the medical practices of nearly half of the participants interviewed, while others said that these differences were relevant to genetics or physiology, but did not have any social importance. The belief that doctors are immune from racial bias was also evident in another study with residents who saw cultural differences as irrelevant to medical practice, and while they were aware that racial bias existed elsewhere, they did not believe it affected their interactions with patients (Lingard, Tallett, and Rosenfield 2002).

A similar finding was noted in Tang and Browne's (2008) study of Aboriginal patients where they found that health-care providers asserted that "everyone was treated the same," inferring that everyone received *equally good care*, regardless of background. However, not acknowledging the role of racial and cultural differences can lead to poorer outcomes for patient care in racialized communities since a patient's social experiences and influences are not factored into the understanding of patterns related to seeking help, access to treatment, and the experiences and outcomes of these processes (Beagan and Kumas-Tan 2009, 27). Tang and Browne (2008, 117) add that by adopting the discourse of sameness, health-care providers may be unknowingly perpetuating further inequities, by discounting processes of racialization and racism in the provision of health care. Such an approach fails to recognize how broader racial inequalities mean that not everyone is equally able to make the same choices, or has the same opportunities.

Research conducted with members of racialized groups in Canada indicates that they do believe there are significant differences in the treatment they receive. Being denied access to health care, having one's illness minimized, or being racially profiled in the clinical setting as a potential troublemaker are common complaints made by Aboriginal patients in Tang and Browne's (2008) study. Upadhya's (2011) study with Indo-Caribbean Canadians found similar results, with some of her participants complaining that they were not offered concrete support, or the kind of support they required. In the *Building Bridges, Breaking Barriers Access Project* (2003), patients also cite language barriers, the lack of outreach initiatives or service promotion for Aboriginal and racialized communities, poor referral relationships, and the lack of awareness of community needs as significant barriers to equitable access to mental health services in Canada. The World Health Organization has also identified several ways in which racial discrimination can occur in the context of providing mental health services. They point to higher rates of involuntary admission, interpreting social and cultural norms of behaviour as signs of mental disorders, involuntary treatment in mental health institutions, and higher rates of arrest of certain populations for minor behaviour problems as some of the exclusionary practices that take place (WHO 2005).

In the UK, where a significant body of research on race and mental illness exists, and where the problem of institutional racism in the mental health system has been openly acknowledged, efforts to address racial disparities have adopted a complex and multilayered approach, with the idea of cultural competency training at the core (Bhui, Ascoli, and Nuamh 2012). In Canada, many mental health organizations, such as the Ontario Federation of Community Mental Health and Addiction Programs, have called for the adoption of a cultural competence approach to better serve racialized communities. This approach involves incorporating anti-racist and anti-oppression standards of inclusiveness, diversity, and the valuing of cultural differences in the provision of mental health care with the aim of improving quality of care and health outcomes for racialized populations (*Embracing Cultural Competence in the Mental Health and Addiction System* 2009). It is not, however, without its critics, as the lack of research, the lack of consensus on defining terms such as "cultural sensitivity" or "culturally appropriate," the lack of knowledge and skills to adequately care for racialized populations, and the reinforcement of biases and stereotypes have been voiced as significant barriers to incorporating this approach into the mental health care system (Gregg and Saha 2006). Others argue that moving toward a cultural competence approach is an ongoing process, but not doing anything is no longer an option, since the impact of discriminatory mental health treatment on racialized communities cannot be ignored.

As the discussion in this section highlights, racism in the mental health sector has deleterious effects on individual mental health as well as the overall health of racialized communities. However, addressing issues of race or ethnicity is not enough, since racism is only one form of bias that distorts our understanding of the mental health system. Sexism and other forms of discrimination also shape experiences and outcomes, and need to be considered alongside racism in the development of mental health policies and practices. Wong and Tsang's (2004) study of immigrant Korean women in Toronto found that a heterogeneity of views, beliefs, values, and practices exist among the women, despite the fact that their research participants shared a lot of demographic similarities. Their complex social and personal realities stress the limitations of universal definitions and criteria for understanding their mental health issues (Wong and Tsang 2004). This claim is particularly salient in the context of understanding the relationship between mental illness, crime, and race.

MAD OR BAD? CATEGORIZING DUAL DEVIANTS

There have been growing concerns in Canada and elsewhere about the prevalence of individuals with mental health issues coming into contact with the criminal justice system. A minority of men and women who commit a crime, but who are also perceived to be in mental distress, end up in the hybrid mental health/criminal justice system for forensic assessment. Most often, the purpose of the assessment is to determine the fitness of the lawbreaker to stand trial—did they know at the time they committed the crime that it was wrong? If the psy assessors find that the accused lacked the *mens rea*, or the intent to commit the crime, they are sent to a forensic facility for treatment, or perhaps released with conditions until they are found fit. A verdict of "not criminally responsible on account of mental disorder" (NCRMD) means that the person is unable to understand the nature of the criminal proceedings and the possible consequences, or is unable to communicate with his or her lawyer (Criminal Code, R.S.C. 1985, c.-46, s. 672.34). However, not everyone who enters the criminal justice system with a mental disorder will be given an NCRMD determination. Sometimes, an accused goes to trial without a psy evaluation and is convicted, but the trial judge requests a forensic assessment before sentencing to determine risks of re-offending and treatment needs.

In Canada, several high profile cases involving dual deviants have increased public awareness of mentally disordered offenders. In some cases, it has led to various campaigns for increased surveillance and regulation of these individuals, and to greater demands for the rights of victims (CBC News 2013c). For example, the cases of Allan Schoenborn and Vincent Li[2] have triggered significant public reaction to concerns that victims in these cases were not adequately acknowledged. They also highlight the oftentimes tense relationship between criminal justice and mental health systems in determining the appropriate management of these individuals.

These dual deviants raise the question of whether being officially categorized as both criminal and mentally ill overrides any other negative identities that an individual has acquired (e.g., gender, racial, sexual), and thereby renders intersectional analysis irrelevant. A considerable body of research suggests that the answer is "no," that it is impossible to explain differential mental health diagnoses and treatments without analyzing the interlocking gender and class differences that underpin them (Chunn and Menzies 1998; Chan, Chunn, and Menzies 2005). Since men are more involved in criminal activity than women, particularly in interpersonal crimes, responses by criminal justice and mental health officials vary. Research has shown that even though there appear to be no overall gender differences in rates of mental disorders, gender assumptions based on normative expectations of male and female behaviour influence criminal justice outcomes and mental health dispositions (Peter 2006; Smart 1995; Offen 1986). Women are more likely to be diagnosed with depression and anxiety disorders, while men have higher rates of substance abuse and antisocial disorders (Mendelson et al. 2008). Women are also more likely to be given a mental health placement, while men are often imprisoned when they commit similar criminal acts (Baskin et al. 1989). Interestingly, Pollack's (2005) study of female prisoners in Canada found that rather than empowering or supporting the women, mental health practices in corrections were often used to regulate women prisoners through the overuse of psychiatric labels, which would then require the female prisoners to complete a treatment regime.

While there is much less research on the relationship between race and mental health assessments in the context of criminal offending, the extant literature indicates that assumptions about race are also important in explaining disparities in the disposition of dual deviants (Thompson 2010; Menzies and Chunn 2012). Statistics in Western Europe and the United States point routinely to higher rates of black offenders being imprisoned or admitted to secure psychiatric facilities (Boast and Chesterman 1995; Hampton, Chafetz, and White 2010; Vinkers et al. 2010). Black men are also more likely to be arrested for behavioural problems and referred for inpatient evaluations (Pinals et al. 2004). Many scholars acknowledge that racial stereotypes about black people, particularly black men, as more prone to violence operate both consciously and unconsciously in diagnostic judgments and in the provision of treatment needs (Abreu 1999; Foulks 2004; Pinals et al. 2004). As a result, there is a greater likelihood of interpreting crimes by black people as criminal and dangerous, rather than as a symptom of mental illness, even though there is evidence to suggest that black people experience higher rates of mental distress than whites (Thomas, Stubbe, and Pearson 1999; Schultz et al. 2000). Massoglia (2008) notes that while imprisoned, many black offenders develop mental health problems that are not addressed, leading to increased likelihood of repeated incarceration after release. The research strongly suggests that differential treatment on the basis of race contributes to the higher rates of confinement of mentally ill, racialized people in either prison or secure facilities. Finally, racial disparities are also evident in the over-representation of black, mentally ill, death-row prisoners in the United States (Cunningham and Vigen 2002).

DIAGNOSING DANGEROUSNESS: MENTAL ILLNESS AND VIOLENCE

Mental illness has consistently been associated with violence over time. The image invoked by the notion of criminal madness is frequently one of an unhinged and unpredictable killer, who is often a racialized man (e.g., the case of Vincent Li). According to Covey (2008–9), these images are entrenched in the popular culture of Canada and other Western countries, and heavily influence public perceptions of dangerousness and the law's treatment of mad criminals. Efforts to understand the connection between mental illness and violent criminality have led to numerous studies seeking to locate various causal factors of violence as well as the prevalence of violence by people who are mentally ill. Most studies agree that people with mental disorders are not at any greater risk of violence than the rest of the population, and, in fact, are more likely to be criminally victimized (Stuart 2003; Peay 2011). Others point out that mental disorders do not cause crime, and that the causes of violence are similar to those experienced by the rest of the population—socio-demographic and socio-economic factors such as age, gender, and class status (Peay 2011, 54). Any link between mental disorder and violent behaviour, according to Monahan (2007), can only be understood in relative terms, since the majority of people with mental illnesses are not violent. Prins (2005) cautions, however, against trying to draw any connections between mental states and crime, since in his opinion the two phenomena are not directly comparable. Definitions of crime and mental illness are not static, and have shifted over time with the prevailing social and political climate (Prins 2005, 335).

For much of the twentieth century, despite all the research conducted, this assumed link between madness and serious violence created a focus on "scientifically" assessing the "dangerousness" of people who commit crimes and exhibit signs of mental distress. In the contemporary context, there is a heavy preoccupation with public protection and implementing measures to manage the mad criminal. The focus has shifted to the assessment of "riskiness," which requires less precision and can therefore be applied to more people than the concept of "dangerousness" allows. Risk management involves identifying, assessing, eliminating, or reducing the possibility of incurring a misfortune (Castel 1991). The result is a widening of the net and what has been called the "syndromization" of society. Ironically, virtually anyone in our society can be linked to at least one of the numerous "syndromes" that have been "discovered" over the past 30 years. Typically, however, it is the "usual suspects"—the poor and members of ethnic and racial minorities—who are most visible in public spaces, and are therefore most likely to come to police attention and end up in the criminal justice and/ or forensic systems.[3] Once in the mental health or criminal justice system, concern about their riskiness makes them more vulnerable to preventative detention and mandatory treatment (Fennell 2002).

Madden (2002) makes a strong case in suggesting that the use of population studies to predict riskiness in psychiatry is fraught with limitations. He argues that regardless of how good the actual data are, it will still be extremely difficult to use the information to accurately predict the behaviour of an individual (Madden 2002, 16). He cites, as one example, how drawing conclusions based on the relationship between ethnic origin and crime— where some ethnic groups are over-represented in the criminal justice system while others are under-represented—would be tantamount to a crude form of racial stereotyping (Madden 2002, 17). Therefore, he asks how it can be any more acceptable to use membership of other groups, such as being mentally ill, to draw conclusions about the criminality or violence of the individual (Madden 2002, 17). Evaluating the risk of dangerousness based on the presence or absence of a mental disorder can lead to serious harm or tragedy for the individual in terms of limitations on personal freedom, and for psy professionals whose perceptions of their clientele can corrode over time (Rogers 2000). It is not surprising to find that many racialized communities, particularly black communities, express mistrust and fear of mental health services (Keating and Robertson 2004). While black communities express a range of reasons for their reluctance to seek mental health support, the fear of psy professionals' typecasting of mentally ill black people as more dangerous, and leading to more restrictive and punitive forms of treatment, is a key source of concern (Keating and Robertson 2004).

Another related phenomenon contributing to the belief that racialized individuals are more violent or dangerous has been referred to as the "psychiatrization" of criminality. Viewing criminal behaviour as a psychological disorder is not new, but the increasing use of psychiatric labels, especially within prisons where racialized people are over-represented, has raised concerns about the misuse of psychiatry (Anderson 1997). Fears that cultural bias, rather than medical considerations, is the driving force behind the application of psychiatric concepts raises questions about the true levels of mental illness, particularly among racialized groups. This is consistent with our analysis in the previous section that racialized groups are either over-diagnosed or misdiagnosed by psy professionals. Blackburn (1998) points out that violence is a key symptom for many psychiatric disorders, such as Anti-Social Personality Disorder, and the high rates of this disorder among prisoners suggest that moral judgments by forensic psychiatrists may be a factor in diagnosis. If violent crime is being increasingly labelled as a mental illness, this will clearly have a disproportionate impact on racialized people, since their social and economic circumstances, combined with racial discrimination, increase their likelihood of contact with criminal justice authorities.

DEINSTITUTIONALIZATION AND THE CRIMINALIZATION OF MADNESS

For much of the twentieth century, individuals who committed a crime and seemed to be in mental distress were initially sent to jail to await a psychiatric examination to determine their (mental) fitness to stand trial. Most often, they were found unfit and sent to a forensic psychiatric hospital as Order-in-Council patients, detained until they were deemed fit for trial and, in effect, serving indeterminate sentences. When deinstitutionalization began to empty psychiatric hospitals in the later twentieth century, psy professionals continued to diagnose dual deviants with mental disorders, but they increasingly found them to be fit for trial and accountable for their crimes (Chunn and Menzies 1990). In many cases, dual deviants have not committed acts of serious violence, and contemporary psy decision makers apparently feel confident that many of these non-violent offenders can serve a community sentence under conditions that address their mental health issues, such as entering an out-patient program, taking the drugs prescribed for their mental disorder, and being supervised by a probation officer or other professional. Lacking adequate socio-economic supports, however, many dual deviants end up living on the streets of large urban centres and come to the attention of police or other authorities when they commit crimes of survival and/or exhibit signs of mental distress, since many symptoms of mental illness are behaviours considered to be anti-social or criminal. In the absence of alternatives, police are arresting people who in earlier times would have been diverted to social services or sent to psychiatric hospitals, and the result is a growing number of people with mental health issues moving in and out of jail. In essence, what we are seeing is the criminalization of madness and the over-representation of racial and ethnic minorities with mental health issues being detained and released from jail in a revolving-door pattern.

Offenders with mental illnesses, many of whom are racialized, now represent a significant and systemic issue for the criminal justice system in many Western countries where deinstitutionalization took place. Arrest has become the default alternative, leading not only to an increased burden on the criminal justice system, but also to increased stress for police officers, who often have no mental health training but are required to manage this population (Coleman and Cotton 2010). Perhaps not surprisingly, then, police are more likely to use force to control people they perceive to be mentally ill. Oriola, Neverson, and Adeyanju (2012) note that Canadian police officers are more likely to use a taser on immigrants, black and Aboriginal people, and people who have mental illnesses and substance-abuse problems. Since police officers approach people with a mental illness and other intersecting identities (e.g., gender, ethnicity, socio-economic status) in the same manner as they would approach a dangerous criminal, there have been occasions where incidents escalate with fatal outcomes, as in the case of Robert Dziekanski (Oriola, Neverson, and Adeyanju 2012). People with a mental illness are more likely to be charged with a crime than those who are mentally healthy, and they are incarcerated for longer periods for the same crime (Lamberti et al. 2001; McNiel, Binder, and Robinson 2005). There have also been several disturbing deaths of defendants with mental health problems in police custody in Canada, many involving Aboriginal people, and several people with mental health disabilities have been lethally shot by police (MacAlister 2012, *Ontario Human Rights Commission* 2012; Cheema 2009).

Wacquant (2001, 98) observes that in the United States, the over-representation of racialized people in prisons is not surprising since the mentally ill along with "the poor, the homeless, the jobless and the useless"—many of whom are African Americans, and all of whom are considered rejects of the market society—have been subjected to mass confinement as the key solution to managing surplus populations and social problems. When racialized offenders are confined in secure psychiatric facilities instead, it is often not by choice, and they tend to be subjected more often to medication, restraint, and seclusion while in these facilities (Hickling 2002; Foulks 2004; Price, David, and Otis 2004). Harcourt (2011) believes that deinstitutionalization is a key factor to the increased racialization of mental health institutions, since only those patients who were deemed "not dangerous" were released. The focus on dangerousness had a disproportionate impact on black people, who were regarded as too dangerous for release, contributing to their over-representation in mental health institutions (Harcourt 2011).

The criminalization of racialized dual deviants has exacted a high price for individuals and communities alike. The overall picture is bleak— fragmented services, with a spatial concentration of people with very complex needs in some of the most deprived areas of Canada, such as Vancouver's Downtown Eastside, and large numbers of prisoners with mental health problems that are not being adequately addressed. Consequently, dual deviants are, perhaps, one of the most excluded groups in Canadian society. In a report by the Ontario Human Rights Commission, numerous barriers to justice were noted by research participants who pointed to the inability to obtain legal counsel, the lack of education and awareness of mental health issues among decision makers, and the overall lack of access to mental health services in the correctional system (*Ontario Human Rights Commission* 2012, 103–6). The criminalization of mental illness also means that people with mental health issues will likely have a criminal record, making it more difficult to obtain housing, employment, and services (*Ontario Human Rights Commission* 2012, 107). When racial differences are included as another barrier to equitable treatment, it becomes clear that much more will need to be done to prevent further exclusion and inequalities.

There is now a rising awareness that the problem of racial disparities in forensic psychiatry and the mental health system cannot be ignored. Psychiatric assessments impact access to treatment, legal standing in criminal cases, the likelihood of involuntary confinement or compulsory detention, and the use of restraint and seclusion in mental health facilities, to name a few. The problem of racial bias is complex, given that many racialized offenders have a variety of risk factors such as poverty, housing, education, and employment exacerbating and contributing to the onset of a mental health problem (Boast and Chesterman 1995). However, the impact of racism, combined with the lack of community mental health facilities, poor staff attitudes, and alienation from psychiatric services, contributes to the likelihood that their mental health conditions will deteriorate. The result is that many racialized individuals end up in the criminal justice system, and then recycled through the justice system on a regular basis due to lack of treatment (Foulks 2004). Racialized non-citizens are at an even greater risk as the criminalization of their mental illness can result in their deportation from Canada (Schizophrenia Society of Ontario 2010). As Morrow and Weisser remind us, "experiences of mental illness and distress, regardless of their origins, take place in a social, cultural and historical context which includes environments of discrimination that are structured through legal, medical and psychological practices and policies" (2012, 29). The ongoing pathologization of racial groups by psy and criminal justice professionals may obscure the web of racism present, but it is painfully obvious to those caught in its strands (Miller and Garran 2007).

In the next chapter, we examine the role of mass media in shaping public perceptions of criminality, mental illness, violence, and criminal justice.

NOTES

1 The DSM is compiled and disseminated by the American Psychiatric Association. It is "the standard classification of mental disorders used by mental health professionals in the United States" (http://www.psych.org/, accessed on November 19, 2013). DSM-1 was completed in 1952 and DSM-5, the most recent edition, was distributed in May 2013.
2 Allan Schoenborn, from Merritt, BC, was found not criminally responsible for killing his three children in 2008 (CBC News 2013d). Vincent Li was also found not criminally responsible for stabbing and then beheading a sleeping, male passenger on a Greyhound bus in Manitoba in 2008 (Gurney 2012).
3 See also the research conducted by and for Across Boundaries, a Toronto-based charity that provides resources and services to racialized and Aboriginal communities, and works with those communities from an anti-oppression, anti-racist framework. Three reports—The Healing Journey Phase I, Phase II, and Final Report—document the experiences of racialized men and women with mental illness and the "run-ins" of some interviewees with the criminal justice system (http://www.acrossboundaries.ca, accessed on August 7, 2013).

DISCUSSION QUESTIONS

What does the literature tell us about the social causes of mental illness?

If you were the federal minister of health, what policies would you adopt to deconstruct the longstanding belief in public culture that mental illness "causes" violence?

Should mental health institutions be restored to avoid having people with mental health problems in the criminal justice system?

Is a crime still a crime when it is committed by someone with mental health problems?

FURTHER READING

Appignanesi, L. 2009. *Mad, Sad and Bad: A History of Women and the Mind Doctors.* New York: W.W. Norton.

Fabris, E. 2011. *Tranquil Prisons: Chemical Incarceration under Community Treatment Orders.* Toronto: University of Toronto Press.

LeFrancois, B.A., R. Menzies, and G. Reaume, eds. 2013. *Mad Matters: A Critical Reader in Canadian Mad Studies.* Toronto: Canadian Scholars' Press.

Menzies, R. 1989. *Survival of the Sanest: Order and Disorder in a Pre-Trial Psychiatric Clinic.* Toronto: University of Toronto Press.

Whitaker, R. 2010. *Mad in America: Bad Science, Bad Medicine, and the Enduring Mistreatment of the Mentally Ill.* Rev. ed. New York: Basic Books.

WEBSITES OF INTEREST

eMental Health—http://www.ementalhealth.ca/
h-madness (History of Psychiatry blog)—http://historypsychiatry.com/resources/
Justice and Mental Health (CMHA)—http://ontario.cmha.ca/mental-health/
services-and-support/justice-services/
Mad Pride Toronto—http://www.madprideto.com/index.html
Mental Health Commission of Canada—http://www.mentalhealthcommission.ca
The History of Madness in Canada—http://www.historyofmadness.ca/

CHAPTER FOUR

MEDIA REPRESENTATIONS OF RACE, CRIME, AND CRIMINAL JUSTICE

As mentioned in Chapter 1, mass media play a profound role in shaping peoples' perceptions of the world, including their perceptions of crime, madness, and criminal justice. The majority of people are reliant on media coverage, as opposed to personal observation or experience, for information on these topics. Thus, crime can be considered analogous to behind-the-scenes, private behaviour, because most people don't routinely see or experience crime as it is taking place. However, the ever-expanding media coverage since the 1960s has made crime increasingly visible, in the same way that people's private lives are increasingly becoming public knowledge (Surette 2010).

For much of the twentieth century, mainstream print media, and newspapers in particular, were the agenda-setters in terms of which social issues were selected and how they were depicted. More recently, social media have had a democratizing effect on the dissemination of information and ideas by enabling the circulation of alternative ways of looking at the world to a global audience. Nonetheless, despite the explosion of "new" media both print and visual mainstream media continue to play an important role in representing social issues. Therefore, it is important to critically interrogate how editors and journalists select and represent the few events and issues out of thousands that potentially could be covered each day or week (Surette 2010, xvi).

NEWSWORTHINESS AND CRIME REPORTING

What makes an issue or event worthy of media attention? Considerable research reveals that the mainstream media are influenced not only by the "objective" importance of a particular story or issue but also by criteria of newsworthiness that are related to the need to be competitive with other media outlets. Editors and journalists have a "professional ideology" of what a good news story is, and they select topics and issues for coverage on the basis of their news value (Hall et al. 1978). Topics and issues that are "out of the ordinary," dramatic, tragic, and so on have "primary" or "cardinal" news value. Under these criteria, crime, particularly violent crime, becomes intrinsically newsworthy. Hence the slogan, "If it bleeds, it leads."

Not surprisingly, then, crime coverage in mainstream media vastly over-emphasizes violent "street" crime. As might be expected, murder is a "staple" of popular tabloid media (Ericson, Baranek, and Chan 1991, 245; Surette 2010), but over the past few decades, all mainstream media outlets have devoted increasing attention to (culpable) homicide, even though it comprises less than one per cent of all crimes in Canada each year (Brennan 2012). Why don't the media focus consistently on behaviours that cause more deaths annually? For example, "there are about six times more deaths from suicide and five times more deaths from road accidents than from homicide" (Perreault 2012, 4). Or why do the media not highlight "violent" conditions, such as unsafe working conditions, that arguably inflict harm on greater numbers of people than a homicide involving two individuals? Corporate actions or omissions that cause death are usually either not a media focus at all, or else are constructed as "accidents," "disasters," and "tragedies," and not as crimes. Consider, for instance, the media coverage of the Westray Mine explosion in Nova Scotia that killed 26 men (McMullan 2005). Ericson and his colleagues suggest that "newsworthiness does not reside in the perceived harm caused by an act or condition of deviance. Rather, newsworthiness is a matter of the type of infractions or rules that have been violated and their relation to symbolic order" (1991, 250). A media focus on corporate homicide would be more threatening to the status quo than a focus on the killing of one person by another. Prioritizing the latter is also a matter of boosting ratings and selling newspapers (Surette 2010).

RACE, CRIME, AND MORAL PANICS

The over-representation of violent crime in mainstream media reflects, in part, the symbiotic relationship between the police and journalists (Hall et al. 1978; Ericson, Baranek, and Chan 1989). Each group has an interest in cooperating with the other. The police talk to journalists in order to disseminate their views of a particular case or of crime and justice in general. Journalists in turn are reliant on police as primary sources of information about crime and justice. While the explosion of new media poses challenges to police control over knowledge about crime, they still arguably remain the first authorities to speak about, and therefore frame, the issues in most mainstream media accounts of crime. This is particularly true of large forces that have a media relations unit to "manage" interactions with journalists and the public. Not surprisingly, both news and entertainment programming over-represent the police relative to other criminal justice actors, with correctional personnel being least evident in media (Doyle and Ericson 1996). Therefore, how the police see themselves, how they think about crime and justice, and who they identify as "real" criminals and "real" victims continues to be extremely influential in shaping media coverage.

Existing research suggests that while police and journalists are by no means homogeneous in their perceptions of the world, to a greater or lesser extent both groups have been guided by mainstream views on crime and criminal justice in carrying out their work (Surette 2010). Historically, both professions have also been comprised primarily of middle- and lower-middle-class white men, and while increased recruitment of women and members of racial and ethnic minorities has occurred since the late twentieth century, white, male police officers and journalists are still over-represented in Canada and other liberal states. Over the past few decades, in particular, news and (to a lesser extent) entertainment media have consistently conveyed a picture of police as they like to see themselves—as "the thin blue line" holding back the criminal tidal wave. A plethora of "reality" television shows including *Cops*, *America's Most Wanted*, among others, construct police as proactive "crime busters" who feel constantly hampered in their work by legal "technicalities," which they believe favour the sleazy, unprincipled, often racialized criminal, who preys on the vulnerable and innocent by selling them illicit drugs, (sexually) assaulting them, and so on (Doyle 2003; Fishman and Cavender 1998). In terms of news programming, this "thin blue line" image is nowhere more graphically illustrated than in media coverage of police who are killed, and their funerals. Likewise, when police wrongdoing (e.g., corruption, brutality) is covered in news media, the focus has tended to be either supportive of the specific police force or targeted at the individual "rotten apples" that must be pulled out of the barrel, rather than presenting a contextualized discussion of systemic institutional bias and wrongdoing (Ericson, Baranek, and Chan 1991).

Given the reliance of news media on the police as sources of information about crime and justice, we should not be surprised to learn that media coverage of crime often directly or indirectly favours the crime control orientation of most police officers (Ericson, Baranek, and Chan 1987, 1991). After all, many journalists share that orientation and the attendant beliefs that members of certain racialized groups are crime-prone and rarely qualify as "real victims" and that a tough "law and order" response is necessary to protect society (Surette 2010). These views are reflected in an over-emphasis on members of racial and ethnic minorities who commit crime, and an under-emphasis on members who are crime victims in mainstream news and entertainment programming about crime and justice (Grenier 1992; Dowler 2004).

At times, these crime-control views underpin and fuel a moral panic about "a condition, episode, person or group of persons ... defined as a threat to societal values" (Cohen 2002, 1). A recurrent type of moral panic is linked with various forms of youth culture associated with deviant behaviour, especially violence, and the demonization of the youth involved as "folk devils" (Cohen 2002; Schissel 1997, 2006; Barron and Lacombe 2005). Sometimes moral panics are also linked to crime waves, or "heavily reported themes in crime which journalists perceive in selecting news" (Fishman 1978, 1). As was discussed in Chapter 1, during the late 1970s, the United Kingdom, the United States, and other Western countries experienced moral panics about alleged "crime waves" that involved the mugging of elderly (white) people by young black men (Hall et al. 1978; Fishman 1980). Bernard Schissel's (1997, 2006) studies of how mainstream media constructed Canadian youth in the mid-1990s, and again a decade later, suggest that no fundamental shift away from the image of youth as "folk devils" has occurred. Expecting to find that the rhetoric surrounding young lawbreakers and youth in general was less inflammatory in the twenty-first century, Schissel was disheartened to discover that "[t]he current journalism of youth is still fraught with stereotypes of race, class, gender and age ..." (2006, 8).

Although not necessarily tied to a moral panic, "gang" violence recurrently becomes the focus of media attention over time. Media coverage is racialized in several ways. First, media stories invariably indicate when the violence is committed by a "gang" comprised primarily or solely of members of racial or ethnic minorities by explicitly referencing racial or ethnic identity (e.g., Indo-Canadian, Somali, Russian, etc.), by naming the gang and the territorial base of the gang, and/or by including usually unflattering pictures of suspects such as police mug shots (Lawson 2013). Second, in conjunction with the overt racialization of violence, mainstream media often inform readers and viewers that the suspected perpetrators of the violence are "known to the police," but they cannot be named or pictured because they are young offenders. These aspects of representation subtly reinforce the image of racialized offenders as being unaccountable for their crimes. Over recent decades in Canada, shooting deaths linked to South Asian, black, and Aboriginal "gangs" have received extensive mainstream media coverage, thereby reinforcing the link between race and violent crime in public culture (Schissel 2006).[1]

Media coverage is particularly intense when inter-gang conflict erupts in parking lots, shopping malls, restaurants, and other spaces open to the general public, and when what were intended to be "targeted" killings result in the injury or death of innocent bystanders. In Canada, several such homicides have occurred in urban centres across the country since the early 1990s. Media representations are particularly dichotomous when the "shooter" is a racialized man and the victim is a white woman. Stark contrasts are drawn between good and evil, guilt and innocence, lightness and darkness, citizens and non-citizens (D'Arcy 2007; Buffam 2009). For example, this dichotomization is unambiguously present in media representations of two killings which took place a decade apart in Toronto and involved a racialized perpetrator and a white bystander victim.

The first, as we discussed briefly in Chapter 1, was the fatal shooting of 23-year-old Georgina Leimonis in 1994 at Just Desserts, a popular downtown café. Ms. Leimonis was sitting with friends when three men, one armed with a shotgun, entered the café and demanded that people hand over their wallets and purses. The gun was fired during the robbery, severely wounding Leimonis, who died a few hours later (D'Arcy 2007, 241). The fact that the men accused of the robbery and killing were black and the victim was white, as well as the sheer randomness of her death, generated "a state of intense and escalating anxiety" among Toronto residents, "as fears spread about violence, crime, and a perceived decline in the safety of Toronto's streets" (D'Arcy 2007, 242; Henry and Tator 2002). Moreover, as one journalist observed, the city's news media contributed to these anxieties and fears by helping the police "whip the population into a panic" (Zerbisias 1994). They did so by drawing a hard line between the image of an innocent, young woman who had her whole life ahead of her and just happened to be in the wrong place at the wrong time, and the "indiscriminately threatening" Jamaican criminals who had no respect for Canadian values and ways of life who killed her (D'Arcy 2007, 248–50). Linking the three accused to another country "othered" them, when in reality, all of them had lived in Toronto from a very young age (Henry and Tator 2002).

The construct of the "Jamaican criminal" was well entrenched in public culture and easily reactivated when another young, white woman was shot to death outside a downtown Toronto shopping mall on Boxing Day in 2005. Jane Creba, a 15-year-old high school student who was shopping with her mother, died during a shoot-out between racialized men from two rival "street gangs." Her killing was the last in a record number of gun homicides in Toronto in 2005, dubbed by journalists "the Year of the Gun" (Buffam 2009, 56). Of 78 homicides recorded, 52 were gun-related and 40 were murders of African Canadian men (Lawson 2013, 2). While the killing of 17-year-old Amon Beckles outside a church at the funeral of a friend murdered earlier that same week heightened public outrage, it was the murder of Jane Creba that shifted "the character and intensity of the 'public' reaction to gun violence in Toronto" (Buffam 2009, 56). She represented the ideal "victim" and "images of the slain teenager displayed across the media

[were] powerful enough to erase in the minds of most Canadians previous images of innocently killed black youth ..." (Davis 2006, 23). Consequently, in media coverage, Creba's innocence and purity made her a poster girl for white femininity, which was consistently juxtaposed with the "threat of black masculinity" manifested by the "Jamaican criminals" who killed her (Davis 2006).

We are not suggesting that outrage and grief are inappropriate responses to the murders of Georgina Leimonis and Jane Creba. On the contrary, such crimes are "heartbreaking and pointless" (Schissel 2006, 8). The issue of concern is the way in which mainstream media representations of serious violence tend to be based on a "hierarchy of victims" that leads to the disqualification of these reactions among the family and friends of young, African Canadian men who have experienced violent deaths (Lawson 2013). Their outrage and grief are tainted because a "Jamaican criminal," or someone who associates with one, is a less worthy crime victim than a young woman who was out with friends or shopping with her mother and was senselessly gunned down. Moreover, the media construction of young, black or other racialized youth as un-Canadian and threatening has "predictable" and unfortunate political consequences, including the implementation of "get tough on youth crime" campaigns "that are supported by all political parties because it would be political suicide to appear to be 'soft' on youth crime" (Schissel 2006, 8; Gosine 2007, 52–53). A sustained media focus on the theme of evil youth and innocent victims in the wake of such killings has helped to legitimize such campaigns and to bolster the "law and order" case for eliminating a separate youth justice system altogether. Increasingly, for example, young offenders are tried in youth court, but then raised to adult court for sentencing.

As well as violent crime, mainstream media have historically devoted considerable attention to the issue of the "sexual endangerment" of innocent, young, white women and girls by predatory, often racialized, men (Brock 2009, 130). During the early twentieth century, many young women moved to cities in search of work and reformers of the day "warned against the dangers of a traffic in women and girls" that allegedly existed in Canada and other nations (Brock 2009, 130; McLaren 1986). For instance, Chinese men who lived and worked in Canada were vilified in media accounts depicting them as evil "Others" who used opiates to lure unsuspecting white women into sexual slavery. Mainstream media thus helped to generate support for the expanded use of criminal law to stop the traffic in women and stamp out the "social evil" of prostitution (McLaren 1988). In the late twentieth century, we see a similar media-fuelled moral panic that focused on child prostitution and street kids and was linked to the (implicit) construction of black pimps as modern "white slavers" (Brock 2009, 131–35).

Over the past two decades, we can also see the emergence of a new media story that illustrates the inter-connectedness of race and sexuality; namely, the criminal prosecution of HIV-positive men who had unprotected sex with women and did not disclose their infection. Media accounts invariably zoomed in on HIV-positive immigrant African men who "infected" white women, drawing on the "old familiar discourse of 'innocent victims' and 'guilty others'" that was so pervasive during the 1980s, except that now it was heterosexuality, not homosexuality, that was at the centre of these stories (Persson and Newman 2008, 633). Similarly, in an Australian study researchers analyzed the coverage of criminal transmission cases in the *Sydney Morning Herald* (considered a "quality" newspaper) over a five-year period, and concluded that, "in these stories, the figure of the African heterosexual man spreading HIV to (white) women through deception comes to stand for a monstrous masculinity that is other to an imagined Australian heterosexuality rendered both vulnerable to and safe from HIV by its presence" (Persson and Newman 2008, 638). This media-constructed image of the "monstrous" thus provides support for "the enforced containment of sexual behaviour and disease through criminalization" (Persson and Newman 2008, 641).

Media depictions of Charles Ssenyonga, a Ugandan immigrant and Canada's most notorious AIDS "criminal," exemplify how "monstrous masculinity" is constructed. Journalists consistently mentioned "his Ugandan origins, his shady dealings at The African Store [his shop], his exotic strain of virus, and his malicious disdain for White middle-class family values" (Miller 2005, 44). Collectively and cumulatively, these media representations constructed Mr. Ssenyonga as "a violent sex-crazed Black man bent on dragging White women ... down into the inferno of African Aids" (Miller 2005, 45). With few dissenting voices, he was also depicted as a man who engaged in criminal behaviour and who just happened to be black (Miller 2005, 45). In short, he was not the victim of racial bias. Although Mr. Ssenyonga died in 1993, before a verdict was handed down in his case, the media representation of him as an exotic "Other" remained influential in subsequent cases (Persson and Newman 2008).

Overall, then, we can see some basic similarities between news and entertainment crime programming in terms of how they define crime and criminal justice, how they depict "real" criminals and victims, how they explain crime, and how they think we should respond to crime. This is extremely important in the contemporary context for several reasons. First, the mainstream media's overemphasis on violent street crime, their over-representation of racialized men and women as "criminal others," and their focus on the need for "law and order" to win the "war on crime" can now reach global audiences on a daily basis. Second, as the distinction between news and entertainment programming becomes more and more tenuous, mainstream media increasingly (re)present crime and criminal justice as spectacle.

CRIME AND CRIMINAL JUSTICE AS SPECTACLE

Since the 1970s, mass media in Canada, the United States, and other liberal democracies have undergone massive restructuring and change. The "tabloidization" of mainstream media, which was in its infancy during the 1970s (see Hall et al. 1978), has become the new "normal" (Surette 2010). Mainstream media content is routinely presented as spectacle. As discussed previously, violent crime is tailor-made for saturation media coverage, and in the age of "tabloidization" the depictions of crime, criminals, and criminal justice in news reporting differ little from those in entertainment programming (or for that matter, in advertising, sports, or any other area of media coverage). The erosion of the line between "fact" and "fiction," exemplified by the traditional distinction between news and entertainment programming, is illustrated by the emergence and proliferation of infotainment, which takes the forms of "reality TV" and "trial as miniseries" on the daily news (Fishman and Cavender 1998; Garber, Matlock, and Walkowitz 1993; Doyle 2003). Reality *is* entertainment, and some fear that Neil Postman (1985) was prescient when he argued, almost three decades ago, that

> Today, we [Americans] must look to the city of Las Vegas, Nevada, as a metaphor of our national character and aspiration, its symbol a thirty-foot-high cardboard picture of a slot machine and a chorus girl. For Las Vegas is a city entirely devoted to the idea of entertainment, and as such proclaims the spirit of a culture in which all public discourse increasingly takes the form of entertainment. Our politics, religion, news, athletics, education and commerce have been transformed into congenial adjuncts of show business, largely without protest or even much popular notice. The result is that we are a people on the verge of amusing ourselves to death. (3–4)

The blurring of the traditional line between reality and entertainment in mainstream media has occurred in all Western countries, and also globally, through the dissemination of American programming in particular. In the US context, mainstream media coverage in 1994 and 1995 of O.J. Simpson's arrest, trial, and acquittal on charges of murdering his ex-wife, Nicole Brown Simpson, and her friend, Ron Goldman, is arguably the penultimate exemplar of real-life crime and criminal justice (re)presented as entertainment spectacle. Dubbed "the trial of the [twentieth] century," it has generated spirited discussion and debate among scholars and the general public in the United States and globally, with media coverage clearly packaging the case as entertainment in the Postman (1985) sense. For eight months, the case was presented as an ongoing soap opera, facilitated by the trial judge's decision to allow cameras in the courtroom, and was inescapable, regardless of whether people tuned in to news, sports, talk shows, "movies of the week," or advertisements. Likewise, the trial was a massive stimulant for commerce (Lipsitz 1997). Below, we illustrate a similar trend toward "tabloidization" in Canada, using an intersectional lens to examine the Reena Virk case as a media spectacle.

Reena Virk, a 14-year-old South Asian girl, was savagely murdered in a primarily white suburb of Victoria, British Columbia, in November 1997. She was invited to "party" with several other teens under a bridge spanning a local waterway, but was instead attacked by a group of seven girls and one boy between the ages of 14 and 17 for allegedly "stealing one of the girl's boyfriends and spreading rumours" (Jiwani 1999, 178). When one of the girls attempted to stub out a cigarette on her forehead, Reena tried to flee, but was "swarmed" by the group and "brutalized" until she was "severely injured and bruised" (Jiwani 1999, 178). Reena's second attempt to flee her abusers also failed, when Warren Glowatski and Kelly Ellard (who by all accounts had never met Reena before) followed her, beat her until she lost consciousness, and allegedly dragged her into the water and "forcibly drowned her" (Jiwani 1999, 178). The body was found eight days later, and an autopsy report concluded that Reena would have probably died from the beating she received before drowning, although the official cause of death was drowning.

The case was an immediate media spectacle. Journalists recounted in excruciating detail the sequence of events leading up to Reena's murder, drawing on experts and other pundits to explain why eight teenagers, seven of them girls, would commit such a vicious crime (Kilty 2010). In 1998, three of the teenage girls pleaded guilty to charges of assault causing bodily harm, and three others were convicted of the same offence, receiving penal sentences from 60 days to one year. Warren Glowatski, who was 16 at the time of the killing and was the only male involved, was convicted of second-degree murder in 1999, sentenced to life imprisonment, and paroled in 2010. Kelly Ellard, who was 15 at the time of Reena's murder, was raised to adult court, had three trials—which, as Byers notes, was "almost unprecedented in Canadian legal history"—and was imprisoned in 2009 after the Supreme Court of Canada upheld her conviction for second-degree murder, thereby nixing her appeal for a fourth trial (Byers 2009–10, 28; Batacharya 2006; CBC News 2009a). She remains in prison, having waived her right to apply for day parole when she became eligible in 2011, and again in 2012, after the Virk family indicated that they would oppose her application (Canadian Press 2012).

Because the administration of criminal justice in this case was drawn out over more than a decade, the initial media framings of the murder were repeatedly reproduced, thus reinforcing them in public culture, while introducing the media spectacle to new audiences. Among other things, this lengthy timeline made the Reena Virk case more marketable, "inspiring" not only the ongoing sensational re-renderings of the murder in the mainstream media, but also several bestselling "true crime" books, and the possibility of producing a Hollywood movie based on these stories (Byers 2009–10; Godfrey 2005).

The initial media framing of the murder is telling. Reena's death was linked to one overarching theme: "girl-on-girl" violence. In the context of the late 1990s, the brutal murder of a 14-year-old girl by a "gang" of "nasty girls" of the same age fed straight into the moral panic about the perceived rise in serious violence committed by young women (Rajiva and Batacharya 2010; Barron and Lacombe 2005), making the story both newsworthy and titillating for local, national, and international media. The focus on the allegedly accelerating girl violence also remained the dominant theme in media coverage, although secondary themes such as the bullying of school children who are "marginalized" because they do not fit the normative expectations of their peers received significant attention as well. Yasmin Jiwani's (1999; 2006) compelling analysis of how print media represented the murder of Reena Virk suggests that the media obsession with "girl-on-girl" violence illustrates how racialized victims of (violent) crime are "de-raced" and "the reality of the violence done to their bodies" is minimized (Jiwani and Young 2006, 901; see also Razack 2000).

For instance, the headshot of Reena, which accompanied many print media and television stories, together with other details of her physical appearance (e.g., dark-skinned, overweight), clearly marked her as a racialized young woman who did not meet hegemonic expectations governing white femininity. Yet, by framing her murder as "girl-on-girl" violence, mainstream media ignored altogether the centrality of race and, in particular, the vulnerability of girls "from racialized immigrant and refugee communities" (Jiwani 1999, 178–79). Overall, Reena Virk's racialized identity was erased in media accounts, and there was a virtual absence of "even the *possibility* that her death was racially motivated" (Jiwani 1999, 181; emphasis in original). As a result, "the structured nature of racism as a system of domination which informs everyday life and constrains the life chances of racialized peoples remains outside the dominant discourse, relegated to the margins" (Jiwani 1999, 183).

The media focus on themes of girl violence and teen bullying also leads to the erasure of agency and the representation of victims "as shy, awkward, immobilized, and silent" (Byers 2009–10, 28). As Tess Chakkalakal (2000, 163) argues, however, this depiction of Reena Virk is inaccurate. Far from being a passive victim, Reena Virk "acted as if she had power, as if she could do things that a girl of her size, colour, and ethnicity was clearly prohibited from doing" (ibid.). Chakkalakal goes on to suggest that media narratives about girl violence and bullying need to be resisted, and in the case of Reena Virk, replaced with narratives that allow the possibility of agency (ibid., 165).

While Reena was "de-raced" and marginalized in media representations of her murder, the two main perpetrators were at the front and centre of media coverage. Warren Glowatski and Kelly Ellard were initially of intense interest to the media because of the seriousness of the crime they were charged with committing (second-degree murder), the fact that they had never met the victim before, their young age, and their major breach of normative expectations governing masculinity and femininity respectively. At the time of the murder, however, Glowatski was closer to being one of the "usual suspects" than Ellard. He was white[2] but far from middle class, living on his own in a trailer park with minimal financial assistance from his father, who had remarried and moved to California. He also drew on the discourse of hyper-masculinity to depict himself as tough, loyal, and so on (Connell 2009). By his own account, inflicting violence made him feel "powerful," a real man, and he was not a "rat," refusing to testify against Kelly Ellard at her first trial (Kilty 2010, 160–61).

Despite his best efforts, Warren Glowatski was not particularly successful in his performance of hyper-masculinity. On the contrary, the media quite quickly began to depict him as "a weak, baby-faced youth" who weighed less than his victim, a "baby man" with "sweet and girlish" features (ibid., 161–62). In short, the media feminized Glowatski, and by questioning his manliness also implicitly questioned his sexuality. As a feminized man who admitted his guilt after he was convicted of Reena's murder, he became much less newsworthy than Kelly Ellard, his co-participant in the crime (Kilty 2010, 163).

Ultimately, Ellard became the centre of media coverage of the Reena Virk case. There is something endlessly fascinating about a young, white, middle-class woman with strong family attachments and support who is accused of a senseless and seemingly motiveless act of lethal violence (Kilty 2010, 161). Why would she do such a thing? Moreover, why would she deny it through three trials and a Supreme Court of Canada judgment that refused her appeal for a fourth trial? Undoubtedly, Kelly Ellard's race and class privilege helped her navigate the criminal justice system, but her egregious violation of the norms governing white femininity ultimately undermined her efforts to avoid conviction. Good girls do not commit acts of senseless violence and then refuse to take responsibility for them.

Just as Warren Glowatski was feminized in media accounts, Kelly Ellard was masculinized. Men's violence is effectively "normalized" since they commit most violent crimes, whereas women who perpetrate acts of serious violence are often viewed as shocking anomalies and demonized for acting like men. In some media accounts, for instance, Ellard was referred to as "Killer Kelly" (Kilty 2010). This depiction was reinforced by media images of Ellard entering and leaving court during her three trials, invariably scowling, swearing, and hiding her face. Her steadfast denial of guilt in the murder of Reena Virk, and the exercise of her legal rights to appeal, are held against her in media accounts. In contrast to Warren Glowatski, who had expressed remorse and had the support of Reena Virk's parents when he was granted full parole, Kelly Ellard will likely remain in prison until her mandatory release date, and face an uncomfortable future when she is released.

As with the O.J. Simpson trial, mainstream media coverage of the trials of those prosecuted for the murder of Reena Virk highlighted the interconnectedness of race, class, gender, and sexuality, and blurred the line between fact and fiction. We turn now to consider how intersectionality plays out in the administration of criminal justice.

NOTES

1 Similar concerns in Britain about racialized, male teenagers killing each other with knives received saturation coverage from the mainstream media about "the growing and apparently unchallenged, threat of 'knife crime' and 'teen gangs'" when the number of such deaths spiked in 2008 (Wood 2010, 97–98). The British government quickly implemented tough legislative measures such as "the increased use of stop and search powers" and the lifting of "blanket anonymity" for accused who were 16 and 17 years old. As a result of both media and government actions, "the 1980s image of Black 'muggers' and 'street robbers'" has now "morphed into one of Black teenage street gangs armed with knives" (Wood 2010, 98).
2 Warren Glowatski had always assumed that he was white, but discovered in prison that he was Metis. He has apparently embraced his Aboriginal ancestry (CBC News 2007a).

DISCUSSION QUESTIONS

Is the concept of intersectionality useful to you for interpreting media representations of crime and criminal justice?

With respect to media coverage of crime and justice, do you agree with Neil Postman's argument that, increasingly, there is little distinction between news and entertainment programming?

Should the mainstream media be held accountable for their contributions to "moral panics" about violent crime, or are they just giving audiences what they want to read or view?

What are the pros and cons of the current ban on media identification of young offenders?

FURTHER READING

Bonnycastle, K.D. 2009. "Not the usual suspects." In *The CSI Effect: Television, Crime and Governance*, ed. M. Byers and M. Johnson. Lanham: Lexington Books.

Doyle, A. 2003. *Arresting Images: Crime and Policing in Front of the Television Camera*. Toronto: University of Toronto Press.

Henry, F., and C. Tator. 2002. *Discourses of Domination*. Toronto: University of Toronto Press.

Jiwani, Y. 2006. *Discourses of Denial: Mediations of Race, Gender, and Violence*. Vancouver: UBC Press.

McMullan, J. 2005. *News, Truth and Crime: The Westray Disaster and Its Aftermath*. Black Point, NS: Fernwood Publishing.

Morrison, T., and C.B. Lacour, eds. 1997. *Birth of a Nation'hood: Gaze, Script, and Spectacle in the O.J. Simpson Case*. New York: Pantheon Books.

WEBSITES OF INTEREST

Canadian Race Relations Foundation—http://www.crr.ca/en/
Media Literacy Week—http://www.medialiteracyweek.ca/en/default.htm
Media Smarts (Canada's Centre for Digital and Media Literacy)—http://mediasmarts.ca/
Race Talk—http://www.racetalk.ca/
The Media Co-op—http://www.mediacoop.ca/
The Race Card Project—http://theracecardproject.com/

PART THREE

ADMINISTERING CRIMINAL JUSTICE

Our focus in this section is the administration of criminal justice. Issues related to policing, prosecution/sentencing, and institutional responses to victimization are well-established areas of research in Western countries, but in Canada, linking these topics to racial groups and communities has received uneven treatment by scholars. Here we attempt to address the unevenness in the literature through an examination of the main institutions in the criminal justice system, and their relationship to racial groups and subgroups. We provide an updated examination of some key issues in the three areas of policing (Chapter 5), prosecution/sentencing (Chapter 6), and victimization (Chapter 7), and demonstrate how they are connected to a particular understanding of racial groups.

Our examination of the administration of criminal justice in Canada will document huge disparities in the ways that legal agents at each stage of the system "hear" accused persons and complainants. What will become evident is how, to a greater or lesser degree, police, prosecutors, judges, and correctional personnel operate with the same commonsense assumptions about who are the most likely "criminals" and victims of crime. We argue that these ideas and images result in the differential treatment of marginalized populations, with the resulting over-representation of racialized men and women accused at every point in the system, and their under-representation as "legitimate" victims of crime.

The systemic nature of this "naturalized bias" stands out in sharp relief when one reads report after report from a Royal Commission or an inquiry that acknowledges the systemic nature of the problem after the fact, makes recommendations for change, and is then put on a shelf to gather dust. As we will highlight, the historical failure of criminal justice reforms to address the systemic inequities in the administration of justice raises even more complex questions: Should criminal sanctions and practices be used to solve non-criminal problems? Is a reliance on criminal law to deal with marginalized populations who need social, healthcare, and other supports and services compatible with the democratic principles that underpin our society? Finally, is the Canadian state at a crossroads where the reproduction of order through containment and/or exclusion of the marginal is more important than the protection of the most vulnerable individuals and groups in Canadian society?

CHAPTER FIVE

RACE, RACISM, AND POLICING

Considerable research reveals that, contrary to many mainstream media portrayals (Doyle 1998; 2003), public police are not the proactive crime-fighters they want to be in real life.[1] Even officers in large urban forces respond most often to citizen calls and complaints, as opposed to "discovering" criminal activity (Ericson 1981, 1982). Moreover, the bulk of police work for most officers relates to activities that are non-criminal or quasi-criminal, including public order offences, driving/traffic violations, calls for assistance, and the paperwork associated with them. Police officers intensely dislike completing paperwork (which has increased exponentially over the last few decades) in part because it reduces their autonomy. They want to be out in the field, preferably as members of a specialized unit dealing with "real" crime (e.g., gangs, homicide, illicit drugs, vice, etc.), and not as paper-pushers tied to a desk (Ericson and Haggerty 1997; de Lint 1998).

But how do racialized Canadians view the police? Critical scholarship in this area is rare. Jackson's (1994) analysis of the relationship between race, crime, and policing in Toronto in the early 1990s found that, after several high-profile conflicts involving members of the Toronto police force and the black community, police–community relations deteriorated, with accusations of police racism by community groups and increased levels of mistrust between police and racialized minorities. Jackson challenged claims made at the time that there was a link between race and crime, and instead redirected the focus back onto the police force, by pointing out that "unequal power relations structure everyday interactions between police and minority communities" (1994, 232). Chu and Song's (2008) study of Chinese immigrants' perceptions of the Toronto police force is more typical of research on police perceptions, insofar as they eschew critique in favour of a quantitative analysis, finding that perceptions were based on whether their respondents' contact with the police was positive or negative. Not surprisingly, more positive contact resulted in more favourable perceptions and vice versa (Chu and Song 2008).

Similarly, Roberts' examination of public perceptions of the criminal justice system found that the public has considerably more trust in the police than they do in the courts or the correctional system (2007, 170). He suggests that, among other reasons, the higher public trust in police reflects the fact that most of the Canadian public tends to share the police orientation toward "crime control," rather than a "due process" model of justice (Roberts 2007, 171–73). However, the literature analyzed by Roberts provided only aggregate findings, making it impossible to determine whether a breakdown of the data by gender, race, age, etc., would illuminate (significant) differences between or among these categories with respect to confidence in criminal justice. He noted that while Canadian polls have "repeatedly revealed that the perceptions of visible minorities are more negative," they do not tell us "whether confidence levels are also lower among visible minorities" (2007, 175).

More recently published studies attempt to address this gap in the literature. Drawing on data from the 2004 General Social Survey of Canada, Liqun Cao (2011) conducted multivariate analyses to determine the impact of visible minority status on confidence in the police. Study results "support the theoretical contention that race structures citizen views of the police: visible minority and non-visible minority members differ significantly in their opinions about local police," even controlling for the effects of perceptions, community contexts, and crime-related variables (Cao 2011, 14–15). In particular, visible minority members in Canada are significantly less likely to believe that police are doing a good job of treating people fairly (Cao 2011, 14–15). Another study based on survey data from black, Asian, and white respondents in Toronto, which also took immigration status into account, revealed that respondents born in Canada and long-time immigrants were "more likely to perceive both police and court discrimination than newcomers (recent immigrants)," and that, in particular, black and Chinese respondents born in Canada perceived "more bias in the Canadian criminal justice system than black and Chinese respondents born in other countries" (Wortley and Owusu-Bempah 2009, 466). These are critical findings, because existing research on other jurisdictions shows that confidence in the police is linked to willingness to report crime, share information about criminal activity, and comply with the law (Cao 2011, 2).

These findings provide strong evidence that attitudes toward the police are most significantly associated with race, although other characteristics such as "previous contact," "prior victimization," and "fear of crime" are also significant (Wortley 1996). Favourable perceptions of and confidence in the police are important because several decades of research reveals that with respect to crime, the public police have historically exercised considerable discretion in their position as the "gatekeepers" to the criminal justice system (Ericson 1981, 1982; Ben-Porat 2008). They decide which citizen calls they will investigate, and which complaints are founded or unfounded. They make crucial decisions about whether suspects will be let go with a warning and spared from official intervention altogether, arrested and criminally charged, or diverted to another system—for example, to the mental health system for psychiatric assessment to determine fitness to stand trial (Menzies 1987, 1989; Godfredson et al. 2011). Race is also heavily implicated in public understandings of who a "criminal" is, with the police playing a pivotal role in shaping this definition. Recognition that police forces need to embrace change has been achieved, although reform itself has been slow. As Canada becomes more diverse racially and ethnically, greater cultural awareness along with more diversity within police forces and the adoption of anti-racism policies has been recommended as necessary policy changes to dispel mistrust and address allegations of over-policing and excessive use of force against racialized communities (Stenning 2003).

Nonetheless, it should be noted that individual police officers have never enjoyed absolute discretion. Political pressure on police administrators, from politicians and citizens' organizations concerned with a specific issue, often results in targeted policing of a particular type of crime, and can dramatically increase the crime rate for that offence, leading to increased surveillance of the "criminals" engaged in it. During the late twentieth century, police crack-downs on street prostitution, illicit drugs, and child pornography (Brock 2009), among others, were carried out regularly in Canada and other Western countries. As was mentioned in Chapter 2, Hall et al.'s (1978) study of the panic around an alleged increase in muggings by young, black people in the UK is a typical example of targeted policing. Police also have been under pressure to strengthen their enforcement efforts in areas such as domestic violence, following the implementation of mandatory charge policies in many Canadian provinces (Pollack, Green, and Allspach 2005).

Policing, and the administration of criminal justice more generally, is always a discretionary process. Even with policies intended to be universal, with no leeway for deviation, such as mandatory charging in cases of domestic violence, police officers still exercise discretion, charging one person and not another for the same offence (Pollack, Green, and Allspach 2005). Ongoing debates about whether some racial and ethnic groups are more "crime-prone" than others, or whether criminal justice agents treat certain racial and ethnic groups more harshly than others, are unavoidable given that racial minorities are over-represented at every stage of the criminal justice system in Canada and other democratic states (Fitzgerald and Carrington 2011). Therefore, it is critical to examine the initial decisions made by police about which lawbreakers or suspected lawbreakers will be pursued.

POLICING UNDER THE RADAR

In a report on policing in Vancouver's Downtown Eastside, a neighbour-hood that has been given the moniker of "Canada's poorest postal code," the authors claim that ample evidence points to systemic abuse of authority by the Vancouver Police Department (VPD) (Pivot Legal Society 2002). They cite routine beatings, torture, unlawful detention, illegal strip searches, illegal entry into homes, abusive language, and unlawful confinement as commonplace in sworn reports by individuals (Pivot Legal Society 2002). Importantly, the study notes that these incidents did not take place within the context of the formal criminal justice system; since none of the victims were criminally charged, the police behaviours were beyond the scrutiny of the courts (Pivot Legal Society 2002). The use of illegal acts in policing the spaces of the inner city to control a marginalized (and often racialized) population has far-reaching consequences for individuals, communities, and police forces alike.

One of the most egregious examples of abuse of power by police officers are the acts variously known as "Starlight Tours," "drop-offs," "dumping," "breaching," and police-initiated transjurisdictional transport (PITT) (King and Dunn 2004; Comack 2012).[2] In short, these activities involve clearing an area of "troublesome" people, including the homeless, the addicted, and the mentally distressed, by picking them up, driving them to another area, and dropping them off to find their way home. For many police officers charged with maintaining order in these "racialized spaces of poverty" (Comack 2012), dealing with people who often need extensive social and healthcare services was not why they chose a policing career. But given that the average patrol officer only makes seven or eight arrests a year, most of his or her time is spent doing what is considered not to be police work. Among other things, then, dumping is a "strategy" for reducing an officer's non-crime-related workload (Comack 2012, 149–50).

While it is a well-established practice, dumping is conducted informally and mainly without any record of the people who are dropped off in another jurisdiction. As a result, there is a gap in the literature on policing, which focuses almost entirely on visible police behaviour such as "stop and search" or the use of potentially lethal force—decisions that are subject to procedural rules such as the "reasonable and probable grounds" requirement for "stop and search" (Comack 2012, 149). Given the "under the radar" character of dumping, then, how did it even come to light, and why is it such a conten-tious practice? The answer seems to be that some "troublesome" people who were dropped off by police in the winter could not find their way home, and froze to death or died of hypothermia. But the real controversy over dumping in Canada arose when it eventually became clear that almost all of the dead were racialized men, raising the spectre of racism (Comack 2012, 115).

In the Canadian context, dumping first came to light in Saskatoon after several young Aboriginal men were found frozen to death on the edge of the city. The first death was that of Neil Stonechild, who was found partially clothed with only one shoe on in 1990. Despite calls for a public inquiry, the Saskatoon Police Service (SPS) conducted the investigation into Stonechild's death and concluded that the death was not suspicious. A decade later, however, the frozen, lightly clad bodies of two more Aboriginal men, Rodney Nastius and Lawrence Wegner, were found on the outskirts of Saskatoon, prompting a fourth Aboriginal man, Darrel Night, to talk to a police officer about his own experience of being dropped off, clad only in a jean jacket and summer shoes, not far from where Nastius and Wegner were found. Fortuitously, Night was able to obtain help (Comack 2012, 115–16).

In combination, the deaths of Nastius and Wegner, along with Darrel Night's story of his "Starlight Tour," generated "a storm of controversy" (Comack 2012, 115). Aboriginal activists and organizations maintained that the "Starlight Tours" revelations pointed to pervasive racism in the Saskatoon Police Service, and they renewed their demands for a public inquiry. Meanwhile, the SPS and their supporters claimed that the tours were "a myth," and denied any police wrongdoing (Comack 2012, 117). Following Night's disclosures, however, the two Saskatoon police officers who "dumped" him were suspended, and later sentenced to eight months in prison for unlawful confinement (Comack 2012, 116–17). As well, in 2003 the Saskatchewan minister of justice appointed the Honourable Mr. Justice David Wright to conduct the Commission of Inquiry into Matters Relating to the Death of Neil Stonechild. Justice Wright found that Stonechild was in the custody of two police officers when he died, "and they tried to conceal this fact when they testified at the inquiry" (Cheema 2009, 91). In his report, he strongly criticized the police investigation into Stonechild's death, describing it as "insufficient and totally inadequate" (Wright 2004, 212, cited in Comack 2012, 117) after concluding "that the police had prematurely closed the investigation because of their suspicion that the lead detective was aware that members of the police could have been involved in Stonechild's death" (Cheema 2009, 91). Subsequently, the two police officers involved in the Stonechild case were dismissed from the Saskatoon Police Service.

But was justice achieved as a result of the revelations about "dumping" by members of the SPS? Some might argue that light was shed on an unauthorized and unacceptable exercise of police discretion, and that the police officers who engaged in the practice were called to account. Others might maintain that simply pulling a few "bad apples" out of the barrel does not address the systemic nature of the discretion that police deploy in efforts to contain and control racialized and other marginalized people across Canada.

The case of Frank Paul provides compelling support for the argument that "dumping" is a systemic, racialized practice that is not confined to the SPS. Paul was a Mi'kmaq man from New Brunswick who had migrated to Vancouver's Downtown Eastside in the early 1980s. He died in an alley in the DTES on a cold, rainy night in 1998 at the age of 47. As a homeless, chronic alcoholic with mental health issues, he was "troublesome" not only for the police but also for other professionals who encountered him on a regular basis.[3] On the day of his death, Paul was taken into custody for being drunk in a public place, confined in a "drunk tank," released, and then taken into custody again by the VPD officer driving the police van that patrolled the DTES. The police sergeant in charge of the lock-up refused to accept Paul a second time and told the van driver to take him "to an area he was known to frequent" in another part of the city (Razack 2012, 909). Although Paul was a large man, he could barely walk at the end of his life, and police video shows him being dragged in and out of the police station. Fate intervened, however, when the van driver encountered a senior police officer and was "advised to leave Mr. Paul in an alleyway" that led to the Vancouver Detox Centre, rather than transport him to another jurisdiction. There, a few hours later, Paul was found dead of hypothermia due to acute alcohol intoxication (Razack 2012, 909).

Almost a decade later, the BC government finally responded to demands for a public inquiry into the death of Frank Paul, appointing William Davies, a retired BC Supreme Court judge, as commissioner. Former Justice Davies conducted "a broad inquiry into the institutions that had responsibility to respond to both the circumstances and the possible responsibility for [Frank Paul's] death," including the VPD, the Coroner's Office, and the Criminal Justice Branch of the Ministry of the Attorney General (Davies 2011, 2). He was critical of them all, but ultimately none were found (criminally) responsible for Frank Paul's death. This finding and the fact that the legacy of colonialism was not central to Davies' investigation elicited disappointment and criticism of his reports from many of those who had pushed for a public inquiry (Razack 2012). Nonetheless, an acknowledgement of how racism and colonialism contributed to the death of Frank Paul was not entirely absent from the reports, as the following passage makes clear:

> It also matters that Frank Paul was a Mi'kmaq man. The circumstances of his life and death are an account in miniature of the risks and struggles faced by many First Nations people of his generation. . . . We cannot know when the psychic injuries of childhood were compounded by the addiction and mental illness of his adult years. We must acknowledge, however, that the tragic arc of his life was that followed all too frequently by the members of the First Nations in our community and that his death speaks

out yet again of our need to revisit and refashion the important relationship between the First Nations people of Canada and the general community. (Davies 2011, 4–5)

This discussion of "dumping" speaks to an issue that often generates criticism of how the police carry out their "visible" work; namely, racial profiling.

RACIAL PROFILING AND POLICE "STOP AND SEARCH" DECISIONS

One of the most common criticisms of contemporary policing in Canada and other liberal democracies is that police decision making is based on racial profiling and, therefore, the criminal justice process is inherently discriminatory. While there is more than one definition, most would agree with David Tanovich that "racial profiling is the practice of targeting racial minorities for criminal investigation solely or, in part, on the basis of their skin colour. It is conduct that is premised on the assumption that the 'usual offenders' can be located within a particular group in society" (2002, 149). In Britain, the United States, and Canada, (young) black men are by far the group most subject to racial profiling, a status captured in the phrase "driving while black" (DWB), which encapsulates why they are being pulled over by police (Tanovich 2002, 147). In Canada, Aboriginal people are also frequently the target of racial profiling, especially in the West (Ontario Human Rights Commission 2003). Moreover, while black and Aboriginal men are the primary targets, racialized women are not exempt from racial profiling, as the case of Stacy Bonds illustrates.

In the fall of 2008, Bonds was walking home from a party when she was stopped by the Ottawa police, arrested "for effectively asking why she had been stopped and questioned by police," and then taken to a police station (Tanovich 2011), where she was formally charged with public intoxication and assaulting police. However, she too was assaulted—kneed in the back, strip-searched by male and female officers, and detained "half-naked" (Tanovich 2011) for more than three hours in a police cell, all of which was captured on a cell block video that was eventually released to the public in the fall of 2010 (CBC News 31 January 2011a). The video generated intense debate about whether the strip search followed proper police procedures or constituted sexual assault (CBC News 2011b). Additionally, since Stacy Bonds is an African Canadian, the incident raised the question of whether race and/or gender factored into the police decision to stop her on the street in the first place, and subsequently to "humiliate her" (Tanovich 2011). After viewing the video several times, prosecutors concluded that Stacy Bonds was not being singled out, and that pursuing the charge of assaulting police against her was in the public interest (Ibid.). When the case came to court, however, the trial judge strongly disagreed. He stayed the charge against Stacy Bonds, after concluding that the police conduct had no basis in law and that what happened to her that night in 2008 was an "indignity towards a human being." In his view, the only reasonable explanation for the officers' conduct was "vengeance and malice" (Tanovich 2011).

Ontario's Special Investigations Unit (SIU) reviewed the conduct of the police with respect to Stacy Bonds, and in March 2011, charged one officer with sexual assault in connection with her arrest and incarceration. Sgt. Steven Desjourdy was the officer in charge of the cell block that night, and it was he who cut off her bra and shirt with scissors after four other officers forced her to the ground and pinned her (CBC News 2011b). In April 2013, the trial judge handed down a mixed ruling. On one hand, he found that Stacy Bonds' arrest constituted a "serious violation" of her Charter rights, that the most likely reason for her arrest was that she "had the temerity to challenge the officer's decision to stop and investigate," and that there was "no plausible reason" to leave her in a cell topless, in soiled pants, for more than three hours. On the other hand, the judge acquitted Sgt. Desjourdy on the grounds that there was no sexual context to his actions, that while he had departed from strip-search guidelines, he had done so in "the least intrusive way," and that the search was not "unreasonable, excessive, or abusive" (Metro News 2013).

Canadian police do have the authority to stop and search someone if they have "reasonable grounds" to think that an individual may be involved in criminal activities, but they are not authorized to use their stop and search powers for fishing expeditions or to punish people like Stacy Bonds for failing to show the expected amount of deference to police authority. The Charter of Rights and Freedoms protects citizens from illegal search and seizure, and the Criminal Code sets out police powers of arrest. The major police services in Canada, however, have always flatly denied that their decision making rests on racial profiling, despite acknowledgement by the courts and community organizations that racial profiling takes place (Henry and Tator 2006). Not surprisingly, then, a series of articles in the *Toronto Star* in 2002, which highlighted the disproportionate use of profiling with the city's black population, "became a new flashpoint for the issue" (Comack 2012, 35). Through a Freedom of Information application, the newspaper gained access to otherwise inaccessible police information about almost 484,000 incidents, dating back to 1996, where Toronto police arrested, ticketed, or charged an individual (Comack 2012, 35). In consultation with York University's Institute for Social Research, the *Star*'s investigative journalists were able to produce an in-depth analysis of how police treat minorities and whites when arrested for two specific offences—simple drug possession and traffic offences. They found that black people were treated more harshly than whites and concluded that Toronto police engaged in racial profiling.

While many black Canadians found that the study's findings were in sync with their own experiences, Henry and Tator (2006) note that a "discourse of denial" was immediately invoked, supported by some black Toronto police officers, the police chief, the mayor; and the Toronto Police Association—who had all strenuously rejected the existence of racial profiling. Alan Gold, a criminal lawyer hired by the Toronto Police Service to conduct an independent review of the *Star*'s analysis, went so far as to dismiss it as "junk science" (Wortley and Tanner 2003, 368). Not only were the findings denied, but the Toronto police force declared that police and black community relations were very good, with no evidence that police discrimination was a pressing issue at the time. Furthermore, if there were any victims emerging from this issue, the police chief claimed it to be the police, since they had become objects of prejudice and discrimination, and their work had been undermined and disparaged as a result of the *Star*'s report (Henry and Tator 2006, 132). Henry and Tator (2006) highlight how these discourses of denial and reverse discrimination, along with discourses of political correctness (in reference to demands from the black community that the police stop profiling) and discourses of otherness (discrediting or silencing black and other oppositional voices), were powerful rhetorical strategies that allowed the police to categorically deny racial profiling. The Toronto Police Association was so incensed, in fact, that they filed a $2.7 billion lawsuit against the *Toronto Star*, along with other countermeasures, in an effort to silence them.

In 2010, the *Toronto Star* published a follow-up series of articles on race and crime, based on the analysis of police data for the years 2003 to 2008, and found the same patterns described in its earlier analysis (Comack 2012, 53). This time, however, police reaction to the newspaper's conclusions about racial profiling was much more tempered. Instead of a flat denial, the police chief, Bill Blair, who had been appointed after the publication of the *Star*'s first series on race and crime, acknowledged the existence of racial profiling. He then went on to soften that admission, emphasizing that police officers are only human, and that humans make mistakes, assuring the public that the Toronto Police Service was working hard to eliminate racial bias from the decision making of its members (Comack 2012, 54).

The fact that police services in Canada may be starting to acknowledge bias in decision making does not, however, put the issue of racial profiling to rest.[4] Unlike their counterparts in the United States and Great Britain, Canadian researchers find it extremely difficult to investigate possible racial bias in the criminal justice system systematically because the virtual ban on the collection and release of all race-and-crime data means that researchers "do not have regular access to official data on the race of people stopped and searched by the police (or any other justice outcome for that matter)" (Wortley and Owusu-Bempah 2011, 396). As we noted in the introduction, being denied access to comprehensive official data on race and crime, some researchers have creatively tackled the issue of racial profiling in a different way, by conducting studies on people's perceptions of and experiences with the police. As a result, there is now a body of Canadian research on police stop-and-search practices, but it consists primarily of small, in-depth ethnographic studies that are difficult to generalize and, like the *Toronto Star* analyses, are often unfairly dismissed as "junk science" or "anecdotal" by police and some academics (Worley and Owusu-Bempah 2011, 396).

Recently, however, some researchers have been able to conduct larger studies based on representative samples to address the issue of racial profiling and police stop-and-search practices. In the fall of 2007, Scot Wortley and Akwasi Owusu-Bempah conducted an interview survey based on a representative sample of 1,522 respondents over the age of 18, who self-identified as black (N = 513), Chinese (N = 504), or white (N = 505), and resided in Metropolitan Toronto (2011, 396–97). Respondents were asked about their perceptions of racial profiling, direct contact with the police, interpretations of police encounters, and indirect experiences with racial profiling (i.e., hearing about the experiences of others). Survey findings showed that blacks were over three times more likely to experience multiple police stops than whites or Asians and were three times more likely to report being searched; that black males were particularly vulnerable to police stop-and-search practices; that blacks were six times more likely than respondents from other racial backgrounds to report that close friends or family members had recently been subject to racial profiling; and that racial differences with respect to both direct and indirect police contact remained statistically relevant, after controlling for other relevant variables such as age, income, education, drug use, community-level crime, driving habits, etc. (Wortley and Owusu-Bempah 2011, 402).

These study results are in keeping with those from the United Kingdom and the United States, where researchers concluded that race influences criminal justice outcomes through processes of racialization and stereotyping (Rose 2002; Warde 2012). As the BC Civil Liberties Association notes, "racial profiling is bad policy," and the costs are high for those who are subjected to harassment and scrutiny on a regular basis (Holmes 2010). Gova and Kurd's examination of the impact of racial profiling by security officials on self-identified Canadian Muslims after September 11 found that most research participants believed that they were being targeted for greater scrutiny and suspicion, compared to other racial or religious groups (2008, 6). The participants stated that they expected to be treated with increased suspicion in all areas of their life—from airport screenings to attending a fundraising event (Gova and Kurd 2008, 8). They were peppered with appropriate and inappropriate questions by security officials about all aspects of their life when they were detained for examination (Gova and Kurd 2008, 8).

Fear of speaking or travelling, practicing self-censorship of one's cultural or religious identity, and retreating from participating in social and cultural events were common responses to the fear of being profiled (Gova and Kurd 2008, 35).

These responses are very similar to those documented in a report by the African Canadian Community Coalition on Racial Profiling (Brown 2004); African Canadians report a sense of injustice, combined with the inability to move around public spaces freely, and a feeling like they are being targeted even when no wrongdoing has occurred (Brown 2004, 36). These emotions exact a toll, particularly for African Canadian male youth, who feel a lack of freedom—that there is no room for making forgivable mistakes without a fear of reprisal (Brown 2004, 38). The report adds,

> When African Canadians feel that they are being profiled by police as anti-social wrongdoers, the sting is all the more sharp because they see themselves portrayed in the same way on TV, in books and in movies. (Brown 2004, 31)

Thus, for many racialized Canadians, their everyday lived experiences of worrying about being stopped by the police, of changing their daily routines to avoid attention, and of the consequences of these fears on their overall physical and mental well-being are substantial. Communities also suffer since their members are less likely to cooperate with police or to report crimes (Ontario Human Rights Commission 2003). Police–community relations often become more strained as levels of trust decline. The need for more action to address this problem has been made clear by numerous community organizations and scholars (Tanovich 2003–04; Holmes 2010). As we discuss in the next section, failure to act may potentially lead to more dire outcomes, such as the increased use of lethal force against racialized individuals.

RACE AND POLICE USE OF FORCE

Just as the public police are state-sanctioned agents with the authority to stop and search people if they have "reasonable" grounds for doing so, they are also mandated to use (deadly) force if necessary under certain conditions that are set out in the Canadian Criminal Code:

> Every one who is required or authorized by law to do anything in the administration or enforcement of the law
>   (b) as a peace officer or public officer, is, if he acts on reasonable grounds, justified in doing what he is required or authorized

to do and in using as much force as is necessary for that purpose.
(R.S.C. 1985, c.-46, s.25)

The interpretation of what constitutes "reasonable grounds" and "necessary" force is often disputed, however, when a civilian is killed, particularly
when the civilian is a racialized person.

Most research on police use of deadly force in liberal democracies has
focused on the United States, and there is now ample evidence that African
American men are "grossly over-represented" in police shootings and other
situations involving police use of force (Black 1976; Terrill and Reisig 2003).
Over the past few decades, high-profile incidents have exacerbated tensions
between racial minority communities and the police, and specific cases of
police violence against racial minorities have "sparked major urban riots in
several cities" (Wortley 2006, 2).

Police use of force has become a contentious issue in Canada as well,
with minority communities alleging discriminatory policing in the wake of
high-profile police shootings in several provinces (Pedicelli 1998; Hodgson
2001; Comack 2012). The use of force to resolve conflict has led some to
claim that there is an epidemic of police brutality (Hodgson 2001). The
report of the Commission on Systemic Racism in the Ontario Criminal
Justice System (1995) found that black people were disproportionately
subject to police shootings. Between 1978 and 1995, 16 black men were
shot by police in Ontario, with none of the police officers convicted for
excessive use of force (Roach 1996; Williams 2001). The victims are usually black and Aboriginal men, or other marginalized individuals, many of
whom are in mental distress at the time of the shooting. But again, as with
police decisions to stop and search, there is no consensus about why this
population is over-represented. The same two polarized positions, among
others, represent the current state of debate. The first is the argument that
black and Aboriginal men (and women) are more predisposed to criminality
and violence than are other racial groups, and that the statistics on lethal
force are representative of their increased contact with police. The second
is the argument that racism is at play, and that black and Aboriginal men,
and especially male youth, are being unjustly targeted. The circumstances
become more precarious when the individuals have mental health problems,
and cannot respond to the police. In contrast to the US, Canada's paucity
of empirical research on the use of lethal force by police officers against
racialized Canadians makes it difficult to assess their motives for the use of
force.

A major reason for the lack of Canadian research is the inability of
researchers to access official data on police shootings and other use-of-force
incidents. While police conduct internal investigations of incidents involving

the use of force, the statistics on police shootings or their non-lethal use of force are not routinely made available. Likewise, government inquiries are often established to look into particularly contentious cases involving police use of lethal force (or other alleged police misconduct), but these investigations usually deal with one particular case or incident, making it difficult to see patterns and trends over time that would support or refute allegations of police discrimination. Moreover, as Brodeur (2003) argues, police use of force is a continuum of behaviours—from mere physical presence on one end to physical contact and deadly force on the other. One of the key difficulties in examining this issue is that there is no shared criterion of what constitutes an occurrence of excessive force (Brodeur 2003, 209). Furthermore, distinguishing between illegitimate and illegal use of force is highly contentious, with definitions differing depending on who is defining the terms (Brodeur 2003, 209). As a result, counting the occasions when force is used is not achievable (Adams 1999).

A report on the use of force by Ontario police was among the first studies to analyze data that had been systematically collected over time. Wortley (2006) examined data from the Special Investigations Unit, which was established in 1990 by the Ontario Attorney General to conduct independent investigations and determine if a crime had occurred in cases when a civilian had been seriously injured or killed during an encounter with police. Because the researchers used a non-random sample, the study results are not definitive with respect to the debate over police use of force, but some of the findings support earlier research, while others point to issues that need further examination. The report noted that African Canadians and Aboriginal people were "grossly over-represented" in police use-of-force statistics, and particularly in police shooting incidents, and that the over-representation of African Canadians was "especially high" in the Toronto Census Metropolitan Area (CMA). Therefore, while police use of force in Ontario seems "quite infrequent," relative to the use of force by police in a comparable American city like Chicago, it appears that when Ontario police decide to use force, "they use it much more frequently against African Canadians and Aboriginals than any other racial groups" (Wortley 2006). Similarly, gender analysis revealed that most of the civilian cases investigated by the SIU involved males and an even greater proportion of the investigations of black civilians involved males (90.4 per cent), as compared to their white (82.5 per cent) and Aboriginal (78.6 per cent) counterparts. A perhaps less-expected, gender-related finding was that women made up almost one-quarter of investigations involving Aboriginal civilians (Wortley 2006, 47). Furthermore, the data showed that police officers are rarely charged for using excessive force, regardless of the racial status of the victims. The researchers suggest that the low charge rate can be interpreted in two opposed ways: either the

Ontario police very rarely use illegitimate force, or the SIU investigations are tilted in favour of the police (Wortley 2006, 50–51).

The existing research does not tell us categorically whether Canadian police engage in racial profiling when they use excessive force, but this has not stopped the general public from protesting against police brutality. The issue has gained more prominence in the wake of large public demonstrations in Canada (e.g., the APEC meetings in Vancouver in 1997, the World Petroleum Congress in Calgary in 2000, and the G20 Summit in Toronto in 2010), with clashes and conflicts occurring between the public and the police (John Howard Society of Alberta 2006). Therefore, periodic concern about the police use of lethal force on minority men—often in the wake of shootings involving black youth in Toronto and Montreal, and Aboriginal men in the Western provinces—has sparked efforts to reform police recruitment, training, procedures, and policies. A relatively recent reform was the introduction in 2001 of the taser[5] or stun gun—a handheld weapon "that deliver[s] a jolt of electricity through a pair of wires propelled by compressed air from up to 10.6 meters away" (CBC News 2011c)—as an ostensibly less lethal weapon for the police "to incapacitate combative or violent suspects who may be resistant to lesser degrees of force" (White and Ready 2007, 170). In Canada, even though there have not been any public policy consultations or discussions on the use of tasers, 129 law enforcement agencies were using them by the end of 2010 (Murphy 2012; CBC News 2011c).

The high-profile deaths of several people who had been tasered raises questions about when tasers should be used, the effectiveness of the taser for police, and the harm (including potential death) to people who are tasered. The death of Robert Dziekanski at the Vancouver International Airport in October 2007, after being shocked five times with a taser by RCMP officers, as well as the subsequent report of the Braidwood Inquiry that "concluded the RCMP was not justified in using a taser against Dziekanski," was the catalyst for a reassessment of the weapon. Canadian police forces appear to be using the taser much more sparingly over the past few years. In 2009, the RCMP watchdog released statistics indicating that in 2008 RCMP officers used stun guns 1,106 times (including incidents when officers drew but did not fire their tasers), about 30 per cent less than in the previous year (CBC News 2011c). However, critics such as Amnesty International argue that police agencies should suspend the use of the taser until the health effects of its use can be further researched (White and Ready 2007, 175). Otherwise, the taser might have simply expanded the lethal weaponry available to the police.

Perhaps it's not a coincidence that the demand for greater accountability in policing comes at the same time that the nature of policing has taken on a harder edge (Brannagan 2011; Murphy 2012). Ultimately, like all dichotomies, the debate about whether police do or do not engage in racial profiling is irresolvable. It echoes the historical debate about whether women were treated more leniently or harshly in the criminal justice system than were men. No across-the-board generalizations can be made because, among other things, racial and gender categories are not homogeneous. There is also a tendency to see racial profiling as a conscious strategy, but in the current context, it is less and less overt (Glover 2007). Improving police services to be more accountable and transparent, particularly in racialized communities that are disproportionately impacted by crime, is an issue that needs continuous attention, if racialized communities are to retain faith in the police force (Roberts 2007).

Elizabeth Comack argues that we should talk about racialized *policing* rather than profiling, because the latter term "has a decidedly individualized focus ... on the exercise of discretion by individual police officers. What is missing in current debates is the need to set the issue within the broader dynamics involved in the encounters between racialized groups and the police as an institution" (2012, 57) that is engaged in the reproduction of order and the status quo. Moving beyond the interpersonal level of analysis would help to illuminate that racialized policing is premised on naturalized assumptions about race, gender, class, and sexuality, which inform the decision making of not just the police, but all official decision makers in the criminal justice system. In the next chapter, we examine how these taken-for-granted beliefs are at play in decision making about prosecution and sentencing over time.

NOTES

1 We focus here on public policing. Private police increasingly outnumber public police (Li 2008), but although this growth and the relationship between public and private police has been extensively discussed in the literature, we have not found any data on the issue of racial profiling and its impacts in relation to private policing.

2 Although we confine ourselves in this discussion to long-standing, well-documented instances of "under the radar" policing strategies that target racialized and Aboriginal men, it is important to bear in mind the strategies that police adopt with racialized and Aboriginal women as well. For example, a recent report by the respected, New York-based Human Rights Watch documents how the RCMP in Northern British Columbia have not only dragged their feet in terms of investigating stories about missing and murdered women, they themselves have subjected Aboriginal women to serious physical and sexual abuse, and in some instances, threatened the women with retaliation if they told anyone about the abuse (Human Rights Watch 2013). See also BCCLA (British Columbia Civil Liberties Association) 2013.

3 The report of the public inquiry into Frank Paul's death noted his "extraordinary use of medical and police services.... He was taken into custody by the VPD on more than a dozen occasions in the months leading up to his death. The BC Ambulance Services responded to 121 calls between April 1996 and December 1998. He was treated at, or admitted to, Vancouver General Hospital 93 times. He was treated at, or admitted to, St. Paul's Hospital 63 times by June 1997.... He had been to the Vancouver Detox Centre 82 times since 1983" (Davies 2009, iv–v, cited in Razack 2012, 917).

4 See, e.g., P. Carrington, ed. 2011. "Symposium on racial profiling and police culture." *Canadian Journal of Criminology and Criminal Justice* 53 (1): 63–131.
5 We use the term "taser" in lower case to refer to a certain type of weapon. We are aware that "Taser" is also a company name, and has significant brand status.

DISCUSSION QUESTIONS

What privileges, if any, do white people enjoy from the police?
Do you agree with the government that we should not be collecting statistics on race and crime?
Is racial profiling something that we can stop?
Should we follow Elizabeth Comack's suggestion to replace the term "racial profiling" with the term "racialized policing"?

FURTHER READING

Doe, J. 2003. *The Story of Jane Doe.* Toronto: Random House.
Henry, F., and C. Tator. 2006. *Racial Profiling in Canada.* Toronto: University of Toronto Press.
Lawson, E. 2013. "Disenfranchised grief and social inequality: Bereaved African Canadians and oppositional narratives about the violent deaths of family and family members." *Ethnic and Racial Studies* (Published online 24 May 2013), http://dx.doi.org/10.1080/01419870.2013.800569.
Mosher, C.J. 1998. *Discrimination and Denial: Systemic Racism in Ontario's Legal and Criminal Justice Systems, 1892–1961.* Toronto: University of Toronto Press.
Tanovich, D.M. 2002. "Using the Charter to stop racial profiling: The development of an equality-based conception of arbitrary detention." *Osgoode Hall Law Journal* 40 (2): 145–87.
Tanovich, D.M. 2011. "Bonds: Gendered and racialized violence, strip searches, sexual assault and abuse of prosecutorial power." *Criminal Reports* (6th): 79, 132–50.

WEBSITES OF INTEREST

Canadian Civil Liberties Association—http://ccla.org/
Pivot Legal Society—http://www.pivotlegal.org/
Race Matters (The Toronto Star)—http://www.thestar.com/news/gta/raceandcrime.html
The Centre for Police Accountability—http://www.c4pa.ca/
Who Killed William Robinson?—http://www.canadianmysteries.ca/sites/robinson/indexen.html

CHAPTER SIX

RACE, SENTENCING, AND IMPRISONMENT

Responses to lawbreakers depend on who they are and how their actions are explained. Viewed retrospectively, it is clear that from the nineteenth century to the present, criminal law and policy in liberal states such as Canada has been framed within the parameters of ideas and discourses about sameness and difference (Deutschmann 2007). Initially, an emphasis on sameness was the dominant influence on criminal law and justice, which was based on several core ideas associated with the classical school of criminology: first, crime is the outcome of a rational choice, albeit a bad one, by both women and men; second, lawbreakers are responsible for their bad choices; and third, they should be punished in proportion to the seriousness of their crimes (Muncie, McLaughlin, and Langan 1996, 4–13). From the late nineteenth century to the 1960s, an emphasis on (gender and age) difference increasingly became the primary influence on criminal law and justice, now premised on key ideas associated with the positivist school of criminology: first, crime is an irrational act by women and men who are afflicted by sex-specific pathologies (e.g., XYY, PMS); second, lawbreakers cannot, therefore, be held fully accountable for their actions; and third, the appropriate response to crime is individualized diagnosis and treatment of the crime-causing pathologies by non-legal experts (e.g., social workers, psychiatrists), rather than punishment (Muncie, McLaughlin, and Langan 1996, 14–39).

From the 1960s to the present, we can track another shift in perspectives on criminal justice as the neo-liberal order took shape. Most liberal states have witnessed the emergence of a criminal justice system that is based on a hybrid of assumptions about sameness and difference, creating what David Garland (2001) calls "the culture of control." Specifically, classical criminological ideas about rational choice, accountability, and punishment are intertwined with positivist ideas about identifying "risky" women and men before they can cause harm, or preventing future harm by working with individuals who can be "responsibilized," while containing those who cannot. As we have noted throughout this book, criminal justice in most contemporary liberal states now rests on a conception of sameness as identical treatment based on the argument that (formal) equality has been achieved. Consequently, differences between and among women and men that are linked to race, gender, class, and sexuality are acknowledged only to pinpoint and control risk, not to develop individualized responses which address the needs of criminalized women and men (Hannah-Moffat 2005; Hannah-Moffat and Maurutto 2010; Swift and Callahan, 2009; Williams 2009; Barron 2011).

GENDERING CRIMINAL JUSTICE

Given the historical gender blindness of research on crime and justice, feminists have been at the forefront of efforts to make the case for gendered analyses of the system. Many American feminists, in particular, became embroiled in an ongoing debate about whether women lawbreakers are treated more leniently or more severely than men in the criminal justice system, generating substantial feminist, as well as non-feminist, literature on gender bias and criminal justice (Moulds 1980). Despite compelling arguments on both sides, the existing literature does not provide conclusive evidence on the issue of gender bias and criminal justice. American researchers have produced a spate of quantitative studies in recent decades that do not demonstrate either across-the-board chivalry toward, or discrimination against, women lawbreakers (Datesman and Scarpitti 1980; Crew 1991; Daly 1994; Grabe et al. 2006; Franklin and Fearn 2008). Sometimes criminal law and the criminal justice system seem to favour women over men, and vice versa.

For some feminists, the conflicting results of research on the chivalry–severity debate suggest that researchers have been asking the wrong questions (Edwards 1989; Daly 1997). Since no blanket legal privileging or repression of women vis-à-vis men has been demonstrated, it is impossible to say that women are always treated either more leniently or more severely than men. The huge and historically consistent gender gap between the numbers of women and men who are criminally charged (Brennan 2012, 20; Rennison 2009) seems to be generally regarded as evidence that women do commit less crime than men, rather than evidence of leniency toward women. Likewise, the gender gap challenges the argument that (criminal) law is merely an instrument of patriarchy, because if men use law to maintain their power over women, why would so many more men than women be criminalized (Daly and Chesney-Lind 1988, 116)?

Nonetheless, it is also evident that while criminal law and criminal justice may not always operate directly in the interests of men, they do work as mechanisms for regulating marginalized populations in Canada and other liberal states, thereby reproducing and maintaining structured inequalities based on social relations of gender, race, class, and sexual orientation, among others. Therefore, researchers need to think about how gender intersects with other social relations to create differences *among* women and *among* men, which privilege some and disadvantage others in criminal law and the administration of criminal justice. In short, the questions researchers should be addressing are *which* women and *which* men are treated more leniently or severely than others in the criminal justice system, and why?

It is generally agreed that the administration of criminal justice is based both on legal factors, including the number of charges, the seriousness of the offence(s), and prior criminal record, as well as extra-legal factors, such as relationship with family, employment status, and the demeanor of the accused. More controversially, many feminists and other critical scholars argue that the administration of criminal justice is a discretionary process, and, therefore, the ways in which legal and extra-legal factors are assessed, and how they influence the processing of women and men lawbreakers, will reflect prevailing ideas about gender and gender relations as well as crime, law, and justice at particular moments in time.

With regard to ideas about gender and gender relations, many feminists have conducted studies that point to what Kathleen Daly has called "familial-based justice" (1989; Eaton 1986; Okin 1989). What their cross-jurisdictional research demonstrates is how the decision making of legal and non-legal agents alike has historically reflected and reinforced, to a greater or lesser extent, a belief that the nuclear family unit, organized around a heterosexual, monogamous-marriage relationship and a sexual division of labour, is the only appropriate form of family (Gavigan 1988, 293). This conception of family incorporates two assumptions about the acceptable relations between women and men, and adults and children. First, "normal" women and men marry, have children, and carry out sex-specific duties and responsibilities that are related to their "natural" roles within the nuclear family—the husband/father as the primary breadwinner/provider and protector of his dependents, and the wife/mother as the primary caregiver/ homemaker and socializing agent. Second, "normal" parents prevent their children from behaving like adults, and they are particularly careful to guard the sexual purity of daughters (Sangster 2001; Myers 2006).

As we discussed in Chapter 2, this means that ideas and discourses about normality are inextricably tied to assumptions about gender roles within a traditional nuclear family unit. Thus, women and men who conform to heteronormative, white, middle-class behavioural norms are more likely to encounter the criminal justice system as agents (e.g., police, prosecutors, judges) than as criminally charged persons; and, if they are charged, such women and men are more likely to receive "lenient" treatment, all other things being equal, than those who cannot or who refuse to conform. Only "bad" mothers and fathers, wives and husbands, daughters and sons go to prison (Daly 1989; Roberts 1993; Swift and Callahan 2009). Over time, for example, we can see that racialized women and men are always present in the "bad" categories in disproportionate numbers, albeit not all racialized groups are targeted at the same moment in time. Arguably, this explains, at least in part, why racialized people are vastly over-represented in the criminal justice systems of all contemporary liberal states (Chan and Mirchandani 2002; Chigwada-Bailey 2003; Carlen and Tombs, 2006; Comack 2012).

Moreover, the currently dominant conception of equal treatment as identical treatment, when there are such obvious differences (of race, class, gender, sexual orientation) among criminalized women and men, works to reproduce and exacerbate those differences, thereby increasing the severity of the criminal justice process for many (Daly 1989; Roberts 1993; Chigwada-Bailey 2003). Studies of women on death row in the United States, for example, show an over-representation of lesbians, or prisoners perceived to be lesbians, who do not project the "hetero-feminine" persona that is critical "in engendering chivalry and leniency" toward criminalized women (Farr 2000, 49; see also Robson 1998, 2004). Rather, they are depicted as "manly and man-hating women," who kill out of rage and an "irrational desire for revenge"; a portrait of "homosexualized ... female evil," which may be an aggravating circumstance in the sentencing of women, particularly for offences that carry the ultimate penalty of death (Farr 2000, 49).

RACE AND THE CRIMINAL JUSTICE PROCESS

Disparities and over-representation of particular racial and ethnic groups are two key issues in the literature on the administration of criminal justice in all liberal states. As we noted earlier, however, Canadian researchers face huge challenges because government publications do not provide information on race and ethnicity, and, in some cases, gender as well, with the exception of Aboriginal people. Moreover, it is not just the statistics on policing that are incomplete or non-existent. Canada lacks comprehensive, longitudinal national data on every stage of the criminal justice process—reporting, policing, prosecution, and sentencing. National court data on convictions and sentencing outcomes are particularly gap-ridden and not up-to-date. While Canadian research often produces findings similar to those of researchers in other jurisdictions who do have access to such data, we know that there are differences as well as similarities across jurisdictions that might only be revealed through access to more complete data sets.

In the meantime, the latest available Canadian statistics tell us that in 2010–11, consistent with police-reported data, 8 out of 10 persons accused in adult criminal court cases were men (81 per cent), 2 out of 10 were women (19 per cent), and less than 1 per cent were companies (Dauvergne 2012a, 9). The main outcome in criminal cases for 2010–11 was a guilty finding (including cases where a guilty plea was entered) in about two-thirds of the cases (64 per cent), a proportion that has been relatively consistent over the last decade. Another 32 per cent of cases were stayed, withdrawn, or dismissed, and 3 per cent resulted in acquittals. The remaining one per cent ended with a different type of disposition, such as "not criminally responsible" (NCR) to stand trial because of mental disorder (Dauvergne 2012a, 9–10).

The rate for adults under correctional supervision in 2010–11 was 616 per 100,000 of the adult population, 7 per cent lower than a decade ago. This decrease reflects a 10 per cent drop in the number of adults under community supervision, and a 5 per cent increase in incarceration. On any given day in 2010–11, there were 38,000 persons in custody (Dauvergne 2012a, 6). Most were incarcerated in provincial facilities where the maximum sentence is two years less a day (29 per cent), or in remand facilities awaiting trial or pre-trial assessment (34 per cent), but 36 per cent of incarcerated people were in federal penitentiaries.

Nonetheless, Canada is not the most punitive liberal democracy. Recent statistics from the International Centre for Prison Studies show that Canada ranks 17th of 34 member countries in the International Organisation for Economic Co-operation and Development, with an incarceration rate of 117 compared with the (first-ranked) United States and the United Kingdom, which have rates of 730 and 154, respectively (Dauvergne 2012b, 7). Still, incarceration in Canada seems to be increasing, and Aboriginal people are already vastly over-represented in custody across all provinces and territories (Correctional Investigator of Canada 2012). In 2010–11, Aboriginal men and women made up 27 per cent of the adults in provincial/territorial custody, and 20 per cent of people in federal custody—about seven or eight times higher than the proportion of Aboriginal people in the adult population as a whole (2012b, 11). This disparity holds true across all provinces and territories, and especially among Aboriginal women, who make up 41 per cent of females in sentenced custody, versus 25 per cent of Aboriginal men in sentenced custody (Dauvergne 2012b, 11).

It is highly possible that some of these prosecutions and penal sentences were based on wrongful convictions, an issue that has garnered much media attention because of a spate of highly publicized cases in recent years (Anderson and Anderson 2009; Keenan and Brockman 2010). Such "miscarriages of justice" were thought to be rare in Canada and other liberal democracies, and it was a surprise to many people to find out that they were not aberrations (Denov and Campbell 2005, 225; Huff and Killias 2008). The majority of highly publicized wrongful conviction cases involve white men, but in light of the stunning over-representation of Aboriginal people in Canadian courts and prisons, it is an issue that needs further study, with a focus on race (Denov and Campbell 2005, 231–32). The case of Donald Marshall Jr., an Aboriginal man who was wrongly convicted and sentenced to prison for life, is a good point of departure for researchers who want to examine how race is implicated in the process leading up to such injustice.

The case began on May 28, 1971, when Donald Marshall Jr., a Mi'kmaq youth, met Sandy Seale, a black youth, by chance in a park in Sydney, Nova Scotia, just before midnight. Both were 17 years of age and barely knew each other. As they walked, they met two white men—Roy Ebsary, aged 59, and James (Jimmy) MacNeil, who was 25. After a brief conversation, the two youths tried to "panhandle" the older men, triggering "a deadly over-reaction in the drunken and dangerous Ebsary. 'This is for you, Black man,' Ebsary said, and stabbed Seale in the stomach" (Hickman 1989, 2). He also lunged at Marshall giving him a superficial cut on the arm. Seale died the next day, and Donald Marshall Jr. was charged and convicted of his murder, and sent to Dorchester Penitentiary to serve a life sentence (Hickman 1989).

Marshall spent 11 years in prison before new evidence supporting his innocence surfaced in the early 1980s, after which the Nova Scotia government finally established a Royal Commission to re-examine his prosecution. After hearing from 113 witnesses over 93 days of public hearings, the commissioners rejected Ebsary's story that Seale was killed in the course of either a robbery, or an attempted robbery, by the two teenagers. Seale had enough money to take the bus home to meet his midnight curfew, and there was no evidence that he had ever been involved in criminal activity. He had no prior brushes with the law. Likewise, while Marshall had a few encounters with the law over minor incidents, he had no history of theft. Ebsary, however, had "a reputation for violence and unpredictable behaviour," and a prior conviction on a knife-related weapons charge (Hickman 1989, 2).

Research has revealed that wrongful convictions are not the result of a single error by one individual. On the contrary, both individual and systemic factors that are inherent to the criminal justice system may singly or in combination contribute to wrongful convictions (Denov and Campbell 2005, 226). These factors include eyewitness error, professional misconduct, false confessions, erroneous forensic science, the use of jailhouse informants, and racial bias (Hickman 1989, 2). In the case of Donald Marshall Jr., the Royal Commission revealed that virtually all of these factors were at play.

Beginning with the police, the commissioners found that the conduct of the Sydney police officers who had initially responded to the report of the stabbing, as well as the conduct of John MacIntyre, the sergeant of detectives who directed the subsequent police investigation, was "entirely inadequate, incompetent and unprofessional" (Hickman 1989, 3). MacIntyre "quickly decided that Marshall had stabbed Seale in the course of an argument, even though there was no evidence to support such a conclusion." The commissioners concluded that MacIntyre shared "a general sense in Sydney's White community at the time that Indians were not 'worth' as much as Whites" (Hickman 1989, 3). His entire investigation seemed to be focused on finding evidence to support his theory of the killing and discounting contradictory evidence. The most damning "evidence" against Donald Marshall Jr. came from two teenage "eyewitnesses," whose statements were based on an acceptance of suggestions made by John MacIntyre. Thus, Donald Marshall Jr. was charged with the murder of Sandy Seale "[l]argely because of the untrue statements MacIntyre had obtained" (Hickman 1989, 3).

The perjured evidence of the two teens was damning, but Marshall's wrongful conviction resulted from the failures of others as well, including the Crown and even the defence lawyer, who had all the necessary resources available, but, among other things, did not perform an independent investigation or request disclosure of the Crown's case (Hickman 1989, 4). The trial judge had also made several errors in law. The cumulative effect of these errors was Marshall's conviction and imprisonment. Ten days after the conviction, Jimmy MacNeil told police he had seen Ebsary stab Seale, but the RCMP officer in charge of the case conducted an "incompetent and incomplete investigation," during which he only spoke with MacNeil once about taking a polygraph test, and filed a report concluding that Marshall had stabbed Seale (Hickman 1989, 3). Information about MacNeil was not passed on to either the defence or the Crown assigned to Marshall's appeal, and was thus never presented to the Nova Scotia Court of Appeal, which would almost inevitably have ordered a new trial. Instead, the appeal was denied.

Ultimately, Marshall's innocence was established only through "an almost accidental series of coincidences" (Hickman 1989, 5). In 1981, Marshall learned that Ebsary had admitted to killing Seale. This time, the RCMP investigation was thorough, but they had also extracted a "confession" from Marshall that went along with Ebsary's version, that the stabbing of Seale was the result of attempted robbery. This statement was used against Marshall later at the Nova Scotia Court of Appeal, when the court quashed Marshall's conviction, but "also inexplicably chose to blame Marshall for his wrongful conviction" (i.e., for a robbery he never committed) (Hickman 1989, 7). The stance taken by the Appeal Court negatively impacted Marshall's negotiations with the Nova Scotia government for wrongful conviction compensation. The Royal Commission concluded that the Appeal Court's decision "amounted to a defence of the criminal justice system at the expense of

Donald Marshall Jr. in spite of overwhelming evidence that the system itself had failed" (Hickman 1989, 7).

In its overall conclusion, the Royal Commission minced no words in condemning the racism that underpinned such a colossal failure:

> The criminal justice system failed Donald Marshall, Jr. at virtually every turn from his arrest and wrongful conviction for murder in 1971 up to, and even beyond, his acquittal by the Court of Appeal in 1983. The tragedy of the failure is compounded by evidence that this miscarriage of justice could—and should—have been prevented, or at least corrected quickly, if those involved in the system had carried out their duties in a professional and/or competent manner. That they did not is due, in part at least, to the fact that Donald Marshall, Jr. is a Native. (Hickman 1989, 1)

The Royal Commission report on the Donald Marshall Jr. prosecution shed light on the systemic nature of wrongful convictions, and several highly publicized cases have come to light since 1989 (Anderson and Anderson 2009). The question is whether these cases represent the full extent of the problem, or whether they are simply the tip of the iceberg. As Myriam Denov and Kathryn Campbell (2005, 226) observe, however, while the exact number of wrongful convictions is unknown, "[t]he fact that wrongful convictions occur at all, points to the importance of studying the contributing factors and underlying causes." Their own small interview study suggests that innocent people are convicted more often than is believed, and underlines the need to address not only the failures of the criminal justice system that lead to wrongful convictions, but also the long-lasting impacts of wrongful conviction. They conducted two- to three-hour interviews with five white, Canadian men, who were wrongly convicted and imprisoned for an average of five years, to obtain their perceptions and experiences of wrongful conviction. All of the men suffered losses of freedom, dignity, credibility, and family, and experienced anger, feelings of aggression (i.e., toward the criminal justice system), and a continued sense of imprisonment upon release (Denov and Campbell 2005, 232–40). It is worth noting that these were men who were able to have their cases reviewed. What of the wrongly convicted who lack the financial (and other) resources needed to clear their names? As Denov and Campbell conclude, clearly the wrongly accused require "a more expedient and more accessible response from the Canadian criminal justice system" (2005, 245).

One suggestion for combating "naturalized bias" in the criminal justice system is to increase racial, gender, and sexual diversity among the legal agents in the system. This proposed reform is based on the assumption that having more women and people of colour working in the criminal justice system, more openly gay and lesbian authorities, and more legal agents with disabilities will broaden the world view of those (middle-class) white men who have historically dominated the administration of criminal justice. Consider the judiciary, for example. There are no national statistics on the number of Canadian judges from racialized groups, but during the mid-to-late 1990s, it was estimated that only two per cent of Canadian judges were Aboriginal or members of visible minorities (Brockman 2003, 161). Thus, even though it cannot be assumed that all visible minorities or Aboriginal people are homogeneous, it is hard to dispute the claim that a more racially diverse judiciary would project a very different image of judging. Kimberle Crenshaw's (2011) analysis of Barack Obama's presidential victory in 2008 is equally applicable to the historic breakthroughs of racialized people in other arenas; namely, that such breakthroughs are necessary, but not transformative of a racist society in and of themselves.

Recruitment of men and women from traditionally excluded groups to broaden the approaches to the administration of criminal justice is difficult, however. Being hired or appointed for positions traditionally monopolized by white men is only the first hurdle. Sticking with such positions is an equally difficult challenge. We can see that white women have made some inroads in terms of obtaining policing, prosecutorial, judicial, and correctional employment, yet they face ongoing backlash from white, male colleagues, as recent revelations about rampant sexual harassment in the RCMP show us (CBC News 2012a, CBC News 2013b). When criminal justice agents are racialized men and women, they experience racial and/or sexual harassment. They also become symbolic representatives for their entire group, and are subject to intense scrutiny for any bias in favour of their "own kind" (Brockman 2003, 161–62). In short, they are accorded "but for" status, which may be lost at any time.

The case of *R.D.S. v. R.* [1997] is illustrative of the constant scrutiny experienced by racialized judges. In this instance, an African Canadian youth-court judge, Corrine Sparks, was accused of bias when she contextualized an encounter between a white police officer and a black youth that ended with the youth's arrest and criminal charges being laid. She found the youth more credible than the police officer, and dismissed the charges. Her oral reasons for the decision to acquit R.D.S. included remarks that led to the Crown's complaint that her comments invoked "a reasonable apprehension of bias":

> The Crown says, well, why would the officer say that events occurred in the way in which he has relayed them to the Court this morning. I am not saying that the Constable has misled the court, although police officers have been known to do that in the past. I am not saying that the officer overreacted, but certainly police

officers do overreact, particularly when they are dealing with non-white groups. That to me indicates a state of mind right there that is questionable. I believe that probably the situation in this particular case is the case of a young police officer who overreacted. I do accept the evidence of [R.D.S.] that he was told to shut up or he would be under arrest. It seems to be in keeping with the prevalent attitude of the day. (cited in Razack 1998b)

Judge Sparks said that, based on her oral reasons and the evidence presented by R.D.S. and Constable Stienburg, she had no choice but to acquit.

On appeal, the lower courts in Nova Scotia agreed with the Crown, but the Supreme Court of Canada upheld Judge Sparks' judgment in a split decision. The majority on the SCC concluded that Judge Sparks did not exhibit "bias," and that she did not tie her comments directly to the race of R.D.S. Rather, she had referenced the historical legacy of racism in Nova Scotia's justice system, which had been exposed by the Commission that reviewed Donald Marshall's wrongful conviction only a few years earlier (Razack 1998b). Judge Sparks survived the attack on her judicial integrity and now sits as a family court judge. But it is easy to see how the prospect of constant sexist and racist backlash might be a deterrent to the recruitment of Aboriginal and visible minority judges (Brockman 2003, 161). Among many other things, R.D.S. raises the issue of how reforms intended to improve the status quo often have an unanticipated downside.

UNINTENDED CONSEQUENCES OF CRIMINAL JUSTICE REFORM

Indeed, the entire history of criminal justice reforms in Canada illustrates the dual-edged nature of reform. Measures aimed at ameliorating the "pains of imprisonment," for example, often have unintended and unwanted consequences, including racialized effects (Hannah-Moffat and Shaw 2000). Similarly, Canadian reforms implemented in recent decades that are aimed at improving police–community relations and reducing imprisonment rates, particularly with respect to Aboriginal people, have clearly been ineffectual (Williams 2009). One of the main objectives of the 1996 sentencing-law reform in Canada was to reduce the overall number of people sentenced to prison. To that end, a remedial section, which instructed judges to consider alternatives to prison for all offenders and, in particular, to pay close attention to the circumstances of Aboriginal offenders, was incorporated in the Criminal Code (SC, c.46, s. 718.2(e)).

The emphasis on Aboriginal people directly addressed their huge over-representation in Canadian prisons. Yet in 2006, a decade after the implementation of the sentencing reform, the incarceration rates for both Aboriginal women and men had increased, while the rates for non-Aboriginal prisoners actually declined (Williams 2009, 80–81). Aboriginal women, who are dramatically over-incarcerated even relative to their male counterparts, are among the most marginalized women in Canada, and are therefore among the least able to meet familial-based, normative expectations, and to achieve self-sufficiency and independence in their lives. But in passing sentence, judges have tended to focus on the individual circumstances and "risky" characteristics of Aboriginal women without considering the broader social context, including the legacy of colonialism, in which they live (Jackson 1999). As a result, sentencing decisions about Aboriginal women in the ten years after 1996 were dominated by a judicial desire to control for risk, with little attention to the ways in which criminalized Aboriginal women are also *at* risk (Williams 2009, 81; Comack 1996; Swift and Callahan 2009; Barron 2011).

The failure of the 1996 sentencing reform to stem the incarceration rate of Aboriginal men and women has been reconfirmed in the Special Report of the Correctional Investigator, which was tabled in the House of Commons on March 7, 2013 (Correctional Investigator Canada 2013). Howard Sapers has emphasized that the "systemic discrimination" toward Aboriginal people in the penitentiary system is evidenced by the "large gaps in correctional outcomes" between Aboriginal and non-Aboriginal prisoners, and the rates of imprisonment for the two groups (CBC News 2013a). He found an almost 40 per cent increase in Aboriginal prisoners at the federal level between 2001–02 and 2010–11, and, additionally, that Aboriginal people receive longer sentences, spend more time in segregation and maximum security, are less likely to be granted parole, and are more likely to have parole revoked for minor problems. At a news conference following the tabling of his report, Mr. Sapers said, "If I were releasing a report card on Aboriginal corrections today, it would be filled with failing grades" (CBC News 2013a).

A second reform with serious and unanticipated consequences is the deinstitutionalization of psychiatric hospitals that began in the 1950s and 1960s, and which accelerated thereafter (Chaimowitz 2012, 1; Scull 1977). Aimed at removing people from "total institutions" and re-integrating them into their communities "with an array of services and supports" (Chaimowitz 2012, 2), the emptying of asylums has turned into a carceral nightmare. As we discussed in Chapter 3, the mass deinstitutionalization of women and men in psychiatric facilities without the provision of adequate community support has resulted in the increased visibility of individuals in mental distress among homeless "street" people, and an exponential growth in the number of people with mental health issues in jails and penitentiaries (Chaimowitz 2012, 1–2; Greenberg and Rosenheck 2008). In Canada, for example, the

2009–10 Report of the Office of the Correctional Investigator shows that 30 per cent of women prisoners (compared with 14.5 per cent of their male counterparts) have experienced hospitalization for some psychiatric reason, and 25 per cent have received a psychiatric diagnosis (Chaimowitz 2012, 3). These unintended effects of the deinstitutionalization reform illustrate the operation of the Penrose principle; namely, that most industrial societies institutionalize "a relatively stable number of people" and therefore if prison populations rise, psychiatric hospital populations will fall and vice versa (Chaimowitz 2012, 3).

The unanticipated and steep rise in the number of Canadian prisoners with mental health issues over the past few decades is difficult to reverse. For instance, it is not enough to argue that women should have the same access to help as men, since resources for the treatment of mental distress have never been adequate in Canada's jails and prisons (Kendall 1993; Pollack 2005, 2008). Moreover, the huge increase in the number of people needing access to treatment and social supports has made it even less possible to provide mental health programming for men and women in need. Instead, correctional services have redefined such prisoners as "risky" rather than "at risk," and have abandoned treatment, slashed social supports and focused squarely on containment through the over-prescription of drugs (Kilty 2012) and/or the reliance on administrative segregation to separate "difficult" prisoners from others (Bingham and Sutton 2012). The Report of the Correctional Investigator for 2009–10 noted that up to one-third of inmates in maximum security settings were in segregation at any given moment, including many with a psychiatric diagnosis. That same year, the daily count for people in segregation in the federal system was 900, with an average of 95 days in solitary confinement (Chaimowitz 2012, 3).

The effects on prisoners are severe. The 2010–11 Report of the Correctional Investigator states that "addressing the criminalization and warehousing in penitentiaries of those who suffer from mental illness is not simply a public health issue, it's a human rights issue" (cited in Bingham and Sutton 2012, 5). A more recent report (Bingham and Sutton 2012), prepared for the International Human Rights Program at the University of Toronto, underscores the racialized effects of these policies. The authors point out that large numbers of federally sentenced women (FSW) have mental health issues related to substance abuse, self-harm and physical and sexual abuse, but "[f]or Aboriginal women, the impacts of post-traumatic stress disorder suffered by inter-generational residential school survivors are compounded by collective cultural and historical trauma and ongoing racial discrimination" (Bingham and Sutton 2012, 5). As well, the vast over-representation of Aboriginal women in penal custody (in August 2010, 174 or 34 per cent of 512 federally sentenced women were Aboriginal) means that the proportion of Aboriginal women with mental health issues is significantly greater than it is for other women prisoners (Bingham and Sutton 2012, 5). The authors conclude that "the Correctional Service of Canada (CSC) responds to FSW with mental health issues in a discriminatory manner, [...] equates mental health issues with increased risk to the institution or public, and responds with excessive use of segregation (sometimes for months at a time), repeated institutional transfers (sometimes over 10 times in a year), and use of force (including restraints)" (Bingham and Sutton 2012, 5–6). They argue that CSC's treatment of prisoners with mental health issues not only violates "their rights under international law" but also has "wide-ranging implications for civil and political rights the world over" (Bingham and Sutton 2012, 6).

In the next chapter, having tracked the differential treatment of many racialized accused in the criminal justice system, we consider how victims of crime, including hate crime, experience the administration of justice.

DISCUSSION QUESTIONS

Do you agree with the neo-liberal argument that equal treatment means identical treatment of all persons charged with a crime?

What safeguards could be implemented to eliminate the wrongful conviction of people who are criminally charged?

Is the diversion of Aboriginal people from incarceration for non-violent crimes a good policy?

Would recruiting more racialized criminal justice agents (e.g., police, prosecutors, judges, correctional officers) eliminate racism in the administration of criminal justice?

FURTHER READING

Anderson, D., and B. Anderson. 2009. *Manufacturing Guilt: Wrongful Convictions in Canada*. 2nd ed. Black Point, NS: Fernwood Publishing.

Barron, C. 2011. *Governing Girls: Rehabilitation in the Age of Risk*. Black Point, NS: Fernwood Publishing.

Denov, M.S., and K.M. Campbell. 2005. "Criminal injustice: Understanding the causes, effects, and responses to wrongful conviction in Canada." *Journal of Contemporary Justice* 21 (3): 224–49.

Garland, D. 2001. *The Culture of Control: Crime and Social Order in Contemporary Society*. Chicago: University of Chicago Press.

Razack, S. 1998. *Looking White People in the Eye: Gender, Race and Culture in Courtrooms and Classrooms*. Toronto: University of Toronto Press.

WEBSITES OF INTEREST

Canadian Association of Elizabeth Fry Societies—http://www.caefs.ca
Justice for Girls—http://www.justiceforgirls.org/
Office of the Correctional Investigator, Canada—http://www.oci-bec.gc.ca/
    index-eng.aspx
Prison Justice—http://www.prisonjustice.ca/index.html
The Association in Defence of the Wrongly Convicted (AIDWYC)—http://www.
    aidwyc.org/
The John Howard Society—http://www.johnhoward.ca/

CHAPTER SEVEN

CRIMINAL VICTIMIZATION AND HATE CRIMES

There are various forms of racial victimization in Canada, including both criminal and non-criminal offences. The one point of commonality amongst these forms of victimization is that they are based on the person's or group's racial or ethnic background. This encompasses a continuum of behaviours, ranging from name calling and expressing insults, to physical and violent assaults. Furthermore, the victimization of racial minorities can be carried out by friends, family members, fellow citizens or agents of the state. In this chapter, we examine the criminal victimization of racial minorities in Canada and the growing problem of hate crimes. We analyze how the state has responded to this phenomenon, the legislation and remedies available to manage this issue, and how the victimization of racialized minorities can be situated within the wider politics of racialization in Canada.

Reliable statistics on the prevalence of racial criminal victimization in Canada are few and far between. The last official survey published on racial minorities as crime victims was in 2004, using victimization data primarily from the General Social Survey (GSS). The report, published by Statistics Canada, concluded that rates of violent victimization for visible minorities were similar to those for non-visible minorities, that Canadian-born visible minorities had higher rates of violent victimization compared to visible minority immigrants and non-visible minorities, that visible minorities had an increased fear of crime at night compared to non-visible minorities, and that visible minorities were less satisfied than non-visible minorities with the police (Perreault 2008b). Finally, visible minorities reported significantly higher rates of discrimination compared with non-visible minorities (Perreault 2008b). Race or ethnic origin was the most commonly cited factor in hate-related crimes (Perreault 2008b, 14).

A related report on immigrants and victimization, also using 2004 GSS data, found that rates of violent victimization for immigrants were lower than rates for the Canadian-born population, and that the characteristics of the violent crimes were similar among immigrants and non-immigrants (Perreault 2008a, 11). Furthermore, the level of satisfaction with the criminal justice system among immigrants was similar to non-immigrants. The proportion of immigrants reporting experiences of discrimination was larger than in non-immigrants, and immigrants tended to have slightly higher levels of fear of crime, even though they were less likely to be victims of violent crime (Perreault 2008a, 14). These two reports, almost a decade old at the time of writing this book, are the most current official studies available in offering a broad picture of the criminal victimization of racialized groups. There has never been annual reporting of victimization statistics on racial groups in Canada. This can be attributed, on the one hand, to the lack of regularly available data, but, arguably, there does not appear to be any political or institutional interest in providing this information on a regular, ongoing basis.

More recently published official reports tend to focus on narrower topics in relation to the criminal justice system and racialized groups. For example, studies on Aboriginal victimization (Scrim 2010), police-reported hate crimes (Dowden and Brennan 2012), and victim services (Munch 2012) are some of the topics covered. The problem of Aboriginal victimization is well documented by both official and scholarly research. Aboriginal communities have, over time, experienced much higher rates of criminal victimization, with Aboriginal women in particular experiencing much higher rates of violent victimization than non-Aboriginal women (Brzozowski et al. 2006). Young Aboriginal women are five times more likely to die from a violence-related event than non-Aboriginal women in Canada (Native Women's Association of Canada 2010). Entrenched racism combined with poverty and marginalization is contributing to the higher rates of violence experienced by Aboriginal women (Amnesty International 2009). Scrim (2010) acknowledges that despite these uncontested higher rates of Aboriginal victimization, the tendency has been to focus on making the criminal justice system more responsive to Aboriginal offending, and little attention has been given to the problem of victimization. In many ways, this position is indicative of state and scholarly responses to criminal victimization more generally. As Walklate (2007) points out, victims of crime were not, historically, part of the political or policy discourse on criminal justice. Hate crime is another area that has only recently garnered more attention, and, as a result, significant gaps remain in our understanding of hate crime victimization.

In Canada, it was not until the 1980s that crime victims began receiving more attention from criminal justice policymakers and that the issue of criminal victimization became politically charged (Stanbridge and Kenney 2009). The emergence of victims' rights occurred through extensive lobbying and awareness-raising on the part of women's groups, service organizations focused on crime victims, criminal justice officials who believed that the inclusion of victims' voices was important, and a public concern regarding rising crime rates (Stanbridge and Kenney 2009, 477). This increased attention created a political opportunity for activism by crime victims, as well as government bureaucrats working on issues of victimization and crime prevention, who seized the opportunity to promote their work (Rock 1988). Victim service organizations also expanded, and continue to be at the forefront of publicizing the multi-layered impact of criminal victimization, which includes emotional, physical, financial, psychological, and social consequences (Canadian Resource Centre for Victims of Crime 2005). The emphasis on helping crime victims through their ordeals, and of challenging stereotypes about victimization, has been an important corollary to official statistics and reports. Yet it is clear that there is still much more work that needs to be done. A study conducted by Justice Canada in 2010 found that almost half of all Canadians (42 per cent) indicated having no knowledge of what services were available for crime victims, and almost the same proportion was unaware of other crime victim programs, such as compensation (McDonald and Scrim 2011). Younger Canadians (18–24) were the least aware of what services were available, and thus, less likely to access the services if criminally victimized (McDonald and Scrim 2011, 7).

As the movement for victims' rights progresses, a more complex understanding of crime victims is also being developed. The increased visibility of crime victims raises further questions about how we define who is a crime victim, how policymakers should respond to them, and how their different experiences of being victimized can be understood (Walklate 2007). For example, the act of defining victims as "crime victims" only if they have engaged with the criminal justice system has been criticized for producing a dichotomous approach to the categorizing of victims (Dawson, Hubbert, and Poon 2010). It is well established that not all victims of crime will report their victimization, for a variety of reasons, but they should not be prevented from accessing victim services (Dawson, Hubbert, and Poon 2010). Furthermore, secondary victims of crime are rarely acknowledged, even though they may share the same experiences of victimization as primary victims (Dawson, Hubbert, and Poon 2010). Although legislation now exists to protect victims' rights (both nationally and internationally), scholars have pointed out that crime victims continue to feel marginalized from the criminal justice process (Wemmers 2012). This has led researchers to argue that a victim-centred approach to policy, research, and practice would be better suited to working with, and meeting the needs of, crime victims (Goodey 2004), particularly for groups such as racialized women, as well as the homeless, immigrants, and Aboriginal youth, who are typically more vulnerable to criminal victimization. A victim-centred approach, which could involve, for example, the inclusion of victim impact statements in court trials, is sensitive to victims, and acknowledges that they have a role in the criminal justice process.

VICTIMIZATION OF WOMEN

Feminist critiques of how women victims, particularly racialized women victims of crime, have been treated by the state and the general public have been intense and harsh. Patterns of criminal victimization in Canada reveal that men outnumber women as victims of crime, except when it comes to violence between intimate partners and sexual assault (Perreault and Brennan 2010). State responses to sexual assault, sexual harassment, and domestic violence—crimes perpetrated primarily by men against women—were often based on an assessment of victim culpability, which could include the extent to which she fought back or resisted her attacker. Early research by victimologists emphasized the victim's contribution to the crime, and consequently, women victims were often blamed, and often blamed themselves, for provoking the attack or being at the wrong place at the wrong time (Britton 2011). There was a belief that victims played a role in causing their own harm, giving rise to notions of victim precipitation and victim provocation to explain victimization (Meloy and Miller 2010, 6). Furthermore, cultural norms about gender were an important factor in assessing victim culpability. If a woman acted outside the bounds of acceptable femininity, for example, by engaging in risky behaviour, she would be regarded as less deserving of state support or protection. Legitimate female crime victims were stereotyped as passive and helpless, as "good" women, resulting in a dichotomy of being either "worthy" and "innocent" on the one hand, or "less worthy" and "bad" on the other.

The highly publicized case of Jane Doe, a woman who was a victim of a serial rapist in a working-class Toronto neighbourhood in 1986, is an example of how "women's worth" played an important factor in the level of police protection provided (Sheehy 2005). Jane Doe sued the Toronto police force for sex discrimination on the basis of failing to protect her from harm (Doe 2003). She argued that she should have been warned about a sexual predator in her neighbourhood, but that sexism on the part of the Toronto police prevented them from taking women's safety seriously (Doe 2003). She also pointed out that women in a nearby middle-class neighbourhood, the Beaches, were warned of a predator and could take preventative measures to avoid being raped, suggesting that she was not deemed worthy by the police (Doe 2003). After 12 years of litigation, Jane Doe eventually won her case, but as Sheehy (2005, 115) points out, it was understood by everyone involved that police responses to male violence against women were unlikely to change as a result of this case. Feminist criminologists routinely cite the re-victimization of women by the justice system as a key factor behind the inaccuracy of official statistics on violence against women, which significantly underestimate the level of women's victimization and fail to capture the magnitude of the problem (Britton 2011).

For racialized women, their experiences of criminal victimization are complicated by the intersection of gender, race, and class—factors that influence their risk of victimization, and how the state responds to the violence they experience (Jiwani 2005). For example, in the context of domestic violence, an intersectional approach challenges monolithic understandings of woman battering by highlighting the role of culture. Sociocultural contexts shape interpretations of what constitutes domestic violence, and they construct risk factors that differentially affect the prevalence of violence as well as the likelihood of disclosure to authorities (Yoshihama 1999, Gill 2004). As a result, generalizations that battering affects all women equally have been dismantled. Cultural traditions and cultural norms about gender impact not just how men and women in racialized communities behave, but also how the state interprets their actions. Within the community, patriarchal expectations, religious influences, and cultural values of family honour can prevent racialized women from calling the police or seeking help (Gill 2004).

At the same time, when police officers and the criminal justice system perceive the violence within racialized communities to be normal or reasonable, battered, racialized women are left with few, if any, options for protection. Adelman et al. (2003) note that multicultural discourses about violence shape how perpetrators justify their violence against women, how women interpret their victimization, and how the police account for the differential responses to it. How we define and measure domestic violence has been sharply criticized for failing to recognize the different social positions that racialized women occupy, and which can create vastly different experiences of victimization. As Richie observes, poor women of colour are "most likely to be in both dangerous intimate relationships and dangerous social positions" (2000, 1136). Acknowledging how gender and racial biases influence our understanding of woman battering is an important step in alleviating the suffering of racialized women.

In a similar vein, racialized and Aboriginal women's experiences of sexual violence point to the persistent problem of racism as a critical reason why victims are not believed when recounting their victimization, and why they do not receive the help they need because their harms have been trivialized (Dylan, Regehr, and Alaggia 2008). Feminist scholars have documented the many instances where trial court judges have made disparaging comments about female complainants of sexual assault in cases involving Aboriginal and racialized minority women (Razack 1998a; Tang 2000). In the case of *R. v. Curley, Nagmalik, and Issigaitok* [1984], Judge Bourassa relied on cultural information, that young Inuit women were ready for intercourse upon menstruation, to proffer a lenient sentence of seven days to three Inuit men for having intercourse with a female under the age of 14 (Razack 1998a, 70). Nightingale argues that in this case, there was little to no consideration given to the violence experienced by the victim or the harm caused to her (1991, 92). Racialized and indigenous women typically do not fit the role of the "ideal" or "authentic" victim of sexual assault because they are less valued in a society characterized by racism (Randall 2010). Women of colour are placed in a sexual hierarchy that holds them in lower regard compared to other women, such that not only are they less likely to be believed, but their perpetrators are more likely to receive lenient sentences, because the harm caused to the women is minimized (Crenshaw 1991).

Colonialism, along with cultural and racial prejudices, has been a critical factor in marginalizing and excluding the victimization of racialized women. Bilge's (2006) examination of the role of cultural difference in Canadian cases of violence against minority women found that judicial interpretations often relied on racialized, gendered, and classed understandings and representations of minorities, thereby reproducing inequalities and hierarchies based on social difference. She argues that the dark side of being sensitive and accommodating to ethnocultural difference in Canada is that cultural information has been used by defence lawyers as a partial defence for violent crimes committed against minority women (Bilge 2006, 174; see also Dick 2011). Thus, while women victims are generally reluctant to report crimes of sexual assault or domestic violence, racialized women, despite higher rates of victimization, are even less likely to seek legal redress through the justice system (Regehr et al. 2008).

In addition, many racialized women's experiences of victimization places them in a dilemma about perpetuating the victimization of men in their communities by a criminal justice system that has historically mistreated racialized men (Cossins 2003). It is not uncommon for many racialized and indigenous women to choose not to contact the criminal justice system if they are criminally victimized, for fear of further exacerbating the victimization of their community by the state (Sokoloff 2008). However, if they do contact authorities, they may be seen as traitors to their community, for revealing the violence and reinforcing dominant stereotypes about their culture's inferiority, which can lead to further racism and discrimination (Crenshaw 1991). Espin (1998) refers to this as the double bind of "gendered racism" and "racialized sexism." Minority women are confronted with the interlocking realities of racism and sexism in society, as well as the problems of sexism and male domination within their own communities. They are forced to decide which option is more important, and they often find themselves penalized for their "choice" (Crenshaw 1991). As a result, minority women's experiences of victimization places them in an untenable position where societal and community interests clash, often culminating in unsatisfactory solutions and responses for ending the violence.

Violence against minority women is as much about racial injustice as it is about gender subordination. This is evident in current debates regarding practices such as honour killings, female genital mutilation, and forced marriages. Beckett and Macey (2001) argue that it is not uncommon for Western states to privilege the sanctity of (male) community rights over the individual rights of (female) victims. Another recent issue that has not involved a victim-centred approach is trafficking women for the purposes of the sex industry, which has resulted in the criminalization of trafficked women, many of whom come from impoverished and marginalized regions of the world, rather than recognizing them as victims (Goodey 2003). Acknowledging and incorporating racial differences into our analysis of women's victimization, and advocacy for victims' rights, will provide a clearer picture of how it may be possible to subvert dominant narratives of women's criminal victimization, while also being attuned to the different manifestations of women's victimization.

RACIALIZED YOUTH AND CRIMINAL VICTIMIZATION

Researchers argue that since the late 1990s, a movement in the criminal justice system has developed, where Canadian youth are increasingly constructed and targeted as problematic subjects in need of greater control and regulation (Schissel 1997; Hogeveen 2005). The introduction of the *Youth Criminal Justice Act* in 2003 was regarded as a watershed moment, where the crime-control model of criminal justice surpassed the due-process approach as the dominant ideology shaping law, policy, and practice. A "get tough" mantra was adopted, and there would now be "meaningful consequences" for serious young offenders (Hogeveen 2005; Alvi 2012). Yet the emphasis on criminalizing youth has not been accompanied by the same level of concern about the criminal victimization of youth, even though rates of violent victimization among youth and young adults (15–24 years old) are higher than they are for older Canadians (Perreault and Brennan 2010).

Ogrodnik (2010) reports that children and youth under the age of 18 are at a greater risk of physical and sexual assault, though a complete picture of their victimization is difficult to obtain. This is because children do not report their victimization, most commonly because they are either unable to or are too afraid to call authorities. Often, perpetrators are family members or friends and acquaintances of the family, and youth are victimized in familiar places, such as the home, in their neighbourhood, or at school (Ogrodnik 2010). Furthermore, child victims are not included in victimization surveys, and research on harmful behaviours against children, such as maltreatment and neglect, is not available (Ogrodnik 2010, 6). As a result, youth victimization is largely overlooked and there is much less scholarly discussion and debate on the criminal victimization of youth when compared to the topic of youth delinquency and offending.

The sparse research in Canada indicates that marginalized and vulnerable youth, such as street youth, homeless youth, racialized youth, and/or youth living in poverty, are more likely to have experiences of criminal victimization, and are also more likely to be at risk of ongoing victimization (Eisler and Schissel 2004; Gaetz 2004; Rossiter and Rossiter 2009). Many vulnerable youth have intersecting identities, including homeless, racialized young women, who, along with Aboriginal children and youth, are at a disproportionate risk of suicide, sexual assault, and other forms of violent victimization (Gaetz 2004; Do 2012). As Eisler and Schissel observe, the victimization of children and youth is conditioned by issues of race, socio-economic status, gender, and geography (e.g., the kind of community one lives in) (2004, 370). Moreover, poverty puts racialized and Aboriginal youth at a further substantial risk of being criminally victimized or witnessing a crime (Eisler and Schissel 2004, 370).

Experiences of non-criminal victimization are a significant problem for racialized youth. Data from the World Health Organization indicates that ethnic bullying and peer victimization are pervasive problems, leading to the social marginalization and social exclusion of many immigrant youth (Craig and Harel 2004; Vitoroulis and Schneider 2009). Similarly, in a 2006 self-report study of delinquency with Toronto youth, research participants noted their experiences of discrimination due to religion, language or skin colour, bullying (e.g., humiliation, exclusion from a group), physical assault, theft (e.g., having property stolen), and threats (Zeman and Bressan 2008).

Fear of youth crime getting out of control, combined with the belief that more intervention is needed to manage "risky youth," led to a study and subsequent report commissioned by the Government of Ontario examining the roots of youth violence (McMurtry and Curling 2008). The report acknowledges how racism can be seen as a risk factor, particularly when young people develop a diminished sense of self-worth as a result of racism (McMurtry and Curling 2008). For racialized youth, the cumulative effects of mistreatment by the police, the lack of role models and opportunities, and the historical exclusion of racial groups in the education curriculum can lead to devastating consequences (McMurtry and Curling 2008). Being the objects of racism can result in racialized youth experiencing higher levels of alienation from mainstream society, becoming more likely to withdraw from mainstream society as a result (McMurtry and Curling 2008). Jackson (2007) adds that for immigrant and refugee girls, they may internalize the dominant culture's view that they are inferior, thereby compounding their difficulties of fitting into mainstream culture. These challenges place racialized youth at risk of engaging in delinquent and criminal behaviour, and, we would argue, at an increased risk of being victimized as well. This is consistent with studies from the US and UK that highlight how racialized youth may have disproportionately higher rates of criminalization than non-racial groups, and higher rates of victimization as well (Muncie 2003; Finkelhor et al. 2005). In this sense, racism is a risk factor for both the criminalization as well as victimization of racialized youth.

The recognition that youth are more likely to be racially targeted within public institutions led the Commission de droits de la personne et des droits de la jeunesse in Quebec to commission a report on the racial profiling of youth in the province (Eid 2011). Since young people occupy and use public spaces more frequently than other age groups, and are more likely to be scrutinized for engaging in anti-social behaviour due to stereotypes about their activities, the Commission believed an examination of the extent to which they are racially profiled and subjected to systemic discrimination was warranted (Eid 2011, 11). The Commission examined the issues of racial profiling and systemic discrimination of youth in the areas of public security, education, and youth protection. The key findings in the report indicate that racialized youth believe they are disproportionately scrutinized by the police and do not receive enough attention when they are victimized; they receive harsher punishment than non-racialized youth for violating rules and policies at school; and they are over-represented in the youth protection system (Eid 2011). These findings are consistent with the experiences of racialized adults insofar as numerous institutions play a role in stigmatizing racialized individuals, such that the problems of racism are, as the Commission notes, systemic in nature since they do not dissipate as youth become adults.

As Muncie (2003) keenly observes, young people are routinely over-controlled and under-protected. There are many examples of the failure to protect and support racialized youth in Canada, particularly Aboriginal youth. Whether it is a police officer allegedly assaulting an Aboriginal girl by punching her in the face (BCCLA 2013), or child protection services failing to protect a young Aboriginal child from abuse and neglect (Representative for Children and Youth 2013), if crime victims are the "forgotten actors" in criminal justice (Goodey 2004), young crime victims are virtually absent in criminal justice considerations. Consequently, like many marginalized adults, marginalized youth have found that one of the best strategies for staying safe is changing their behaviour, rather than relying on the state for protection, to avoid further victimization (Gaetz 2009).

The victimization of racialized youth, both criminal and non-criminal, occurs in a context where racism plays a direct and indirect role in both public and private settings. Racialized youth are victimized as a result of discriminatory practices, but they are also victimized because their racialized status leaves them more vulnerable to other forms of criminal and non-criminal victimization. Given the over-representation of Aboriginal and racialized adults in the justice system, many scholars have expressed concerns about the future of racialized youth in Canada. Without adequate intervention, the fear is that racialized youth will continue to perpetuate the crime and victimization patterns of racialized adults (Totten 2009). Bania (2009, 107) argues that a "coordinated approach that addresses underlying issues of child poverty, inadequate housing, barriers to education, unemployment, mental health, racism and discrimination" is needed if we are to move beyond simply "blaming the victim." Although community justice principles, such as the use of community programming, were incorporated in the *Youth Criminal Justice Act*, it remains to be seen whether these practices will result in meaningful change for Aboriginal and racialized young offenders *as well as* victims of crime.

HATE CRIMES IN CANADA

Research on hate-crime victimization in Canada is sparse to say the least. As an area of criminological discussion, it only started to receive more scholarly attention after September 11, when Muslim and Arab groups were identified and targeted for victimization. However, the phenomenon of hate-motivated victimization, in Canada and elsewhere, has a long history and is interwoven into the evolution and development of many Western societies. Discriminating against the cultural practices of Aboriginal people, restricting the entry of racialized immigrants into Canada, segregating African Canadians in Ontario public schools, and criminalizing homosexuality are just some of the practices that are part of Canadian history (Canadian Race Relations Foundation 2003). As the phenomenon of hate became more public globally, evident in the rise of right-wing propaganda and violence in Europe and the US, like other nation-states, Canada developed legislative measures to officially recognize hate-motivated crime in 1996, although there has been legislation against the promotion of hate of an identifiable group since 1970 (Janhevich 2001, 7).

Hate crime in Canada refers to a wide range of behaviours, from state-sponsored practices of genocide, to crimes by hate-motivated groups and individuals committing property and violent crimes (Janhevich 2001). Two key characteristics of hate crimes are that victims are targeted based on a recognized feature of their social identity, and that the victims are easily replaced by another member of the same group since their victimization is based on holding a particular characteristic that is shared across the group (Al-Hakim 2010, 344). Current legislation governing acts of hate can be found in various sections of the Criminal Code. The oldest hate-related offences are the hate propaganda provisions set out in sections 318 and 319. They provide definitions of what it means to advocate genocide, of "identifiable groups" in the public incitement of hatred, and of the willful promotion of hatred. In *R. v. Keegstra* [1990], a highly publicized case of hate propaganda in Canada, the accused, an Alberta schoolteacher, was charged with promoting hatred against an identifiable group for making anti-Semitic statements to his students in class. The Supreme Court of Canada stated that the seriousness of Keegstra's statements could not be justified under the Charter of Rights and Freedoms and therefore, the criminal code provisions were upheld. In section 718.2, guidelines are provided requiring courts to consider motivation when sentencing offenders whose crimes were motivated by bias, prejudice, or hate. The case of *R. v. Miloszewski* [1999] relied on this provision when sentencing five men for the death of Nirmal Singh Gill, a caretaker at a Sikh temple in Surrey, BC. Substantial weight was given to Gill's race, national or ethnic origin, colour or religion as an aggravating factor in the attack. Finally, section 430 (4.1) recognizes mischief to religious property as a hate-motivated offence, and is included in section 718.2 for the purposes of sentencing.

· According to international reports, hate crimes are on the rise globally (Human Rights First 2008). This is true even in Canada, a country which many regard as more tolerant and multicultural than others. Official statistics on the nature and prevalence of hate crime in Canada indicate that there were 1,410 cases of hate-related crimes in 2010, the latest year for which official figures are available (Bowden and Brennan 2012, 7). This is a decrease from previous years, which saw the rates increase steadily between 2007 and 2009, reaching a high of 1,473 reported incidents in 2009 (Bowden and Brennan 2012, 7). The three primary motivations for police-reported hate crimes were race and ethnicity (52 per cent of all hate crimes in 2010), followed by religion (29 per cent) (Bowden and Brennan 2012, 5). Black people were the most commonly targeted racial group, while attacks against the Jewish faith are the most common type of religiously motivated hate crimes (Bowden and Brennan 2012, 5). The most common type of hate crime, mischief (e.g., vandalism and graffiti), accounts for over 50 per cent of all hate-motivated crimes in 2010. This is followed by minor assaults (11 per cent) and uttering threats (9 per cent) (Bowden and Brennan 2012, 8). Hate crimes are typically committed by a stranger, which is contrary to the general pattern of violent crimes, which are committed by someone the victim knows (Bowden and Brennan 2012, 14).

The publication of annual statistics and related reports on hate crimes suggests that the Canadian government has, in recent years, been more attentive to this problem. Al-Hakim (2010) surmises that the reason why governments are taking a greater interest in this issue is due to their desire to ensure social stability by lessening conflict between groups and reducing potential threats to individual citizens. He notes that hate crimes "threaten the realization of the ideals of multicultural liberalism, as they target indi-viduals specifically for their group-based identities" (Al-Hakim 2010, 344). Dixon and Gadd (2006) add that the flurry of legislation in many Western states criminalizing hate-motivated behaviour is about sending a strong mes-sage to the general public that racial violence and other forms of hate-related activities will not be tolerated. However, they raise an important issue when they ask whether or not all this legislation will in fact curb the incidence of hate-motivated crime (Dixon and Gadd 2006).

The policing and prosecution of hate crimes in Canada has been challeng-ing due to several issues. First, although hate crimes account for less than one per cent of all reported criminal code offences in Canada in 2010, it is consid-ered a highly under-reported crime, with estimates that only one-third of hate crimes are reported annually, and therefore the true extent of the problem is unclear (Dauvergne and Brennan 2011). Roberts (1995, vii) adds that "of all forms of criminality, hate crimes are likely to be among the most unreported of offences." He cites fear of additional victimization, fear that the criminal justice system will not take victim reports seriously, and fear of stigmatization on the basis of homophobia, particularly by gays and lesbians, as contributing factors to the problem of under-reporting (Roberts 1995, vii). Second, there is a lack of consensus over the definition of hate crime in Canada. Unlike the United States, Canada does not have a national definition of what con-stitutes a hate crime. An Ontario report by the Hate Crimes Community Working Group (2006) pointed out that it is difficult to mobilize against hate activity if there is no clear and common definition about how to identify and name it, since people are unable to recognize and deal with it. Finally, unlike many other crimes, hate crimes create many secondary victims because of the underlying motivation for committing the offences. By attacking the victim's identity, that is, who the person is rather than what he/she may have done, others who share similar characteristics are equally afraid and insecure (Hate Crimes Community Working Group 2006). It is not uncommon that when feelings of victimization are projected onto an entire community, the com-munity feels vulnerable and tense (which can lead to polarization within the community), with trust in the police declining (Pruegger 2009, 11). The lack of successful prosecutions in this area suggests that these barriers, along with the lack of resources, the lack of experience applying the hate crimes provi-sions in the Criminal Code, and the high burden of proof, have significantly hindered the criminal justice process (Pruegger 2009, 12).

Racialized communities have been particularly traumatized by hate- or bias-related behaviour. As noted earlier, they are the most common targets of hate activity in Canada. After September 11, several studies have illustrated the high degree of suffering experienced by Arab and Muslim communities (Henricks et al. 2007; Poynting and Perry 2007; Disha, Cavendish, and King 2011). Strong anti-Muslim and anti-Islamic discourse from political and media elites resulted in a significant backlash that included a dramatic rise in hate crimes, hate speech, and daily experiences of discrimination. Arab and Muslim people in many Western countries were racially profiled, denied access to human rights, and in some cases arbitrarily detained. Their treatment by both members of the public and state officials has been based on their representation as "inherently foreign, essentially unassimilable and a potential enemy within" (Cainkar and Maira 2005, 4). Disha, Cavendish, and King (2011, 40) report that while hate crimes against other racial groups declined after September 11 in the United States, crimes against Arabs and Muslims increased sharply. A similar trend was noted in Canada, where the Canadian Islamic Congress (2003) reported a 1,600 per cent increase (from 11 to 173 cases) in the number of anti-Muslim hate incidents after September 11. A survey conducted in 2002 found that people of Muslim heritage reported that their lives had worsened since September 11, that they didn't think Canadians liked them, and that they were fearful about their own safety and that of their family members (Helly 2004). As we discuss in Chapter 8, their victimization was made worse by the criminalization of Muslim and Arab communities based on presumptions of deviance and inferiority.

Aboriginal communities have also been deeply affected by a legacy of hate activity directed at their members in Canada. The Ontario-based Hate Crimes Community Working Group noted that hate crimes in these communities are often unreported and unacknowledged (2006, 22). Since racism, discrimination, and hate are common daily experiences for Aboriginal people, they no longer see the point of reporting the incident only to find that the police or other state officials will not believe them (Klaszus 2007). Systemic racism across many social institutions, such as the justice system, has also contributed to the continued perpetration of hate crimes against Aboriginal peoples (Hate Crimes Community Working Group 2006, 22). The many cases of missing women in Vancouver, which includes a high proportion of Aboriginal women, is one tragic outcome of the state not taking seriously the victimization of Aboriginal peoples. It has been well documented that Aboriginal communities have some of the highest rates of youth suicides, the shortest life expectancies, and high levels of violence when compared to non-Aboriginal communities (Hate Crimes Community Working Group 2006, 22). Brzozowski, Taylor-Butts, and Johnson (2006) found that overall, Aboriginal people were three times more likely to be a victim of a violent crime than non-Aboriginal people.

The impact of hate-crime victimization affects, as we noted earlier, not just the individual targeted, but entire communities. For this reason, they have been considered by scholars and policymakers to be "message crimes"—a warning to the entire community—that the harm can extend to others in the victim's community (Ignaski 2001). Like crimes in general, hate crimes produce a wide array of victim effects, including shock, anger, fear or vulnerability, and a sense of inferiority (Perry and Alvi 2012). A central motivating factor for offenders is to "reaffirm their dominant identity, their access to resources and privilege, while at the same time limiting the opportunities of the victims to express their own needs" (Perry and Alvi 2012, 65). For the victim and other members of the victim's community, fear of victimization or re-victimization often leads to changing one's behaviour, such as routine activities and habits. Since hate crimes are attacking the victim's identity, the consequences of hate-crime victimization can be more severe or longer lasting, with the period of recovery enduring much longer than in non-hate crimes (Dauvergne, Scrim and Brennan 2008, 15).

Intervening and mobilizing against racist violence and other types of hate crimes involves recognizing that hate activity is not simply the act of individuals or small groups. Taking this perspective, as Ray and Smith point out, situates the problem of racism and violence "as the result of the presence of pathological individuals, rather than as embedded in institutional practices and offending communities, in locales and habitual ways of dealing with the world, and especially of dealing with problematic situations" (2001, 221). They call for an understanding of race-based hate activity that involves recognizing multiple issues of bias, cultures of violence, exclusion, and marginalization in developing broad preventative strategies (Ray and Smith 2001, 221). This is similar to the Hate Crimes Community Working Group (2006, 73) recommendation that the Ontario government "recognize and respect the unique historical, constitutional and current position of Aboriginal people" as a goal for addressing hate crimes against Aboriginal people. Thus, while legislation is important, it is equally important to "disrupt the institutional and cultural assumptions about difference that condition hate," since the responsibility for addressing and preventing hate crimes has to be shared by all (Perry 2003).

Research on the victimization of racialized and Aboriginal people in Canada is still in its infancy. As a result, there are many more questions than there are answers with regards to the patterns and prevalence of victimization in minority communities. As Janhevich, Bania, and Hastings (2008) note, we know more about issues of discrimination in the criminal justice system, and overt forms of racism such as racial profiling and hate crimes, than we do about the victimization of racialized groups. The available research in Canada suggests that a continuum of harmful behaviours characterizes the many types of victimization people can experience. For racialized and Aboriginal people, their racial identity and background places them at a higher risk of criminal and non-criminal victimization, as well as direct and indirect forms of racist victimization.

DISCUSSION QUESTIONS

Is Canada doing enough to address the problem of hate crimes?

Which stereotypes play into the view that some crime victims are "asking for it"?

How much of a role should crime victims be given in the legal processing of their perpetrators?

Should gender and racial characteristics determine the legitimacy of a crime victim? Why is it often considered?

FURTHER READING

Christie, N. 2010. "Victim movements at a crossroad." *Punishment and Society* 12 (2): 115–22.

Cossins, A. 2003. "Saints, sluts and sexual assault: Rethinking the relationship between sex, race and gender." *Social & Legal Studies* 12 (1): 77–103.

Dick, C. 2011. "A tale of two cultures: Intimate femicide, cultural defences, and the law of provocation." *Canadian Journal of Women and the Law* 23 (2): 519–47.

Perry, B., ed. 2003. *Hate and Bias Crime: A Reader.* New York: Routledge.

Weinrath, M. 2000. "Violent victimization and fear of crime among Canadian Aboriginals." In *Race, Ethnicity, Sexual Orientation, Violent Crime: The Realities and the Myths,* ed. J. Pallone. New York: Haworth Press.

WEBSITES OF INTEREST

Canadian Crime Victim Foundation—http://www.ccvf.net/

Stop Racism and Hate Collective—http://www.stopracism.ca/

The FREDA Centre for Research on Violence against Women and Children—http://fredacentre.com/

Victims of Violence—http://www.victimsofviolence.on.ca/rev2/

PART FOUR

CRIMINALIZING RACIAL GROUPS

In this section, we take a closer look at three contemporary issues in the criminalization of race in Canada. The number of racialized communities that have been constructed and identified as sites of particular problems offers little room for optimism about curtailing the tentacles of state control over the lives of everyday Canadians. Our examination of three groups who have been targeted for control will highlight how race intersects with nationality, immigration, and class to produce "undesirable" subjects of criminalization, illegalization, marginalization, and exclusion. We point to the ways in which the criminal justice system has influenced the development of other state agencies, as well as their policies and practices. The tendency to criminalize behaviour that is deemed problematic by invoking the use of criminal sanctions for non-criminal behaviours, or framing the discourse of terrorism, immigration, and poverty through the lens of criminality, should give pause to those concerned about equality and social justice. Research continues to show that racialized groups that have long been the focus of state policing (such as First Nations and black communities) remain the central focus of police attention. More recently, Muslim and Arab people have been charged with possessing criminogenic tendencies, and are thus liable to attract the attention of law enforcement. They are joined by a variety of other groups—refugees and migrant workers in particular—who, in this global climate, have come to be regarded as potentially threatening to the security of the state.

Throughout the chapters in this section, we argue that while contemporary Canadian society eschews overtly racist attitudes and behaviours, and a wide array of organizations are involved in racial and ethnic monitoring that has resulted in greater awareness of race issues, discriminatory practices within state agencies persist nonetheless. Racism continues to shape social and economic outcomes for many, and while the institutional policies that undergird the disadvantage that racialized people experience may not employ or explicitly use racial language, they nevertheless perpetuate and (re)create racism's structural and ideological forms (Ostertag and Armaline 2011, 267). By examining the structural entrenchment of contemporary racism in policies of national security, immigration, and the welfare state we demonstrate how, by offering a more thorough understanding of the problem, it is the state, rather than racialized people, that should be confronted about their practices. In times of economic and political uncertainty, racialized groups are easy targets for fiscal restraint or demonstrations of state force and power. This has been most clearly evident in the period after September 11, when a wave of unbridled racism against "brown-skinned" people reigned over many Western states. The chapters in this section demonstrate the need to remain vigilant in highlighting the problems of racial inequality and exclusion, with the hope that greater sensitivity about race issues will find its way into policy and practice.

CHAPTER EIGHT

THE RACIALIZATION OF NATIONAL SECURITY

Recent global events have given rise to a dynamically changing social, political, and economic context, and this has significantly influenced how racialized groups are perceived, managed, and integrated into Canadian society. Although Aboriginal and black communities continue to attract higher levels of criminal justice attention, more recently, South Asian communities (especially Muslim communities) have also come under greater scrutiny. South Asian cultural differences, once regarded as an effective form of informal social control, have been reconstituted as a criminogenic factor (Smith 2008). Research demonstrates the many different ways that this community has become the primary target of surveillance and marginalization post–September 11. This chapter examines the treatment of Arab and Muslim communities in Canada. We pay particular attention to the legislative changes that resulted in increased powers for security and intelligence organizations, often at the expense of human rights and fair, equitable treatment within these communities.

In the aftermath of September 11, Canada's response was to implement a set of legislative policies that would create new powers for law enforcement officials while also enhancing existing provisions for preventing terror in Canada and abroad. Concerns about national security were given top priority, overriding questions of fairness, due process, and respect for human rights. Since the hijackers identified in the September 11 attacks were all of Arab descent, government officials claimed that racial and ethnic profiling was now regarded as an acceptable law enforcement strategy, despite the lack of clarity over who, exactly, would be profiled—Arabs, people of Middle Eastern descent, or Muslims (Choudhry 2001). Correspondingly, in the mainstream media, Middle Eastern communities came under relentless attack through constant negative media coverage. Middle Eastern people were not only being subjected to intense criminalization by state authorities, but their cultural identities were being reconfigured into a single, homogenous identity where being Middle Eastern was synonymous with being a "terrorist." In this chapter, we explore these issues through an examination of how the treatment and representation of Arab and Muslim communities in Canada have been reshaped by the events of September 11. What becomes apparent is that in both the political arena and in the mainstream media, the demonization, racialization, and criminalization of Arab and Muslim communities, and those communities perceived as being Muslim,[1] has been all-encompassing.

LEGISLATIVE CHANGES

Several security initiatives were taken by the Canadian government following September 11. First, the *Anti-Terrorism Act* was introduced in October 2001 to address the issue of terrorism and terrorists, and it includes measures to prosecute, convict, and punish terrorists. Those individuals and groups defined and designated by the government as terrorist groups, or suspected of engaging in terrorist and terrorist-related activities, would be subjected to increased surveillance, preventative arrests and detention, and stiffer penalties (Bhabha 2005). Key features of the act include criminalizing a broad range of activities that would aid in the advancement of a terrorist act, allowing elected ministers to designate certain groups and individuals as terrorists, expanding police powers to allow for preventative arrests of up to 72 hours,[2] and giving state agents the ability to compel a person to answer questions relating to terrorist activities (Roach 2005).

The speed with which this legislation was passed by Parliament, and received royal assent (December 2001), did not go unnoticed, and was criticized by legal scholars for placing the security of some over the security of (racialized) others (Roach 2005; Goldsmith 2008). To date, three people have been charged under the *Anti-Terrorism Act*, and all three are alleging that the definition of terrorist activity is unconstitutionally broad and violates the Charter of Rights (CBC News 2012d). A report by the International Civil Liberties Monitoring Group on Canada's *Anti-Terrorism Act* raised concerns about the lack of an oversight mechanism, the lack of transparency, and the potential for abuse of power, noting the adverse impact which all these legal policies would have on non-governmental organizations (ICLMG 2003).

The second key set of policies implemented in response to September 11 can be found in the *Immigration and Refugee Protection Act* (IRPA), which has been the most frequently used provision against suspected terrorists. Roach (2005, 521) points out that immigration law is attractive to authorities in dealing with suspected terrorists because "it allows for procedural shortcuts and a degree of secrecy that would not be tolerated under even an expanded criminal law." The key anti-terrorism provisions contained in IRPA are as follows: the ability to exclude non-citizens from entering Canada on the grounds that they pose a security risk; the use of preventative arrest and an unlimited period of detention of a non-citizen who is inadmissible and deemed a danger to the public; the use of security certificates to declare that a non-citizen is inadmissible to Canada on security grounds, which allows the person named to be detained indefinitely, and prevents the person from appealing their removal or making a refugee claim; the use of secret proceedings (the person named and his/her counsel is absent) to review the reasonableness of the security certificate; the signing of the Safe Third Country Agreement, which stipulates that asylum seekers in Canada and the United States would not be allowed to make an asylum claim if they arrived through the other country (Bell 2006; Roach 2005; Lowry 2002).

Critics of the enforcement provisions in IRPA have pointed out how increasing the powers of discretionary treatment available to the government will result in the mistreatment of racialized immigrants and refugees who are seen as threats to national security (Chan 2004, Bell 2006). Immigration reform is now less about building citizenship and importing economic capital, and more focused on law and order and security issues. Russo (2008) claims that by situating immigration issues in the context of a terrorist threat, the government is able to mobilize the public's fear and resentment to create a sense of urgency, and to garner support for the crafting and implementation of their reforms. The problem, however, is when the response to this threat of terrorism becomes a permanent state of affairs for how immigration is governed (Russo 2008). Such an approach, if not remedied over time, can compromise the independence of law by eroding the principle of the rule of law (Bell 2006).

In addition to the above legislative changes, in April 2004, the Canadian government introduced its new national security policy. This policy outlined the framework for how Canada would address national security interests in an "increasingly complex and dangerous threat environment" (PCO 2004, vii). Although Canada had been engaged in counter-terrorist operations before September 11, Rudner (2004) observes that this policy, along with significant changes to the organization of the intelligence community, demonstrates how the government moved from a passive, reactive mode to a proactive one. Giving priority to national security and intelligence led to a sizeable expansion of the intelligence community that included "a sharpening of its legislative weaponry; the intensification of its international intelligence cooperation; and the reorganization of government responsibilities around the new Department of Public Safety and Emergency Preparedness Canada" (Rudner 2004, 17). The new policy, bolstered by an $8 billion investment, enhanced the operating budgets of policing and intelligence-gathering organizations, bringing together new (e.g., the National Security Advisory

Council) and existing agencies, and expanding the scope of institutions involved, including the creation of a Public Health Agency of Canada to deal with potential threats to health with the aim of explicitly identifying Canada as an active member in the "war on terror" (Wark 2004).

These developments represent the most significant changes that have taken place in response to September 11. They are not, however, the only changes adopted. Other initiatives were also implemented to enhance security and intelligence activities. Abroad, Canada contributed militarily to the US-led campaign in Afghanistan, and domestically, Canada signed the Smart Borders Accord with the United States. This agreement expanded the integrated border enforcement teams, and coordinated visa-control policies between the two countries (Chute 2005). There was a strong belief that terrorism was an imported problem, and that the best way to stop terrorism was to prevent terrorists from entering Canada (Public Safety and Emergency Preparedness Canada 2004). The case of Ahmed Ressam, a terrorist who had trained with al-Qaeda in Afghanistan, known also as the Millennium Bomber, reinforced the view that more security was vital for protecting Canada and the United States. Ressam was found guilty of engaging in a terrorist plot to blow up the airport in Los Angeles (Johnson 2012). He was found by customs agents with a trunk full of explosives as he attempted to cross into Washington State from Canada (Johnson 2012). Allegations by the American government that Canada's borders were too porous and that terrorists were entering the United States through Canada, as exemplified in the Ressam case, led to the increased securitization of Canada's borders.

The general argument made in support of these counter-terrorist legislative developments and changes in Canada and elsewhere has been the protection of public safety from further attacks (Goldsmith 2008). However, the rush to provide solutions and quell public fears has raised questions about the efficacy and legitimacy of these policies. Bell (2006, 148) argues that like its Western allies, Canada's security agenda post–September 11 does little to safeguard civic freedom, and heightens policing of perceived risk areas and groups while arguing simultaneously that such measures are necessary to protect these freedoms. Bhabha (2005) concurs, claiming that while states are expected and required to protect the security of their citizens, they must do so within the bounds of human rights norms. Canada's war on terror, both at home and abroad, has failed to observe these rights, and consequently, racism and stereotyping have flourished post–September 11.

THE NEW ENEMY

The key targets of these new national security priorities have been Canada's Arab and Muslim communities, who were increasingly regarded as terrorists and threats in references and discussions about national security (Kruger, Mulder, and Korenic 2004). These communities have been the primary targets of government surveillance and policing since the terrorists of September 11 were identified as Muslim men. Said (1979) notes that in many Western states, this type of treatment is not new, since Arab communities have been, historically, the objects of demonization and control. Many scholars concur, pointing out that when the foreign policies of many Western states are examined closely, the construction of Muslims as dangerous and threatening may have intensified after September 11, but was not a product of it (Ha-Redeye and Simard 2010; Lazar and Lazar 2004).

Prior to September 11 in Canada, Arabs and Muslims were mostly regarded as long-time, peace-loving, contributing citizens and residents. However, after September 11, they became increasingly viewed as a key threat to Western societies, who regard their race, ethnicity, and religion as incompatible with Western values and traditions (Hanniman 2008). Zine adds, "being part of a common framework of citizenship and 'Canadianness' quickly became a fragile reality" (2004, 111). Many scholars argue that the result of such popular beliefs and attitudes has been nothing short of catastrophic for Arab and Muslim communities. For example, organizations like the Canadian Muslim Civil Liberties Association and the Canadian Islamic Congress reported a dramatic rise in incidents of racism, Islamophobia, and anti-Muslim/anti-Arab sentiments after September 11. The Toronto Police Hate Crimes Unit found a spike in racially and religiously motivated hate crimes immediately following September 11 (Toronto Police Services 2002). Reports of widespread discrimination, mosques being vandalized, death threats being issued, constant harassment, and racist abuse became commonplace in Arab and Muslim communities across Canada, as the backlash and increased security reinforced the discrimination and oppression experienced by these communities (Zine 2004). Similar incidences were reported in the United States and Europe. Despite calls for tolerance and respect for diversity, it was clear that Arab and Muslim Canadians would be scapegoated and made to pay the price for having the same racial, ethnic, and/or religious affiliations as the perpetrators of September 11.

The response by the Canadian government was no less damaging. Arab and Muslim people found themselves subjected to multiple layers of screening at Canada's borders, giving rise to the phenomenon of "flying while brown." Pre-entry assessments, fingerprinting, and interviews with security or border officials would become common routines for many. Stories of people being denied access onto a plane, removed from planes for praying, denied visas to other countries, or questioned extensively about their "Canadian identity" played out in a context where public sympathy was in short supply and recourse to fair treatment was not a priority. The belief that Arab and Muslim communities were now groups to be feared made it easier for politicians to amplify their exclusion. However, these incidents would pale in comparison to the treatment of several Arab and Muslim Canadians who would suffer unfathomable injustice as a result of the government's national security agenda.

THE EXCEPTIONAL STATE?

The incarceration of Canadian Omar Khadr, a child soldier, at Guantanamo Bay, and the unwillingness of the Canadian government to advocate for his repatriation to Canada, illustrates how very different life would now be for Arab and Muslim Canadians. Khadr has been repeatedly branded as a "war criminal" and a "convicted terrorist," even though he was never charged with US criminal offences or internationally recognized war crimes (Toronto Star 2012). His treatment has been described as "offending the most basic Canadian standards about the treatment of detained youth suspects" (Toronto Star 2012). Although many international organizations urged Canada to repatriate Khadr, since he represented the "classic child soldier narrative: recruited by unscrupulous groups to undertake actions at the bidding of adults to fight battles they barely understand," Canada ignored these pleas (Toronto Star 2012). In an act of desperation, Khadr entered into a plea agreement with US prosecutors in October 2010, accepting an eight-year sentence in addition to time already served, in an effort to secure the possibility of transferring to a Canadian prison after serving the first of eight years (Jiwani 2011). In September 2012, after being imprisoned for more than a decade and having never received a fair hearing, he finally returned to Canada (Toronto Star 2012). As Jiwani observes, Omar Khadr is "an exemplar of the profound criminalization, isolation and abandonment of those who are considered deviant, disposable and dispossessed Others" (2011, 15).

Khadr was not alone, however. In two other cases, we see how fear of the "internal, dangerous foreigner" would trump citizenship status and rights, leading to a nation's banishment of its own citizens (Dhamoon and Abu-Laban 2009). Approximately one year after September 11, Maher Arar, a dual Canadian and Syrian citizen, was detained at JFK airport in New York while on his way home to Ottawa from a vacation. He was accused by US officials of being linked to al-Qaeda, and was deported to Syria where he was imprisoned for 10 months, during which time he was beaten, tortured, and forced to make a false confession (Commission of Inquiry 2006). A Commission of Inquiry into his case found that Arar was clear of all terrorism allegations. Prime Minister Stephen Harper issued an apology to Arar and $10.5 million in compensation for his ordeal.

Abu-Laban and Nath (2007) argue that while Arar's story has been represented as a simple tale of guilt versus innocence, with Arar portrayed as an innocent man wrongfully accused, there are several other ways to read this story. A more critical reading of this situation highlights how Arar's treatment, despite being a Canadian citizen, is neither exceptional nor anomalous (Abu-Laban and Nath 2007). During the course of Arar's ordeal, citizenship and law took on multiple meanings where, for example, Arar's status shifted between being a Canadian and a Syrian, depending on the context of debates and media coverage (Abu-Laban and Nath 2007). The exercise of structural and racialized violence against Arar by the state highlights the challenges of protecting human rights and ensuring human security when the state operates from a position of fear in moments of crisis. The combination of foreignness, security, and racialization legitimized state actions against Arar, and while redress was made, he was, nonetheless, severely penalized for occupying the role of the racialized foreigner. Thus, allegations by Canadian Arabs and Muslims that the government has failed to respect their citizenship rights when they were most needed is difficult to refute in light of the Arar case.

In a similar case, another racialized Canadian citizen has been subjected to suffering in the name of protecting Canada. Abousfian Abdelrazik's case raises many troubling questions about the continued mistreatment of Muslim Canadians. Abdelrazik, a black and Muslim Canadian citizen, was accused of being a supporter of al-Qaeda, as well as a terrorist, during a trip to Sudan in 2003 to visit his sick mother (Brown 2008). He was jailed and tortured for nine months without charges, and then arrested again in November 2005, to be released in July 2006 (Brown 2008). The Sudanese government formally exonerated him in 2005, finding that there was no evidence of any links to al-Qaeda or terrorism (Koring 2011). Despite this pronouncement, his name was placed on a United Nations security council blacklist, and the Canadian government refused to renew his passport or issue travel documents to him. As a result, he languished for six years in Sudan before finally returning to Canada in June 2009, after the Federal Court of Canada ruled that his Charter rights had been violated (Koring 2011).

After a long and public campaign, his name was removed from the UN blacklist in November 2011, allowing for the release of his assets and the ability to travel internationally again (Koring 2011). Abdelrazik sued the government for punitive and aggravated damages, and Foreign Affairs Minister Lawrence Gordon for malfeasance in public office (Koring 2009). Like Arar's case, Abdelrazik's citizenship has been irregularized and rendered inoperable insofar as the rights associated with state membership had been removed (Nyers 2011). His irregularity is the result of both exclusion and racialization. Nyers observes that "once race is overlaid on the spectrum of citizenship statuses, we see that irregularization is not a general phenomenon, but one that threatens certain kinds of racialized subjects more than others" (2011, 186). The assumption that Abdelrazik's citizenship would protect him fails to recognize the culture of fear that marks this era of heightened securitization, and how it is racialized and casts racialized bodies as eternal outsiders (Walia 2012). Whitaker (2011–12) adds that Abdelrazik's experiences demonstrate the stark deficiencies in accountability, where various government organizations actively blocked, stalled, and impeded Abdelrazik's ability to return to Canada because they did not regard him as truly belonging to Canada.

BOLSTERING DOMESTIC SECURITY

A decade after September 11, and with increased public awareness of these cases of injustice and inequalities, the national security narrative has largely remained unchanged—strengthen security and ignore accountability (Whitaker 2011–12, 157). The racialization and securitization of Arab and Muslim people continues both at home and abroad. While the above cases highlight the dangers of travelling as a Muslim Canadian, those at home have not been any safer from the heightened anti-terrorism security and surveillance policies and practices. In the enforcement provisions of the *Immigration and Refugee Protection Act* (part 1, division 9) are sections that grant the Minister for Citizenship and Immigration Canada the authority to issue danger opinions and security certificates against individuals deemed a security threat to Canada. The process of issuing a security certificate to a permanent resident or foreign national begins with the signatures of two ministers who deem the person named in the certificate inadmissible to Canada, for reasons of national security or criminality (Berger 2006). The security certificate process is meant to be an immigration proceeding, to ensure "the removal from Canada of non-Canadians who have no legal right to be here and who pose a serious threat to Canada and Canadians" (Public Safety Canada 2012). Once the certificate has been approved by a federal court judge as reasonable, this process allows the state to detain the person indefinitely, without judicial recourse, and to deny the defendant access to the evidence used to support their indefinite detention. It also allows the government to eventually deport the individual from Canada (Berger 2006).

Given the government's assertion of sovereign power, and the one-sided nature of this policy, it is not surprising that the use of security certificates as a counterterrorism measure is regarded as one of the most controversial practices employed by the government. Many concerns have been raised about the detention process, the use of secret evidence, and the dissolution of habeus corpus (the rule of law) by the state in these cases.[3] The use of protracted or indefinite immigration detention has been shown to cause mental and physical trauma for the detainee. Steel, Silove, Brooks, Momartin, Alzuhari, and Susljik found that long-term detention can cause sadness, hopelessness, intrusive memories, attacks of anger, and physiologic reactivity (2006, 63). Duffy and Provost (2009) argue that since security-certificate detention can result in a person being permanently deprived of liberty, the proceedings and standards for determining detention should more closely resemble the process used in criminal proceedings, where the standards for fairness safeguards are higher than in immigration proceedings. They state that "fundamental to the concept of fairness is the idea that a detainee must know what evidence is being used to justify a detention in order to adequately rebut that case" (Duffy and Provost 2009, 556).

As mentioned earlier, the current approach does not allow the defendant or the defendant's lawyer to see the evidence used to justify a detention order, and this constitutes a significant gap in protecting the constitutional rights of the defendant. In challenging the state's case, the defendant has access only to a summary of the intelligence dossier against them, and must rely on a special advocate who has access to the defendant's limited case file, but not to the defendant. Whether or not the defendant's rights can be overridden in times of national security, and to what extent, has been intensely scrutinized by legal scholars. Bell (2006) contends that the denial of basic legal protection and judicial impartiality to security certificate detainees compromises the rule of law and has been questionably rationalized under the imperative of fighting terrorism. She states,

> With an absence of judicial checks, and no structural imperative to balance the rights of the accused with their accuser ... the security certificate process has effectively rendered the courts an investigative tool of CSIS and is part of a larger representational process that certifies immigrants and refugees as security risks. (2006, 64)

The many layers of secrecy, combined with the state's ability to invoke the privilege of national security, highlight the problematic nature of security certificates and why critics refer to the proceedings as "secret trials."

Although 27 people have been subjected to security certificate proceedings since 1991, the treatment of Muslim non-citizens after September 11 has generated the most significant attention. After the events of September 11, at least five men have been detained indefinitely in Canada, as a result of being issued a security certificate for being suspected of some sort of terrorism affiliation (CBC News 2009c). The "Secret Trial 5," as they have been called, include Hassan Almrei, Adil Charkaoui, Mohamed Harkat, Mahmoud Jaballah, and Mohammed Zeki Mahjoub. All five men are of Muslim origin and were living in Canada with their families. They have been detained for periods of two to seven years, and face the possibility of torture if deported to their countries of origin (CBC News 2009b). Three of the men accused—Mohamed Harkat, Adil Charkaoui, and Hassan Almrei—challenged the security certificate process on constitutional grounds (CBC News 2007a). In February 2007, the Supreme Court of Canada issued a unanimous judgment that struck down the security certificate system on the basis that it violates the Charter of Rights and Freedoms. Furthermore, they stated that the detainees had a right to not be arbitrarily detained and to see and respond to the evidence against them (CBC News 2007a). This ruling, however, did not bring an end to the use of security certificates. Instead, the system was amended to include the addition of a special advocate (as mentioned above) who would act as watchdog and test the evidence against the accused (CBC News 2007b).

The men were not freed as a result of the SCC ruling. Instead, they were moved from prison to house arrest and given some of the strictest conditions in Canadian history.[4] For example, they live in homes with security cameras everywhere, their phones are wiretapped, they must wear a tracking anklet 24 hours a day, and they cannot leave the house unchaperoned.[5] All five of these cases are disturbing, but perhaps none more so than the case of Mohammed Mahjoub, an Egyptian who came to Canada in 1996 as a Convention refugee. He has endured two security certificates in relation to his involvement with a banned political organization while he lived in Egypt. He was detained for six and a half years, but never formally charged, and subsequently placed under house arrest. While under house arrest, he requested that a judge return him to prison because the conditions were too damaging to his family.[6] The five men, who have spent a combined total of 26 years in prison, have never been charged. Aitken (2008) claims that while their numbers are few when compared to the thousands detained globally, the experiences of these men are striking in terms of the mistreatment they have suffered, and the use of extraordinary powers by the state.

Narratives of security and threat have dominated the political landscape since September 11. Men of Middle Eastern, Arabic, and Muslim backgrounds have borne the brunt of this fixation on national security and the fears of insecurity. The extent to which, as a result of racial and ethnic profiling, ethnic minorities associated with Islam have been subjected to negative attention from police and other security forces has been well documented across the United States, Canada, the United Kingdom, and Australia. The arrest of 24 South Asian men in Toronto in 2003, under a joint RCMP–Immigration Canada operation known as Project Thread, is illustrative of racialized targeting. The 24 men were in Canada on student visas, studying at the Ottawa Business School. When the school closed suddenly, and the owners fled the country, the students were stranded in Canada with invalid visas (People's Commission on Immigration and Security Measures 2007). They were targeted on suspicions of being part of an al-Qaeda sleeper cell, and thus a threat to national security (Shephard and Verma 2003). The evidence used against them included living together in clusters, having a minimal standard of living, being in possession of pictures of aircrafts and strategic landmarks (one man had a photo of the CN Tower), and having connections to or being from the Punjab province in Pakistan, allegedly known for Sunni extremism (Odartey-Wellington 2009, 28). A week later, all the charges were dropped for lack of any links whatsoever to terrorism, despite initial claims by the police that there was "strong" evidence to support the allegations (Shephard and Verma 2003). While media outlets reported widely on the allegations made against these men, as well as their arrests, much less attention was given to the fact that these men were not terrorists, or that they were detained for up to five months in a maximum security prison for possessing invalid visas (People's Commission on Immigration and Security Measures 2007, 19). This sensational case devolved into one of immigration fraud, even though the men insist they were not aware of the legitimacy issues surrounding the school, and had paid for their education in good faith (Shephard and Verma 2003).

Eventually, 13 of the men were deported to Pakistan, where they continue to live under the shadow of suspicion, and the remaining men have applied for refugee status in Canada, in the hopes of avoiding a similar fate (Shephard and Verma 2003). Some of the men reported on the impacts this has had on their lives, including broken families, unemployment, estrangement from family and friends, and the trauma of detention (none of the men had been imprisoned before) (Shephard and Verma 2003). Razack observes that what made the men's situation particularly vulnerable was "not simply the racist power of the cluster theory and its capacity to win support for the state, but crucially, the anomic zone into which non-citizens are plunged once they are profiled" (2007, 113). Racism provided the strength for the assumption of pathology, and the idea that the men might have been poor students pooling together their resources while studying in Canada was overridden by the belief that people from the Punjab province of Pakistan are all suspicious (Razack 2007). Operation Thread highlights the dangers of racial profiling and stereotyping in a post–September 11 environment that emphasizes security above individual rights and liberty.

The formation of the generic "Arab–Middle-Eastern–Muslim other," whose politics, histories, societies, and cultures are reduced to a unified negative conception, has been made possible by inextricably linking discussions about Islam and Muslims to terrorism (Semati 2010). The rise of Islamaphobia has positioned "the Muslim other" or the category of "brown" as the antithesis of the Euro-American identity, and in so doing, has pathologized a wide swath of people while also legitimizing their marginalization. The ongoing securitization of Muslim and Arab communities underscores the potential for innocent and defenceless ethnic minorities to find themselves at risk, and to be unprotected from state counterterrorism measures.

It was not by chance that after September 11 Middle Easterners became the targets of retribution and redemptive violence. Kumar's (2007) historical analysis highlights how complex genealogies and discursive contexts have, over time, constructed different racial groups from various parts of Asia as "cultural others," culminating in the post–September 11 racialization of Asian identities. Being brown skinned was no longer just about being from a different territory or culture, it now linked Muslims with "terrorists" (Kumar 2007, 17). In a similar vein, Poynting and Mason (2006) observe that while September 11 did not mark the beginning of "othering" for Arab and Muslim communities, it did dramatically heighten and intensify the negative attention law enforcement agencies paid to these communities. That is, police and security officials were now focused on rooting out suspicious individuals in these communities, rather than acknowledging and responding to the escalated levels of hate crimes, victimization, and racism that they were experiencing. Spivak (2004) concurs, noting that the racism directed at Arab and Muslim people post–September 11 invoked genealogies of the Self and Other, of colonized and colonizer, East and West, where racial and ethnic difference is fetishized and manifested. It is less a response to a particular event and more accurately "an entire culture of imperative ideology of self, including all its attendant manifestations, that existed years before September 11, which was merely strengthened by the anxiety manufactured in the aftermath of the attacks" (Salaita 2005, 166).

To date, there are no mechanisms in place to adequately assess the impact of the war against terrorism for racialized and ethnic minorities. As acts of discrimination and violence against Arab and Muslim communities in Canada persist, all we have are assurances by the Canadian government that the balance between individual rights and collective security is adequate. The consequences, both intended and unintended, suffered by Omar Khadr, Maher Arar, Abousfian Abdelrazik, the Secret Five, the men of Project Thread, and the many other racialized minorities in Canada, suggest that their suffering is not inconsequential. The lives of these men have been shattered by a national security agenda that allows the terrorist label to be applied to citizens as easily as it is applied to non-citizens. Bahdi (2003) argues that while some people may find that the harms endured are justified as part of the price paid for fighting terrorism, the consequences, when viewed from a community perspective of systematic exclusion and marginalization, are not insignificant. Acts of discrimination fuel the belief that members of Muslim and Arab communities are the dangerous internal foreigners, despite their citizenship status (Dhamoon and Abu-Laban 2009). As Bahdi states, "those who turn to racial profiling as an anecdote for uncertainty will find neither solutions nor comfort. Racial profiling will produce only illusions of security while heightening the disempowerment and sense of vulnerability of racialized groups in Canada" (2003, 317).

Furthermore, the treatment of Arab and Muslim people as potential threats and convenient scapegoats is a cautionary reminder about what is being given up in the name of security. As many critics point out, the war on terrorism effectively served a wider political agenda that sought to manufacture consent, through the evocation of fear, to allow for intrusive surveillance, routine frisks, and limitations on personal freedoms (Bell 2006; Russo 2008; Aitken 2008). Altheide (2006) observes that when the rituals of control become pervasive and institutionalized, they are much more easily accepted by a fearful public. Anti-terrorism legislation and practices affect citizens and non-citizens alike, creating a context where all opposition is regarded as a security threat, and politically opportunistic racism prevails. This approach does not solve the problem of feeling less secure in an insecure world, nor does it adequately protect us from future risks and threats.

NOTES

1 Sikh, Hindu, and Tamil communities in Canada were also targeted after September 11.
2 Preventative arrest means that the person arrested has not yet committed a criminal offence. The concern is that they may commit an offence in the future, and their arrest is to prevent the crime from occurring.
3 Habeas corpus refers to a legal action, which can be addressed to a prison official, demanding that a prisoner be brought before a court of law to determine if he or she is serving a lawful sentence, or whether they should instead be removed from custody. The writ of habeas corpus is frequently used by detainees who are seeking relief from unlawful imprisonment, and is generally regarded as an important instrument for the safeguarding of individual freedom against arbitrary state action. It has been commonly used in immigration matters to challenge unlawful decisions resulting in deportation (Kurzban 2008).
4 www.secrettrial5.com
5 www.secrettrial5.com
6 www.secrettrial5.com

DISCUSSION QUESTIONS

Is it appropriate to detain people indefinitely because they may be terrorists? What role should human rights play here?
Should racial profiling in the context of terrorism be banned?

Are you worried that your citizenship status no longer protects you from state torture? What safeguards should be in place? Is Canada safer now that we have many policies in place to combat terrorism?

FURTHER READING

Daniels, R., P. Macklem, and K. Roach, eds. *The Security of Freedom: Essays on Canada's Anti-Terrorism Bill*. Toronto: University of Toronto Press.

Dowling, J., and J. Inda. 2013. *Governing Immigration through Crime: A Reader*. Stanford, CA: Stanford University Press.

Jiwani, Y. 2011. "Trapped in the carceral net: Race, gender, and the 'War on Terror.'" *Global Media Journal* 4 (2): 13–31.

Odartey-Wellington, F. 2009. "Racial profiling and moral panic: Operation thread and the Al-Qaeda sleeper cell that never was." *Global Media Journal* 2 (2): 25–40.

Poynting, S., and V. Mason. 2006. "Tolerance, freedom, justice and peace? Britain, Australia and anti-Muslim racism since 11 September 2001." *Journal of Intercultural Studies* 27 (4): 365–91.

Semati, M. 2010. "Islamophobia, culture and race in the age of empire." *Cultural Studies* 24 (2): 256–75.

WEBSITES OF INTEREST

Canadian Network for Research on Terrorism, Security and Society—http://www.tsas.ca/

GlobalResearch—Centre for Research on Globalization—http://www.globalresearch.ca/

Project Censored—http://www.projectcensored.org/

Stop NATO—http://rickrozoff.wordpress.com

Strategic Culture Foundation—http://www.strategic-culture.org/

The Secret Trial 5—http://secrettrial5.com/

CHAPTER NINE

THE RACIALIZATION OF IMMIGRATION SURVEILLANCE

This chapter focuses on how the changing patterns of migration and immigration have increased cultural diversity and complexity, and in the process, reshaped our understanding of the relationship between immigration and crime. The unprecedented numbers of people migrating around the globe today has led to Western states shutting down their borders, in an effort to curtail the number of migrants settling in. At the same time, immigration to Canada has become increasingly difficult for those without significant resources. In Canada and other Western states, a key strategy adopted for preventing unwanted migrants and immigrants from entering their respective countries has been to criminalize their activities. In this chapter, we examine the use of criminal justice practices in dealing with immigration matters (which are seen as administrative) and highlight some of the central issues within these debates.

The reality of living in a globalized world means that it is not only people in high-risk groups (such as potential terrorists) who are subjected to state surveillance and control. Mobility itself has increasingly become the object of surveillance and regulation due to concerns about global threats such as human trafficking, pedophilia, and crime by immigrants and refugees. As migration becomes synonymous with risk, many developed nations have securitized their borders as a strategy for managing contemporary anxieties and fears arising from the effects of globalization, such as increased poverty and income inequality. A variety of control technologies have been implemented to sort, select, and exclude border crossers. In this neo-liberalized world order, it is much more difficult to travel internationally, unless one is willing to pay for the privilege of mobility. Those who are globally connected can move with ease around the world (e.g., Nexus[1] travellers), while travellers designated as illegitimate will find their mobility restricted. Social characteristics such as race, class, and citizenship are the key markers used by states to differentiate these two groups. In the process, immigrants and refugees are constructed as either "desirable" or "undesirable," and this tactic has been instrumental in legitimizing punitive immigration policies and practices, aimed at excluding those who do not belong. The increasing criminalization of immigration taking place in many Western nations is the result of immigration and criminal justice practices merging to fend off a perceived common enemy—the "criminal alien" (Kanstroom 2005).

In Canada, racialized groups of immigrants and refugees have been increasingly constructed as unworthy and criminal, and as illegitimate border crossers. For example, the former minister of immigration, Jason Kenney, repeatedly used the word "bogus" in reference to failed refugee claimants, particularly those from countries he deemed to be safe (Levine-Rasky 2012). For Kenney, they are the "queue jumpers," the economic migrants who are "abusing" Canada's refugee system because they do not apply for immigration through normal channels (Showler 2009). In the mainstream media, it is not uncommon to find refugees being depicted as the cause of chaos and disorder, posing a danger to the rest of Canada by virtue of their troubled backgrounds and cultural differences (Bradimore and Bauder 2011). In the last two decades, several high-profile cases of refugees arriving in Canada through irregular means have crystallized the belief that few, if any, refugees are truly deserving of Canada's generosity. This has made it possible to enact reforms to Canada's refugee program that dramatically deny or limit the amount of support available (NOII 2012).

Immigrants have not fared much better. As the Maytree Foundation puts it, the pace and scope of change to Canada's immigration policies in the last five years "can leave one breathless," and it is difficult to believe that such fundamental change can occur so rapidly (Alboim and Cohl 2012, 1). In an effort to lure only the most productive and desirable immigrants to Canada, the government has made it more difficult for older individuals to immigrate, has made it easier to deport "foreign criminals," has closed immigration offices overseas, has imposed visa requirements on more travellers, and has expanded the discretionary powers of the minister, allowing them to make decisions and changes without going through a parliamentary process (Alboim and Cohl 2012). Through various news releases and press announcements, the government has stated that preventing fraud and abuse of the immigration and refugee system is a main priority in immigration reform.

Recent policies have been crafted in such a way that immigrants who do not fit the image of being worthy or desirable are portrayed in the role of a criminal, making it easier to punish them for their outsider status. For example, the passage of a recent parliamentary bill seeking to expedite the process of removing "foreign criminals" has been criticized for suggesting that

Canada is "overrun with foreign terrorists, escaped convicts, war criminals and the like" (Huffington Post 2012). Furthermore, critics point out that the government makes no distinction in the bill between serious criminals that should be deported and those that should be given more leniency, such as people who have lived in Canada most of their lives and commit a minor offence (Toronto Star 2012b).

MIGRATION SURVEILLANCE

A wide range of changes to immigration policies and practices has perpetuated the perception that not all immigrants and refugees are "desirable," and as such, the need to differentiate between these groups is imperative for managing complex issues such as violent crime, social disorder, clandestine migration, and international terrorism (Walters 2011). Various technologies of surveillance, identification, and regulation have proliferated to control borders and migrants, as the globalization of security has taken hold (Walters 2011). For example, biometric technology in the form of e-passports, transnational fingerprint databases, and a permanent resident card (PRC) highlights a preoccupation with the security and surveillance of mobility. Biometrically enhanced passports were introduced as part of the 30-point action plan agreed upon by Canada and the United States in the Smart Border Declaration, which was signed shortly after September 11. According to the Canadian government, the vision behind this plan is to advance the movement of people and security based on the belief that "national security and economic security are not competing objectives" (Public Safety Canada 2008). Both governments have hailed the program as a success, with Canada pointing to the increased levels of inadmissibility and detention as evidence that high-risk travellers are being screened out (CBSA 2007).

The development of transnational biometric databases is another approach that has generated significant interest from many governments. The increasing harmonization of border and immigration principles demonstrates how various Western countries are being drawn together to create security perimeters. Canada, Australia, and the United Kingdom quietly signed an agreement in October 2009 to share their fingerprint databases in order to combat immigration fraud (Blanchfield 2009). The Canadian government declared this a "landmark initiative," noting that the agreement will give Canada the ability to identify foreign nationals who are seeking entry into the country, but trying to hide their past from authorities (CIC 2009). Yet, the privacy commissioner of Canada and the president of Australian Lawyers for Human Rights both expressed concerns about the agreement, particularly with regards to how the information would be used and whether or not the information would be adequately safeguarded (Blanchfield 2009).

Finally, one of the first measures to be implemented when the *Immigration and Refugee Protection Act* (IRPA) took effect in 2002 was the introduction of a high-tech identity card for landed residents to replace the Record of Landing document. The Permanent Resident Card (PRC) is required for re-entry into Canada, and is considered to be "secure" proof of the landed immigrant's status since it is the world's first optical memory card to comply with the standards of the International Civil Aviation Organization (Browne 2005). As an identity document, the PRC is able to "nationalize immigrant bodies by codifying place of birth and county code," sorting "citizens" from "permanent residents," and fragmenting individuals by reducing them to bodies and body parts, all for the purposes of conducting surveillance and managing immigration (Browne 2005, 425).

The increasing need for identification has fuelled the development of these security regimes, and "ubiquitous biometrics" is viewed by both corporations and government-regulated agencies as the solution for greater efficiency and security (Lyon 2008). Although unsuccessful, efforts by the former minister of citizenship and immigration, Denis Coderre, to implement a national identity card program that would be issued to all Canadians was based on the belief that "identity has taken on new prominence," and that a national ID card would provide the opportunity "to clarify what it means to be a citizen, a Canadian" (Browne 2010).

Biometric technologies are highly attractive because they are able to "categorize the mobile body as a biological body, stripped of its connection to the body politic and the large geopolitics of mobility," with the aim of producing low-risk subjects who can then safely travel to meet the needs of global capitalism (Rygiel 2011, 144–45). Lyon adds that biometric solutions are seductive because they are sufficiently dramatic in addressing dramatic risks (Lyon 2008, 503). Yet, biometric technology is not without its problems. As the Science and Technology Division of the Parliamentary Information and Research Services has pointed out, some of the technological limitations of biometrics include the possibility of inaccurate readings and the system's vulnerability to damage or attack (Acharya 2006). The report also cited concerns with privacy issues, particularly the trend toward mass surveillance, the use of data (which is collected for one specific purpose but subsequently used for another unintended or unauthorized purpose), the lack of or inadequate legislation to protect privacy rights, and the cost of implementing and running these systems (Acharya 2006).

In the context of immigration, biometric information is specifically sought from those who are most disadvantaged, with the aim of identifying them for control. For example, in Europe, asylum seekers are fingerprinted to ensure that applicants are not applying for asylum in more than one country (Lyon 2008). As Magnet (2007) comments, making "suspect" or "othered" bodies newly visible is a central intent of biometrics. She adds that since these technologies were developed in large part due to anxieties around racialized suspect bodies, biometrics, far from circumventing racism, was intimately connected to problematic assumptions about race, class, and gender (Magnet 2007). Rygiel (2011) concurs, arguing that e-border surveillance efforts continue to target those groups of people who have been historically the objects of surveillance at borders for reasons of race, nationality, religion, and class. Thus, non-citizens from the Global South, asylum seekers, migrant workers, and international students are more likely to experience increased surveillance than other groups.

PREVENTING AND DETERRING UNWANTED MIGRATION

Along with biometrics are many other security measures used to control and regulate immigrants and refugees in Canada. The *Immigration and Refugee Protection Act* contains a long list of preventative and deterrent provisions designed to strengthen government control over non-citizens, and to police the external borders (Crépeau and Nakache 2006). Preventative measures include visa regulations, or requiring a non-citizen to have a visa before entering a country; carrier sanctions, or the imposition of fines and penalties for airline, shipping, and railway companies that transport foreign nationals without proper documentation; and interdiction and interception mechanisms, or the use of immigration officers at key overseas locations to screen travellers before they depart (Crépeau and Nakache 2006). From a government perspective, these preventative measures are important and beneficial because they allow the government to limit the movement of people in a manner that does not draw attention from its critics; this is because these measures are executed outside of Canada, making it more difficult to monitor the treatment of migrants (Crépeau and Nakache 2006). Furthermore, when the legitimacy of these mechanisms is based on the discourse of migrants as dangerous or threatening, it is more difficult to present a compelling counter-discourse. For example, Villegas' (2012) examination of the newly imposed visa requirement for Mexican nationals describes how opposition to the visa requirement by Mexican officials, business interests, and several Canadian politicians failed to counteract government claims that Mexican migrants were irresponsible and required containment. Fears about Mexicans overstaying their visits and applying for refugee status were repeatedly made by government officials to highlight their illegitimate status and the impact this would have on Canada if no action was taken (Villegas 2012). In this respect, the visa regime plays an important role not only in controlling access to the border, but also in the criminalization and illegalization of racialized migrants.

Working in tandem with preventative mechanisms, deterrent measures are also aimed at discouraging "undesirable" migrants from entering Canada. Crépeau and Nakache (2006, 14) suggest that the intent behind deterrent measures is to make the costs of entry so high, and the benefits so low, that migrants do not make the journey. Many of the measures involve reducing the privileges or entitlements available to migrants and refugee claimants, leaving critics lamenting the state of human rights for some of the world's most disadvantaged and marginalized people. The increased use of immigration detention is one measure that has drawn significant criticism in relation to the unjust treatment of non-citizens, particularly in light of historical practices such as the internment of Japanese Canadians during World War II.

Debates on contemporary practices of detention coalesced around the treatment of hundreds of Sri Lankan asylum seekers who arrived by cargo ship on the West Coast of Canada in the summer of 2010. All 492 asylum seekers, including 63 women and 49 children, were detained in provincial prisons for several months (Naumetz 2011). In response to this event, the Conservative government introduced legislation—the *Protecting Canada's Immigration System Act*—that would impose mandatory detention without access to appeal rights for "irregularly arrived" non-citizens, because, as the minister of public safety has stated, "the federal government must ensure that our refugee system is not hijacked by criminals or terrorists" (Derosa 2012). The minister raised the possibility that members of the Tamil Tigers, a known terrorist organization, could be part of this group of migrants or involved in this smuggling operation (Derosa 2012). As a result, along with mandatory detention, irregular arrivals have reduced access to health care, and delayed access to permanent residency status, family reunification, and travel documents, even if they are found to be bona fide refugees (Alboim and Cohl 2012).

The attempt to control migration to Canada by restricting refugee claims has been widely condemned by many nongovernmental organizations. The Canadian Bar Association points out that while it is legitimate to focus on criminalizing human smugglers who take advantage of desperate people, many of the government's policy changes are directed at asylum seekers and refugees (CBA 2010). Removing or limiting the rights of refugees will do little to curb human smuggling and irregular migration. Furthermore, the representation of the Sri Lankan asylum seekers as posing a very real threat by virtue of being "different from us," underscores how poverty and racial difference, disguised as dangerousness, are mobilized to justify the violation of human rights.

DETENTION AND DEPORTATION

According to the Global Detention Project, Canada remains one of the few industrialized countries in the world to make widespread use of prisons to confine non-citizens for administrative detention (Global Detention Project 2012). They do not regard mixing immigrant detainees with the regular prison population an appropriate practice, nor are they impressed with the lack of any independent monitoring of detention conditions or the lack of time limits (Global Detention Project 2012). An earlier report by the Auditor General, evaluating the detention and removal of individuals by the Canada Border Services Agency (CBSA)—the key institution responsible for immigrant detention and deportation—raised concerns that the detention of immigrants was not being monitored adequately to determine whether or not individuals were receiving consistent and fair treatment (Auditor General 2008). The report pointed out that while standards of treatment are in place, there was no mechanism to ensure that these standards were being met (Auditor General 2008).

As we noted in the previous chapter, the most contentious use of immigration detention has been in cases where non-citizens are detained indefinitely for national security reasons. This situation can be attributed to the lack of oversight and transparency of law enforcement agencies. In addition, although the detention of immigrant children should only occur as a last resort, children have been detained by the CBSA, a practice that has been heavily criticized by the Canadian Council for Refugees (CCR), and other nongovernmental organizations, as highly inappropriate and failing to address the interests of children first (CCR 2009a). Both of these situations are important reminders of the need for adequate monitoring in applying fair treatment to all immigrant detainees, to ensure that the use of detention is not driven by the desire to punish and criminalize migrants and asylum seekers.

The Canada-US Safe Third Country Agreement is another deterrent measure that has not been well received by advocates and supporters of asylum seekers. The agreement, which came into effect in 2004, prevents asylum seekers from making a refugee claim if they arrived in one country by way of the other through a land port of entry (CCR 2005). This agreement is another example of the ongoing harmonization of immigration policies and practices that Canada is undertaking with other nations. Kent (2011) suggests that American criticism of Canada's lax refugee policies has influenced Canada's participation in this agreement. Since 2004, as a result of this agreement, the number of Canadian refugee claims made at land borders has dropped significantly (Kent 2011). The Canadian Council for Refugees has argued that the US is not a safe country for refugees, and with far fewer people making a refugee claim from Canada to the US, the agreement is more about preventing asylum seekers in the US from travelling to Canada in order to claim refugee status (CCR 2005).

Some of the serious concerns over the treatment of asylum seekers in the US are in relation to lengthy periods of detention and the practice of sending people back to countries where they are at risk of torture (CCR 2007). While a lengthy legal challenge by the Canadian Council for Refugees, Amnesty International, and the Canadian Council of Churches has taken place, it failed to have the US declared an unsafe country for refugees (CCR 2009b). Critics argue that the Agreement is a form of interdiction that punishes asylum seekers and results in human rights violations, as asylum seekers are prevented from finding protection (Macklin 2005). Like other forms of interdiction, asylum seekers who are caught in the Safe Third Country rule are rendered invisible in the country of intended asylum since they never arrive (CCR 2005, ii). When they do make it to Canada, as was the case of the Tamil refugees in 2010, it is often through irregular means, resulting in the further victimization and exploitation of asylum seekers, heightened concerns around security, and subsequent intensification of border-security measures. Since Canada shares one of the world's longest borders with the US, Macklin (2005) believes it is somewhat naive to think that instruments like the Safe Third Country Agreement will deter desperate and determined migrants from seeking entry. MacIntosh (2012) suggests that the Safe Third Country Agreement has not only failed, but has also increased irregular or illegal border crossings through the development of an illegal market in human smuggling. As the Tamil refugee case illustrates, one adverse outcome of this has been the rebranding of refugees as security and criminality risks.

One of the permanent deterrent mechanisms in place to discourage unwanted migration is the practice of deportation by nation-states. Non-citizens found to be inadmissible to Canada, according to the criteria set out in the IRPA, are subject to deportation or what the government euphemistically calls "removal proceedings." Terrorist suspects, non-citizens with a criminal record, failed refugee claimants, and undocumented migrants have increasingly been managed through the use of deportation. An evaluation of the Canada Border Services Agency's removal program found that removals from Canada have increased by 10 per cent between 2004 and 2009 (CBSA 2010), with greatest priority given to the removal of high-risk persons, such as those considered to pose a national security threat, organized criminals, and people who commit serious crimes. More recently it was reported that 2011–12 was a "milestone year" for the CBSA, insofar as they deported a record number of foreign nationals and permanent residents due to criminality or failed refugee claims (Cohen 2012a). Public support for deportations has been high, and various law enforcement agencies have taken the opportunity to request additional monies, totalling $27 million, to bolster the work associated with removing targeted individuals (Cohen 2012b).

The ability to accelerate deportation proceedings for more people has been made possible through various policy changes. For example, the government has extended its discretionary powers over the *IRPA*, giving themselves the authority to designate a non-citizen as a "danger to the public," which then allows for the detainment of the designated person indefinitely as well as their removal from Canada, regardless of how long they have resided in the country (Russo 2008). Second, under the *Protecting Canada's Immigration System Act*, which came into effect in June 2012, failed refugee claimants not only have their rights severely curtailed (as mentioned earlier), their deportations are also expedited if they do not voluntarily self-deport. As one immigration spokesperson has claimed, these measures will "put a stop to foreign criminals, human smugglers and bogus refugees abusing our generous immigration system" (Cohen 2012b). Third, restricting removal appeals and limiting judicial discretion as well as discretionary appeals, such as humanitarian and compassionate claims, has perhaps been the most effective policy change in fast-tracking the deportation process.

A recently passed bill to force the deportation of non-citizens or "foreign criminals" who have been convicted of a crime and sentenced to imprisonment for six months or more has been described as an American-style "one strike and you're out" policy (Godfrey 2012). A key criticism of this policy is in regards to the removal of long-time permanent residents who have lived in Canada since childhood but never applied for citizenship. Legal scholars question whether justice is being served by deporting these individuals to unfamiliar countries, and breaking up families and communities for what are in some cases summary or driving offences (Godfrey 2012). It has even been suggested that this policy could fall within the ambit of the Charter's ban on "cruel and unusual punishment," and one lawyer has accused the government of "attacking and destroying the immigration system" with these changes (McKiernan 2012). Yet as Bosworth (2011) observes, foreign offenders often have limited numbers of supporters, and, as a result, governments seldom experience any qualms about disrupting social relationships or violating human rights.

Deportation practices reinforce and reproduce the boundaries between citizen and non-citizen, between those who belong and those who do not, and they offer us a particular vision of national identity that is embraced by the Conservative government. Anderson, Gibney, and Paoletti (2011) point out that freedom from deportation is one of the few remaining privileges that separate citizens from non-citizens. Those without an unconditional right of residence, particularly those who are deemed "undocumented," "irregular," or "illegal," are conventionally depicted as quintessentially deportable. De Genova (2011) suggests that there is no such thing as "illegal migrants" in a general, universal sense—they only exist as a result of particular political and legislative histories. As Canadian historians have demonstrated, these histories are, and continue to be, a melting pot of immigration policies and racial politics that have routinely denied basic rights to racialized groups defined as outsiders (Roberts 1988).

As more people are displaced from their homes in this globalized economy—for reasons of war, environmental disaster, or economic turmoil, with many of these events caused by the policies and practices of governments and multinational corporations—and as the distinction between "economic migrant" and "political refugee" becomes indistinguishable, Western governments are anxious to bolster exclusionary policies like detention and deportation. The increased use of deportation for asylum seekers, "economic migrants," and criminal offenders has become a necessity for all governments that need to demonstrate that they are in control of migration and borders. Gibney and Hansen (2003, 2) characterize deportation as "the noble lie," arguing that deportation is "both ineffective and essential" insofar as it is a central practice of state sovereignty despite the fact that it is actually very difficult to deport people. Western states, in promising more than they can deliver, exacerbate the sense of crisis, allowing the enactment of extraordinary measures to appear normal and justifiable (Bloch and Schuster 2005, 509). For example, in Canada there has been a long backlog of removal orders. Only by denying immigrants access to the appeals process has it been possible to hasten their deportation. This has been a key strategy for increasing the number of deportations, and for closing the gap between government rhetoric and the reality of immigration control. The practice of deportation reveals the extent to which the state relies on the use of violence, through the forcible banishment of foreigners, to defend narratives of national belonging.

THE RISE OF ANTI-IMMIGRATION

The contemporary treatment of "undesirable" non-citizens is rooted in a politics of exclusion and an inequality of treatment that are spurred on by growing suspicions of, and resentment toward, immigrants and refugees. While the phenomenon in Canada is not new, since there have always been groups of immigrants and refugees who have been the targets of intolerance and xenophobia, the increasingly harsh criminal consequences attached to violations of immigration rules and policies are striking. Like many Western states, Canada has incorporated criminal law practices into immigration proceedings while denying procedural protections of criminal adjudication to immigrants and refugees. For example, the recent omnibus bill *Protecting Canada's Immigration System Act* expands the minimum mandatory sentences for those convicted of human smuggling, even though critics argue that the penalties are already at unprecedented levels (van Liempt and Sersli 2012). Furthermore, migrants who arrive in Canada without adequate documentation for whatever reason can find themselves detained until their identities are sufficiently proven. Thus, fleeing persecution is now redefined as unlawful entry. These types of measures repackage immigration control as a form of crime control, despite the fact that undocumented migration to Canada is not a crime. The theme of immigrant criminality in policy debates has become so prevalent that processes of criminalization and illegalization are now relatively uncontroversial (Keith 1993, 198).

The linkage between migration and crime is also evident in the discursive framing of immigration issues through the use of terms like "bogus" or "illegal." Angel-Ajani (2003) claims that anti-immigrant rhetoric is saturated with the language of national citizenship, class, gender, and race. It is not uncommon, for example, for the public to regard eastern European women as responsible for the problems of sex trafficking and prostitution (Angel-Ajani 2003, 437). A recent campaign by the immigration department to crack down on immigration fraud by denationalizing Canadians citizens if their citizenship application, upon review, is deemed to be fraudulent, is another example of how immigrants are represented, first and foremost, as illegitimate (Bell 2012). What the government's media release about this campaign doesn't mention is the fact that the number of fraudulent citizenship applications submitted is actually very low—half of one per cent, according to one critic's calculations (Decoste 2012). This means that, contrary to harsh negative representations, over 99 per cent of the time, immigrants are obeying the rules and are law-abiding. Melossi (2003) argues that the mythical figure of the deviant immigrant has come to embody the dangers, insecurities, and perceived risks of a rapidly changing global environment. Increasingly, foreignness has been constructed and treated as a criminal threat, illustrating how law and language have conflated and reinforced the connection between migration and crime.

The racially motivated stereotype of migrants as the cause of crime and disorder is the basis upon which immigration policies have become more punitive and restrictive. The crime–immigration nexus has fuelled public distrust of immigrants, such that when an individual immigrant is found guilty of a crime, they are seen to be committing not one, but two offences (Sayad 2004). They are guilty by virtue of their immigration status, which is then compounded by their criminal delinquency (Sayad 2004). As Sayad posits, "any trial involving a delinquent immigrant puts the very process of immigration on trial, first as a form of delinquency and second as a source of delinquency" (2004, 282). The former immigration minister, Jason Kenney, has repeatedly invoked the image of migrants and refugees as criminals in his justification for harsher immigration enforcement measures. It is a practice that is not unique to Canada, as criminalization of immigrants has spread across many Western states. In Europe there has been a dramatic rise in the incarceration of foreigners and non-nationals (Wacquant 2005a), while in the United States, asylum seekers and "illegal" immigrants are routinely jailed and denied bond if they are considered a security risk (Welch and Schuster 2005b).

Even as crime rates have declined in the industrialized world, the crusade against immigrants and refugees persists, leading to their ongoing penalization, stigmatization, and marginalization. For women migrants, their criminalization exacts a heavier toll, as they are, typically, a more vulnerable group. Female immigrants risk losing custody of their children if incarcerated, have fewer opportunities for employment, and can become dependent on abusive spouses or be exploited in the underground economy if they lack proper working documents (Hartry 2012). These circumstances make women more susceptible to being criminalized by immigration policing practices.

The creation and enhancement of criminal sanctions for immigration violations demonstrate how the regulation of migration has moved from the civil to the criminal sphere. Violations of immigration law now trigger a range of proceedings, with criminal consequences. The intertwining of immigration control with criminal justice is a phenomenon that Stumpf (2006) describes as "the crimmigration crisis." It refers to the ways in which politicians like Jason Kenney speak about immigration issues as well as to the many policy reforms that seek to prevent and deter immigrants and refugees through the use of mechanisms such as mandatory detention, offshore processing, and deportation. Legomsky (2007) adds that crimmigration is an asymmetric process insofar as enforcement mechanisms have been imported into the immigration system, but the bundle of procedural rights involved in the adjudication process found in criminal proceedings has not been incorporated.

The lack of adjudication fairness in immigration proceedings is premised on the belief that immigrants and refugees are "different from us," or that they violate the nation's "core values" with their cultural and/or racial difference. Stumpf (2006, 27) believes that the decision to deny constitutional rights to non-citizens is much easier when we see them as unworthy or excludable. As a result, in Canada, there has been virtually no effort on the government's part to protect the due process rights of immigrants and refugees who are undergoing immigration proceedings. In fact, some critics argue that procedural protections are actually declining in the government's attempt to "fast-track" proceedings and "crack down" on illegitimate claimants (Showler 2012). For example, the new timelines for processing refugee claims clearly illustrate how the desire to accelerate the process results in claimants being denied the right to a fair hearing and the ability to obtain proper legal representation (Lindell 2012).

Immigration lawyers anticipate that this approach will not save the government any money, and will likely result in lengthy court challenges (Lindell 2012). The activist group No One Is Illegal claims that these changes to the refugee process in Canada create a "racist and discriminatory two-tier system of asylum [that] increases incarceration, denies and revokes legal status, and violently targets and expels refugees and migrants from Canada" (NOII 2012, n.p.). Certainly, many of the harshest reforms in Canada have targeted asylum seekers, the most vulnerable group of migrants and the most vilified. Their desperation has been interpreted as cause for suspicion and fear, resulting in their demonization for a host of social problems. It is by representing asylum seekers and other non-citizens as criminals that detention and deportation can be presented as "natural" solutions in controlling immigration.

The Canadian Civil Liberties Association (2010) has released a report reminding Canadians that immigration status cannot be easily separated from race and ethnicity, and that any policy that seeks to deny rights and entitlements on the basis of immigration status needs to carefully examine whether or not racism and xenophobia lurk beneath the justification of differential treatment. They contend that distinctions between immigration status and race or ethnicity are razor-thin, and that protecting immigrants and refugees against discriminatory treatment also involves acknowledging the problems of racism and xenophobia, which fuel the mistreatment (CCLA 2010). Many scholars agree, arguing that issues of race and racism are deeply embedded in discussions about immigration control (Ibrahim 2005; Barmaki 2009; Palidda 2011). Feminist scholars point out that gender and class are also prominent markers of the desirability and undesirability of migrants (Brion 2011).

Debates over the "welfare burden" of migrants, and the problems of sex trafficking and exploitation, highlight the interplay of race, gender, and class in demarcating excludable groups. Their perceived cultural differences, understood primarily through their criminality and supposed dependency on the state, are fodder for politicians and the media, and concerns about the "flooding" or "invasion" of Canada. For example, a 1999 newspaper headline about Fujian Chinese migrants reads: "Canada could face a much larger tide of humanity" (Bedeski 1999). Bradimore and Bauder (2011) found similar headlines in media coverage of the Tamil migrants a decade later. Typically, it is racialized migrants that are perceived as "illegal" or "bogus," while white migration is invisible, and thus de-problematized (Tesfahuney 1998). Tesfahuney (1998) points out that white migrants bear the "right colour" and the "right culture," and therefore pose no recognizable threat or risk. She contends that it is not migration that is the problem, but the identity of immigrants (i.e., who and where they come from) that shapes understandings of desirability and legitimacy (Tesfahuney 1998). The case of Maher

Arar, along with other cases in which racialized Canadians are mistreated by the government, exposes the role of race as a key factor in determining how migrants are constructed and subsequently treated.

For racialized Canadians and non-citizens, being subjected to ongoing scrutiny and surveillance is a reminder that their membership in the nation is always provisional. Pratt (2010) posits that we can understand the securitization and criminalization of non-whites as part of a broader crime-security nexus, in which the racial stratification of immigration control is rationalized through concerns over criminality and the integrity of the nation. The production of "undesirable" migrants is a highly racialized undertaking, which identifies non-whites—and particularly Middle Eastern, West and South Asian, and Muslim people—as objects to be feared, scapegoated, and criminalized. In this sense, contemporary immigration enforcement is very much a "racial project" that combines overtly race-based hostilities with a set of institutional practices (such as criminalization, confinement, and the denial of basic services) to produce an "immigrant other" that is perceived as threatening (Provine and Doty 2011).

According to Bauman, racialized migrants and refugees "evoke a new form of xenophobia: a mix of old and new ethno-racial suspicions, fear for personal safety and crime victimization, terrorism, and institutional uncertainties and insecurities of contemporary liquid existence" (2003, 119). As a result, questions regarding the nature of state behaviour and the exclusionary treatment of immigrants and refugees are obscured by the notion that the state has the ultimate right to assert its sovereignty and protect its citizens. The control and surveillance of immigrants and refugees demonstrates the changing modes of "risk thinking," where national identity, race, class, and gender intersect in multiple ways to inscribe specific notions of "otherness" and suspicion onto the globally less privileged.

NOTE

1 Nexus travellers are low-risk, pre-approved border crossers. As such, with their Nexus pass, they are eligible to travel in the expedited lane when crossing the border between Canada and the United States.

DISCUSSION QUESTIONS

Should it be a crime for an asylum seeker who is fleeing persecution to arrive in Canada without proper documentation?

If an immigrant has lived most of their life in Canada, should they be deported from Canada for minor crimes? For major crimes?

What would be an acceptable level of border security? How much is too much?

Refugees and asylum seekers are some of the most vulnerable people globally, yet we are reluctant to help them. Why?

FURTHER READING

Dauvergne, C. 2008. *Making People Illegal: What Globalization Means for Migration and Law*. New York: Cambridge University Press.

Finn, R. 2011. "Surveillant staring: Race and the everyday surveillance of South Asian women after 9/11." *Surveillance & Society* 8 (4): 413–26.

Hartry, A. 2012. "Gendering crimmigration: The intersection of gender, immigration and the criminal justice system." *Berkeley Journal of Gender, Law and Justice* 27 (1): 1–27.

Macklin, A. 2005. "Disappearing refugees: Reflections on the Canada–US safe third country agreement." *Columbia Human Rights Law Review* 36: 365–426.

Palidda, S. 2011. *Racial Criminalization of Migrants in the 21st Century*. Burlington, VT: Ashgate.

Roberts, B. 1988. *Whence They Came: Deportation from Canada, 1900–1935*. Ottawa: University of Ottawa Press.

Rygiel, K. 2010. *Globalizing Citizenship*. Vancouver: UBC Press.

WEBSITES OF INTEREST

Border Criminologies—http://bordercriminologies.law.ox.ac.uk/

crImmigration—http://crimmigration.com/

Immigration and Refugee Board of Canada—http://www.irb-cisr.gc.ca/Eng/Pages/index.aspx

Migrations Map—http://migrationsmap.net/#/CAN/arrivals

No One Is Illegal—http://noii-van.resist.ca/

Open Borders: The Case—http://openborders.info/

CHAPTER TEN

THE CRIMINALIZATION AND RACIALIZATION OF POVERTY

Punitive measures to manage issues of immigration and national security are also being adopted in the domestic context to deal with issues of welfare administration and poverty, highlighting the transformation of state practices in many different areas of governance. These practices are not unrelated, since many poor, racialized people are also immigrants and refugees. People of colour suffer the most from punitive state policies because they are more likely to live in poverty and to experience a range of discriminatory treatment by public actors (welfare workers) and private actors (landlords, employers). In this final chapter, we interrogate the ongoing stigmatization of poor, racialized people through an examination of state policies and practices that result in their continued penalization.

The increasing penalization and criminalization of poor, racialized people is situated within the context of an eroding welfare state and within public and policy rhetoric that blames poor people of colour for their situation. Both provincial and federal governments in Canada have dramatically reduced benefits, restricted eligibility, and increased the levels of surveillance and policing associated with obtaining and receiving welfare support. According to Wacquant, current approaches to regulating the poor involve a three-pronged strategy that includes "amputation of its economic arm, the retraction of its social bosom and the massive expansion of its penal fist" (2009, 4). To a greater extent, poor people are being denied state support and protection while simultaneously being portrayed and treated as deviants for failing to be economically stable. The expanded use of workfare programs, snitch lines, fingerprinting, and imprisonment for fraudulent behaviour highlights how disciplinary systems have taken on a greater role in governing poverty. Patterns of penalization are also affected by the interplay of race and gender, since women and racialized minorities are more susceptible to being poor and are thus more likely to be subjected to disciplinary measures.

For these groups, the spread of neo-liberal policy-making into the welfare system has had a detrimental effect, as welfare policies have become much more punitive toward the poor.

It is a well-documented phenomenon that poverty in Canada is deep and persistent, and has not improved in the last several decades (National Council of Welfare 2010; Citizens for Public Justice 2012). The economic marginal-ization of many individuals and families in Canada can be attributed to the continuing impact of the 2008 economic recession, to declining welfare state provisions, and to a globalized, neo-liberal marketplace. In the last decade, welfare benefit rates have decreased dramatically, in many cases falling well below the levels required for basic subsistence (Klein and Pulkingham 2008). Other social support programs for low-income earners have also been dramatically reduced, and some eliminated. Contrary to popular opin-ion, "welfare is not, and has never been, 'generous'" (Klein and Pulkingham 2008, 8). Low-income Canadians are unable to survive on current welfare benefits, and, as a result, their day-to-day lives are focused on struggling to meet basic needs such as food, shelter, health, and personal safety (Klein and Pulkingham 2008, 10). At the same time, income inequality has grown, with the wages of middle-class and working-class people either stagnating or declining (Ivanova 2009). These problems are profoundly gendered and racialized. Family responsibilities, the lack of access to affordable childcare, and discrimination in the labour market make it more difficult for women and racialized individuals to obtain economic security. As a result, they have higher rates of unemployment, and if they are employed are more likely to be in part-time, temporary, or precarious work arrangements.

Various studies have affirmed the problems that racialized people encounter in securing full-time, permanent employment (Citizens for Public Justice 2012; Pruegger, Cook, and Richter-Salomons 2009). With the exception of people who identify as Japanese and Filipino, racialized men are 24 per cent more likely to be unemployed than non-racialized men, and racialized women fare even worse, with a 48 per cent greater likeli-hood of unemployment than non-racialized men (Block and Galabuzi 2011, 4). Furthermore, while racialized workers have contributed to the growth of Canada's economy, they have not reaped the benefits insofar as their incomes did not grow significantly (Block and Galabuzi 2011, 4). Hence, labour-market discrimination is reflected in both employment incomes and rates of unemployment. As a result, economic inequality continues to plague racialized communities, where many people struggle with low incomes and are unable to meet basic survival needs. The 2006 census showed that while the overall poverty rate in Canada was 11 per cent, the rate was 22 per cent for racialized people, compared to 9 per cent for non-racialized people (National Council of Welfare 2012). Within the group of racialized people, recent immigrants to Canada have fared the worst, with poverty rates rising continuously in the last two decades (National Council of Welfare 2012). This is due primarily to the lack of recognition of their international education and credentials, the devaluing of their non-Canadian work experience, and racial discrimination, leaving new immigrants to face an uphill battle upon their arrival to Canada (Block and Galabuzi 2011).

ROLLING BACK STATE SUPPORT

As Canadians struggle to adapt to the changing nature of work and the economy, the Canadian government has also responded by restructuring and retrenching the welfare state. Poverty reduction strategies are now based on neo-liberal principles of smaller government, carefully targeted social programs, and greater reliance on families and the private sector for services and support (Baker 1997, 1). These ideas are viewed by politicians of all political stripes as the solution to managing the problems of rising program costs, increasing numbers of claimants, and structural changes in the labour market. As a result, in most provinces, program entitlement has shifted from the principle of "guaranteed annual income" to the view of social support as temporary and needs-based, designed to encourage independence and self-sufficiency (Baker 1997, 2). Current polices emphasize work ethics and personal responsibility, with blame and guilt placed squarely on poor people if they fail to meet the expectations of the marketplace. This neo-liberal shift in the welfare system sees poverty as the failure of individuals to make good decisions for themselves, rather than the consequences of structural changes to the labour market or inadequate government support (Brodie 2008, 148). As a result, poor people who cannot demonstrate success in the labour market are recast as undeserving and unworthy of welfare benefits (Breitkreuz 2005).

This has been the dominant approach that Western governments have taken in reducing high public debt and the cost of providing welfare support. Many welfare systems have shrunk, following reforms that involved slashing programs as well as reducing the number of people entitled to benefits on the assumption that many recipients were either not worthy or morally suspect, and that welfare dependency is harmful. Sossin (2004) adds that while governments benefit politically from demonstrating fiscal restraint and getting "tough" on welfare, they also reap subtle benefits from restructuring the welfare system. These include "providing a ready supply of inexpensive and available labour to low-wage industries, winning the 'race to the bottom' against other jurisdictions so as not to become a haven for social assistance recipient migrants, and reinforcing moral norms which value independent and self-sufficiency as the hallmarks of citizenship"

(Sossin 2004, 4). Implementing policy changes to achieve these goals has not been difficult, since the targets of these changes—single mothers, racialized people, and people with disabilities—are some of the most disenfranchised, and often lack the ability to fight back effectively.

The erosion of the welfare state has left vulnerable groups without a safety net. The most recent poverty-trends scorecard in Canada revealed some disturbing findings (Citizens for Public Justice 2012). The report noted that there has been only minor progress in reducing the poverty gap, that many Canadians are finding it difficult to move beyond their low-income status, that the gap between rich and poor continues to widen, and that poverty and disadvantage is increasingly concentrated among certain groups, notably Aboriginal peoples, recent immigrants, racialized communities, and persons with disabilities (Citizens for Public Justice 2012, 4). For these vulnerable groups, economic disadvantage, combined with discrimination and exclusion, has a direct impact in creating more insecurity. They are much more likely to suffer from poor health, are less likely to attain high levels of education, and will have weak community ties (Citizens for Public Justice 2012, 14).

Limiting access to state support will only exacerbate these problems. As mentioned earlier, welfare benefit rates across most provinces are so low that recipients cannot meet basic needs (Caragata 2003; Gordon 2005). For example, the National Council of Welfare (2009) estimated that the welfare income of a single person considered employable in 2009 was at best only 62 per cent of the income needed to reach the poverty line. Modest welfare increases over the last several years have not kept up with the increase in inflation, and in some cases welfare incomes have decreased by 20 per cent or more (National Council of Welfare 2009). Most recently, the Conservative government has decided not to renew an employment insurance program in regions of Canada with high unemployment (CBC News 2012c). Local politicians and poverty advocates point out that this change will have devastating impacts on many poor Canadians, who have no other source of income given the limited opportunities available in those regions (CBC News 2012c). As one advocate points out, "it seems every step the government takes, every announcement, it's another slap at the poor people" (CBC News 2012c).

In addition to reduced rates, numerous restrictive rules now accompany access to state benefits. In British Columbia, changes to welfare policies in 2002 included the introduction of time limits, and claimants are now required to wait three weeks and to be actively searching for employment before they are permitted to submit an official application (*BC Employment Act* 2002). Benefits are now only available for two out of every five years (unless an exemption is granted) and an applicant cannot apply for welfare until they have proven to be financially independent for two consecutive years (*BC Employment Act* 2002). This last rule requires that claimants provide documentation to show that they have worked at least 840 hours or earned at least $7,000 for two years in a row (*BC Employment Act* 2002). For younger applicants, this two-year independence test is seen as harsh, since many will not have been in the labour market long enough to pass the test (Wallace, Klein, and Reitsma-Street 2006, 30). The Canadian Centre for Policy Alternatives argues that these measures are deeply punitive, and exemplify how the government is concerned only with reducing welfare caseloads, at any expense (Klein and Long 2003, 27).

Similar trends have been taking place in Ontario, where, since the mid-1990s, a well-established workfare program has been in place to ensure that welfare recipients are not simply "passive" claimants that are becoming too dependent on welfare. Ontario Works is a compulsory, welfare-to-work program that focuses on helping claimants develop labour-force attachment, through participation in job searches and other related activities (Lightman, Herd, and Mitchell 2008). In interviews, participants in these workfare programs refer to the programs as "dehumanising, degrading and demoralizing" (Herd, Mitchell, and Lightman 2005, 73). Critics observe that these programs did not move participants out of the low-paid, insecure work they had previously engaged in, and many continued to rely on welfare benefits and undeclared work to survive (Lightman, Herd, and Mitchell 2008, 256). Their labour-force attachment was anything but strong, as participants continued to struggle with hunger and ill health after leaving the programs (Lightman, Herd, and Mitchell 2008, 256). For single mothers, the impact of mandatory participation in workfare programs has been particularly harsh, since program expectations do not take into account their status as lone mothers or their lack of access to childcare (Gazso 2012).

Critics contend that current welfare provisions are symbolic of a government that is deeply contemptuous of poor people, for failing to rise to the challenge of labour market changes. It doesn't matter if the type of work available to the unemployed in today's labour market pays poorly, if it is insecure and alienating, or if family responsibilities limit one's ability to work outside the home. According to government rhetoric and policy, paid employment in any job is preferable to dependency on the state. Thus, lone mothers in BC, with children as young as three years old, must make "reasonable efforts" to seek employment (Klein and Long 2003). Furthermore, efforts are underway in BC to recover welfare overpayments, which involves taking welfare recipients to a small claims court (Hodson 2010), and claimants with outstanding criminal warrants are denied access to welfare (CBC News 2009a). These practices, which the government argues are necessary to protect the public purse, highlight the punitive treatment of poor people. As one newspaper editorial pointedly notes: "Certainly, income assistance rates should encourage people to seek employment. Some might argue that those on welfare are paying the price for bad choices. But people do not choose to become disabled. Children do not choose to be born into poverty. And B.C.'s assistance rates are so inadequate as to be destructive" (Victoria Times Colonist 2011). Thus the balance between providing support for people in times of need and maintaining proper fiscal management of public funds has become overwhelmingly one-sided as the economy is restructured to meet the needs of employers, and poor people are required to endure the harsh consequences of recent policy reforms.

THE "UNDESERVING" POOR

Despite the inadequacies of welfare support, politicians and the media continue to promote the message that cuts to welfare programs are needed in order to make welfare so unpleasant that people seek alternatives (Gordon 2005, 60). Based on neo-liberal ideology, "rolling back" the welfare state and labour regulations, while "rolling out" disciplinary programs, will encourage poor people to get back into the labour market (Wacquant 2009). A key feature of welfare disentitlement is the ideological construction of poor people as either "deserving" or "undeserving." Welfare recipients are portrayed as individuals with moral or psychological deficiencies, to the extent that the term "welfare" generally connotes deeply held negative emotions and associations (Fraser and Gordon 1994). A recent study found that while Canadians continue to support spending on social services for the poor, they favoured reduced spending on welfare (Harell, Soroka, and Mahon 2008). The researchers claim that the way welfare has been framed—in terms of need—typically evokes negative images, and thus support is lessened when there is a belief that recipients can "control" their situation (Harell, Soroka, and Mahon 2008). As a result, groups that are seen as the most deserving— children, disabled people, and the elderly—are given greater support than others who are on social assistance (Harell, Soroka, and Mahon 2008, 55). However, the "deserving" can easily fall into the ranks of the "undeserving" (Little 1998). For example, lone mothers have been attacked and vilified for failing to be independent, responsible, and self-sufficient (Fraser and Gordon 1994; Seccombe, James, and Walters 1998; Quadagno 2000; Sidel 2000; Coulter 2009).

People of colour have been similarly portrayed as predominantly undeserving. Racialized imagery of poor people continues to shape attitudes about welfare, and has promoted the belief that poor people of colour live in poverty because they prefer to live in a culture of dependency (Quadagno 1994; Gilens 1996; Harell, Soroka, and Mahon 2008). Racialized and feminized constructions of poverty emphasize the pathological nature of being poor. One of the most enduring myths about women of colour is that they are hypersexed and promiscuous, resulting in a belief that they have children in order to obtain welfare money (Abramovitz 2006). As a result, many jurisdictions have reduced welfare benefits for women with children, or have implemented earlier cut-off times, as the three-year limit in BC demonstrates. Immigrants and refugees have also been targeted by reforms, with immigrants in Canada being denied access to welfare benefits upon arrival, due to restrictions in sponsorship arrangements, and with refugees being consistently portrayed as undeserving recipients of Canada's "generosity" (Razack 2000; Pratt and Valverde 2002). Finally, Aboriginal people in Canada have been stigmatized for decades due, in part, to their high rates of participation in the welfare system (Kendall 2001).

This phenomenon is not restricted to Canada, and can be seen in many advanced democracies. For example, during the 2012 election campaign in the US, the Republican Party characterized American citizens as either "makers" or "takers," suggesting that those in the former group are hard-working Americans (read: white), while those in the latter group want the government to pay for everything (read: non-white). These racially coded categories and the racism they invoke illustrate how poor people are demonized for being poor, female, and racialized (Menendian 2012). Stereotypes of the "welfare queen," "bogus refugee," and "lazy immigrant" are prevalent in many nations with an advanced welfare system, and they continue to shape public attitudes and policy discussions regarding access and entitlement to welfare (Seccombe, James, and Walters 1998; Sidel 2000). Empirical studies have found that many people assume that racialized individuals are receiving assistance illegitimately, despite ongoing racial inequities and inequalities in the welfare system (Neubeck and Cazenave 2002; Mirchandani and Chan 2007).

Perhaps the most damaging stereotype about poverty is the assertion that the values held by the poor are the major source of their problems and life circumstances—in other words, that they live in a "culture of poverty." Specifically, this perspective claims that poor people are different from mainstream society insofar as they lack a work ethic, they have improper family values, and they are comfortable with dependency (Jones and Luo 1999, 440). This explanation emerged in the 1960s, and has gained prominence, particularly in the United States, in explaining why poverty exists (Piven and Cloward 1987). Poor people were seen as dysfunctional and pathological, with women and racialized groups epitomizing the images of welfare dependency. The feminization and racialization of poverty were built on ideologically distorted ideas that women were more likely to have dependent personalities, and that poor, racialized families were the result of "children having children" (Fraser and Gordon 1994, 326).

Nelson's (2011) study of black communities in Atlantic Canada during the 1960s found that Canadian policy-makers attributed the poverty found in communities like Africville[1] to assumptions about family life, gender, and moral codes. Critics of the "culture of poverty" thesis point out that culture became a proxy for race and "gave those who were uncomfortable with frankly racist stereotypes a way to embrace a fundamentally racialized theory of the defective poor while avoiding the stigma of racism" (Bennett and Reed 1999, 189). Nelson (2011) elaborates, stating that it is all too easy to overlook the particularities of racialized poor people (including the problems of discrimination and marginalization) when racism is subsumed in the problems of poverty. Thus, calls for the state redistribution of wealth and higher minimum wages were not seen as potential solutions to poverty, but as ways of giving in to the inadequacies of the poor, at the expense of the wealthy (Finkel 2002).

Although the "culture of poverty" argument did highlight the complexity of poverty, it has been widely discredited by many poverty scholars for labelling poor people as pathological, making them personally responsible for their circumstances, and failing to adequately capture the dynamic forces of impoverishment (Gans 1995). The erroneous assumptions and unsubstantiated claims found in the "culture of poverty" thesis simply made it easier to target vulnerable groups like women and racialized communities, and to justify their increased discipline and regulation. The negative construction of poor people as "scroungers" and as "undeserving" is, thus, part of a broader political campaign to reinforce the myth that welfare is "too generous," that it encourages laziness and irresponsible behaviour, and that welfare recipients are getting something they do not deserve at the expense of hard-working taxpayers (Power 2005). They are the "undeserving poor," the "deviant," and the "irresponsible" (Sidel 2000) who are often discredited as illegitimate and unworthy, and, in some cases, as criminals. According to politicians and the mainstream media, the only recourse available in the management of poor people is to take a "tough love" stance through draconian measures, to ensure that their continued dependency on the state will cease (Seccombe, James, and Walters 1998). As Sidel aptly points out, these designations leave no room for the considerable variation and complexity that characterizes people's lives, and the fact that many of us have relied, to varying degrees, on the state for support of one kind or another (2000, 75).

In the neo-liberal context, these views have intensified as politicians have become more pessimistic about solving the problems of poverty, and have focused instead on the dangerous and undeserving nature of the poor. Therefore, even as poverty rates in Canada continue to climb, and as the gap between the rich and the poor sharpens—particularly between racialized and non-racialized communities—the dominant discourse of poverty portrays welfare recipients as "cheaters" with bad habits and inadequate self-control (Reid and Tom 2006, 403). As many scholars argue, they have been constructed as the "never-deserving" poor (Crookshanks 2012; Gazso and Waldron 2009; Chunn and Gavigan 2004).

PENALIZING AND CRIMINALIZING POOR PEOPLE

Stigmatizing poverty has made it possible to enact policies and practices that minimize the role of the state in providing support, and to place more attention on treating poor people as a population in need of social control. The penalization and criminalization of poor people and their activities has become commonplace, as their social exclusion from full participation in social, political, and economic life leaves few options available to governments managing an ever-increasing pool of surplus labour. Many Canadian municipalities have passed bylaws and legislation criminalizing the activities of poor people (Hermer and Mosher 2002). These policies, ironically named the *Safe Streets Act* in BC and Ontario, are anything but "safe" for poor people. Activities such as panhandling, squeegeeing, sleeping in public, and loitering have been reconstituted as "disorderly" activities that can result in criminal sanctions (Hermer and Mosher 2002). Reports conducted in various Canadian cities illustrate how, as a result of discriminatory enforcement, street youth and homeless people are disproportionately targeted (VIPIRG 2011; O'Grady, Gaetz, and Buccieri 2011). They are more likely to receive tickets and fines for minor offences, are more likely to be stopped and searched, and are at increased risk of incarceration (Douglas 2011).

The highly discriminatory and differential treatment of poor people is also clearly evident when compared to the treatment of other groups in receipt of state benefits (Henman and Marston 2008, 192). It has not been suggested, for example, that unemployment insurance recipients ought to be fingerprinted or subjected to mandatory addiction screenings, whereas these proposals have been considered for welfare recipients (Bobier 1998; Berger 2001). These latter practices are often accompanied by campaigns to combat the alleged problem of welfare fraud in many provincial welfare programs. Despite evidence that the problem of welfare fraud is not significant, politicians have asserted that the problem is a major threat to the welfare system when justifying the implementation of harsh sanctions and the increased surveillance of claimants (Mosher and Hermer 2005). The use of snitch lines, unannounced home visits, biometric surveillance, and criminal sanctions for repeat violations are just some of the current practices and penalties that welfare recipients face. Claimants can also have no expectations of personal privacy, as they are required to provide all manner of personal information to apply for and continue receiving benefits. Welfare recipients report that this level of scrutiny leaves many of them feeling as if they are criminals, even when they have not done anything wrong (Mirchandani and Chan 2007, 70–76). They point out how the whole process of accessing welfare benefits can be degrading and dehumanizing (Mirchandani and Chan 2007, 76). Nonetheless, governments claim that welfare should only be available for those who are most in need, and that sanctions are necessary to deter and prevent fraud by people who want to take advantage of the system.

Although the policing of poor people is not a new phenomenon, in the past, punitive practices were tempered by social programs and services that sought to reintegrate welfare recipients back into the labour market (Wacquant 2009). However, in the last several decades, as services and programs have withered away, and as well-paying, secure jobs have become harder to come by, the task of regulating and disciplining the poor has fallen onto an expanded police and penal system. According to numerous research studies, the level of surveillance experienced by welfare recipients in receipt of government assistance has reached unprecedented levels (Maki 2011; Magnet 2011; Gilliom 2005). One Canadian study of women on social assistance found that the women felt guilty for every little thing they did, and that the loss of personal privacy due to the high levels of surveillance resulted in the loss of human dignity (Collins 2005, 23). To ensure claimants were conforming to the rules, surveillance occurred at the point of determining eligibility, and throughout their time on assistance. However, the women also noted that they were required to release all kinds of personal information, which could then be scrutinized regardless of whether it pertained to welfare rules or not (Collins 2005, 23). Other researchers found similar comments by welfare recipients, noting that their research participants felt humiliated on a daily basis, and experienced high levels of anxiety, paranoia, and stress from worrying about their actions and whether they would result in being denied support or being criminally punished (Seccombe, James, and Walters 1998; Power 2005; Gilliom 2005; Gilman 2008). Gustafson (2009) claims that recent welfare reforms have been rewritten in such a way as to assume a latent criminality among the poor. Many of the punitive measures implemented in the welfare system borrow from the "get tough on crime" approach used by the criminal justice system (Gustafson 2009). Wacquant concurs, stating that a key characteristic of current welfare policy is the presumption that welfare recipients are "guilty until proven innocent," that their conduct needs to be closely supervised and remedied by restrictive and coercive measures, and that deterrence and stigma are necessary to modify the behaviour of welfare recipients (2009, 79).

For street-involved people and those who are homeless, assumptions of criminality are even more prevalent. As a result, they tend to experience regular interactions with the police and other security agents for displaying visible signs of poverty or marginality. Furthermore, the social and racial profiling of public spaces shapes how law enforcement determines when standing in a public space becomes an act of loitering (VIPIRG 2012). A key theme to emerge in a study of policing practices in Victoria, BC, was the increased likelihood of experiencing discrimination and lack of fair treatment among people who use drugs, homeless and poor people, and First Nations people (VIPIRG 2012). Other studies have confirmed that these groups are often identified as problematic by law enforcement agents and are subjected to increased surveillance (Douglas 2011; O'Grady, Gaetz, and Buccieri 2011). The treatment of First Nations people is particularly alarming given that, in Canada, this community has been the most racially discriminated against for decades.

The consequences of increased surveillance are many. Along with the continued demonization of poor people, the reinforcement of disadvantage and discrimination, and the dehumanizing impact of surveillance, recent studies suggest that now, more than ever, the social exclusion of poor people is cemented through a punitive approach that permeates both penal and welfare institutions (Beckett and Western 2001; Mosher and Hermer 2005; Mirchandani and Chan 2007). This neo-liberal approach to poverty governance has transformed the way we think about poor communities, and it has led to the emergence of practices that seek to discipline poor people into becoming good neo-liberal subjects. In Ontario, a significant restructuring of the province's welfare programs, which included increasing and investing in welfare surveillance, was justified on several grounds (Maki 2011). The government cited the need to demonstrate integrity in the system by preventing criminality and fraud, the need to reduce welfare caseloads, and the need to ensure an accountable, efficient, and cost-effective system for taxpayers as reasons for intensifying levels of surveillance (Maki 2011, 48). Yet as Maki notes, in the context of servicing the neo-liberal state, welfare surveillance is a direct assault on poor people (2011, 51). Hartmann claims that the increased level of control over the lives of welfare recipients is the deliberate outcome of neo-liberal rationalities, which seek to discipline poor people into self-governing in the name of individual initiative and responsibility (2005, 69). Thus, poverty is not just an economic condition; it is also a socio-political experience, a state of being, and an identity (Spencer-Wood and Matthews 2011).

Clearly, welfare policies, and the practices that accompany them, are anything but neutral. Groups more likely to experience higher levels of poverty, such as single mothers, older women, people with disabilities, and people of colour, are thus more likely to be impacted by punitive welfare reforms. Welfare and punishment are now part of a broad policy regime that manages labour and inequality, with welfare acting as the carrot and punishment the stick (Haney 2004). In an effort to educate Canadians about the realities of welfare, and to dispel myths about the welfare system, anti-poverty advocates have held various campaigns to demonstrate the consequences of income inequality. One such campaign took place in January 2012, when a provincial politician in BC took up the challenge of living on welfare for one month. During that time, he lost a considerable amount of weight, accumulated debt, and had to sell his possessions to buy a transit pass so he could return home (Klein, Copas, and Montani 2012). Unfortunately, since many political parties have been heavily influenced by the tenets of neo-liberalism in policymaking, efforts to reduce poverty are limited to market-driven goals and practices (Weaver, Habibov, and Fan 2011). In fact, many scholars argue that the purpose of welfare reforms was never about alleviating poverty but had more to do with reducing the dependency of individuals and families on state support (Mosher 2000; Sidel 2000; Gordon 2005; Wacquant 2009). The effort to reduce welfare rolls has been a key strategy of neo-liberal welfare policy reform, since, for the government, reducing the number of people eligible to receive welfare benefits constitutes a savings.

In a 2010 speech, the former leader of the New Democratic Party of Canada, Ed Broadbent, noted that social and economic rights are the cornerstones of human rights (Broadbent 2010). During the mid-twentieth century, many Western governments believed that it was important for the state to intervene in the economy by ensuring that their citizens were adequately supported during difficult times. The belief was that a just society would emerge through the provision of equality-building measures and the implementation of new social rights (Broadbent 2010). Fast-forward to the start of the new millennium and most of the gains of these hard-fought policy debates have been either dismantled or watered down significantly across many liberal democracies. Reductions in health, education, welfare, and housing benefits are not only a direct attack on social rights, they also deepen the economic, social, and political stratification of nation-states. Siltanen questions whether we were really all that generous to begin with: "Was there *ever* a commitment to the social rights of citizenship in the social policy of the Canadian 'welfare state'?" (2010, 398). In her view, we have simply gone from "mean and lean, to meaner and leaner" under neo-liberal governance (Siltanen 2010, 397).

The implications of increased inequality are many. Osberg (2012, 27) states that inequality in market incomes will likely produce more financial volatility in an economy that is peppered with periodic financial crises, which will have long-lasting effects in the economy overall. As a result, poor people will continue to find it more difficult to move up the economic ladder, labour standards will decrease, and wages will likely remain low paying and insecure. Accessing affordable housing will be more challenging as municipal exclusionary zoning practices, such as restrictions on minimum lot sizes or unit sizes, "will severely discriminate against the poor" (Makuch et al. 2004, 200). Moreover, poor people who fail to integrate into mainstream society will confront an expanded security net, with public and private policing organizations seeking to ensure that streets are safe and clean through the demonization and criminalization of their activities. Gustafson wryly remarks that while policymakers appear to be unwilling to spend more tax dollars on improving the conditions of the poor, they are more than willing to spend money on policing the poor, even when this appears economically inefficient or ineffective (2009, 677). Finally, failing to address fundamental social divisions of gender and race, which can result in discriminatory and marginalizing treatment, will exacerbate the harms of living in poverty, and accelerate the social exclusion of women and racialized people.

The decline of social citizenship in the context of neo-liberal practices and policies makes it clear that the model "universal" citizen is far from being neutral or inclusive (Fraser 1992). While the idea of welfare support was meant to be available to all those in need, access to support has always been partial and selective, and based on notions of entitlement that are gendered, racialized, and cultural. The convergence of penal and welfare practices suggests that harsher treatment will be the *de facto* state response, as the particularities of the poor are dismissed as individual pathologies, and a discourse of sameness and meritocracy prevails. The neo-liberal welfare state rejects the existence of racism (and sexism), believing instead that any-one willing to work hard can be incorporated into the marketplace, with no barriers to their participation in the economy (Davis 2007). In the process, the realities of racism are dismissed as possible explanations for racial ineq-uities. Chesney-Lind and Pollock (1995) refer to this situation as "equality with a vengeance." For poor, racialized people, having racism dismissed and undermined will do little to facilitate their departure from poverty, or to address the underlying conditions that perpetuate their impoverishment.

NOTE

1 Africville (1761–1969) was a seaside village in Nova Scotia. It was populated primarily by people of African descent who were former slaves, escaped slaves, and free people looking for a better life in Canada. See www.africville.ca.html for more details.

DISCUSSION QUESTIONS

Poverty is not a crime, but poor people are required to find creative means to survive. Should they be punished for doing so?

Who is responsible for the problems of poverty? Who is responsible for solving these problems?

Should welfare rates be increased? What are some of the pros and cons of increasing welfare rates?

Why do we stigmatize poor people? Why are some poor people more ac-ceptable than others (e.g., poor children vs. single, racialized mothers)?

FURTHER READING

Chunn, D., and S. Gavigan. 2004. "Welfare law, welfare fraud, and the moral regulation of the 'never deserving' poor." *Social and Legal Studies* 13 (2): 219–43.

Gazso, A., and I. Waldron. 2009. "Fleshing out the racial undertones of poverty for Canadian women and their families: Re-envisioning a critical integrative approach." *Atlantis* 31 (1): 132–41.

Kendall, J. 2001. "Circles of disadvantage: Aboriginal poverty and underdevelopment in Canada." *The American Review of Canadian Studies* 31 (3): 43–59.

Mirchandani, K., and W. Chan. 2007. *Criminalizing Race, Criminalizing Poverty.* Black Point, NS: Fernwood Publishing.

Wacquant, L. 2009. *Punishing the Poor. The Neoliberal Government of Social Insecurity.* Durham, NC: Duke University Press.

WEBSITES OF INTEREST

Canada without Poverty—http://www.cwp-csp.ca/
Canadian Centre for Policy Alternatives—http://www.policyalternatives.ca/
Canadian Council on Social Development—http://www.ccsd.ca/
Peacock Poverty—http://www.peacockpoverty.org/
Poverty and Race Research Action Council (USA)—http://www.prrac.org/
Povnet—http://www.povnet.org/
The Poverty and Human Rights Centre—http://povertyandhumanrights.org/

REFERENCES

Abramovitz, M. 2006. "Welfare reform in the United States: Gender, race and class matter." *Critical Social Policy* 26 (2): 336–64.

Abreu, J. 1999. "Conscious and nonconscious African American stereotypes: Impact on first impression and diagnostic ratings by therapists." *Journal of Consulting and Clinical Psychology* 67 (3): 387–93. http://dx.doi.org/10.1037/0022-006X.67.3.387.

Abu-Laban, Y., and N. Nath. 2007. "From deportation to apology: The case of Maher Arar and the Canadian state." *Canadian Ethnic Studies* 39 (3): 71–98.

Acharya, L. 2006. *Biometrics and Government*. Ottawa: Library of Parliament, Parliamentary Information and Research Services, Science and Technology Division.

Adamoski, R., D.E. Chunn, and R. Menzies, eds. 2002. *Contesting Canadian Citizenship: Historical Readings*. Toronto: University of Toronto Press.

Adams, K. 1999. "A research agenda on police use of force." In *Use of Force by Police: Overview of National and Local Data*, ed. K. Adams, G. Alpert, R. Dunham, J. Garner, L. Greenfield, M. Henriquez, P. Lanagan, C. Maxwell, and S. Smith. Washington, DC: National Institute of Justice Research Report.

Adelberg, E., and C. Currie, eds. 1987. *Too Few to Count: Canadian Women in Conflict with the Law*. Vancouver: Press Gang.

Adelberg, E., and C. Currie, eds. 1993. *In Conflict with the Law: Women and the Canadian Justice System*. Vancouver: Press Gang.

Adelman, M., E. Erez, and N. Shalhoub-Kevorkian. 2003. "Policing violence against minority women in multicultural societies: 'Community' and the politics of exclusion." *Police and Society* 7: 105–33.

Adler, F. 1975. *Sisters in Crime: The Rise of the New Female Criminal*. New York: McGraw-Hill.

Aitken, R. 2008. "Notes on the Canadian exception: Security certificates in critical context." *Citizenship Studies* 12 (4): 381–96. http://dx.doi.org/10.1080/13621020802184242.

Alboim, N., and K. Cohl. 2012. *Shaping the Future: Canada's Rapidly Changing Immigration Policies*. Toronto: Maytree Foundation.

Al-Hakim, M. 2010. "Making room for hate crime legislation in liberal societies." *Criminal Law and Philosophy* 4 (3): 341–58. http://dx.doi.org/10.1007/s11572-010-9095-4.

Altheide, D. 2006. "Terrorism and the politics of fear." *Critical Studies–Critical Methodologies* 6 (4): 415–39. http://dx.doi.org/10.1177/1532708605285733.

Alvi, S. 2012. *Youth Criminal Justice Policy in Canada.* New York: Springer. http://dx.doi.org/10.1007/978-1-4419-0273-3.

Amnesty International. 2009. *No More Stolen Sisters.* London: Amnesty International Publications.

Anderson, B., M. Gibney, and E. Paoletti. 2011. "Citizenship, deportation and the boundaries of belonging." *Citizenship Studies* 15 (5): 547–63. http://dx.doi.org/10.1080/13621025.2011.583787.

Anderson, D., and B. Anderson. 2009. *Manufacturing Guilt: Wrongful Convictions in Canada.* 2nd ed. Black Point, NS: Fernwood Publishing.

Anderson, M. 1997. "Mental illness and criminal behavior: A literature review." *Journal of Psychiatric and Mental Health Nursing* 4 (4): 243–50. http://dx.doi.org/10.1046/j.1365-2850.1997.00061.x.

Angel-Ajani, A. 2003. "A question of dangerous races?" *Punishment and Society* 5 (4): 433–48. http://dx.doi.org/10.1177/14624745030054004.

Arat-Koc, S. 2005. "The disciplinary boundaries of Canadian identity after September 11: Civilizational identity, multiculturalism, and the challenge of anti-imperialist feminism." *Social Justice (San Francisco, CA)* 32 (4): 32–49.

Auditor General. 2008. *Report of the Auditor General of Canada to the House of Commons: Chapter 7—Detention and Removal of Individuals—Canada Border Services Agency.* Ottawa: Office of the Auditor General of Canada.

Avery, D. 1979. *Dangerous Foreigners.* Toronto: McClelland and Stewart.

Backhouse, C. 1999. *Colour-Coded: A Legal History of Racism in Canada, 1900–1950.* Toronto: University of Toronto Press.

Bahdi, R. 2003. "No exit: Racial profiling and Canada's war against terrorism." *Osgoode Hall Law Journal* 41 (2&3): 293–317.

Baker, M. 1997. *The Restructuring of the Canadian Welfare State: Ideology and Policy.* Social Policy and Research Centre (SPURC): Discussion Paper No. 77.

Balfour, G. 2008. "Falling between the cracks of retributive and restorative justice: The victimization and punishment of Aboriginal women." *Feminist Criminology* 3 (2): 101–20. http://dx.doi.org/10.1177/1557085108317551.

Balfour, G., and E. Comack. 2006. *Criminalizing Women: Gender and (In)justice in Neo-Liberal Times.* Black Point, NS: Fernwood Publishing.

Bania, M. 2009. "Gang violence among youth and young adults: (Dis)affiliation and the potential for prevention." *IPC Review* 3: 89–116.

Bankey, R. 2001. "La donna é mobile: Constructing the irrational woman." *Gender, Place and Culture* 8 (1): 37–54. http://dx.doi.org/10.1080/09663690120026316.

Banton, M. 1998. *Racial Theories.* Cambridge: Cambridge University Press. http://dx.doi.org/10.1017/CBO9780511583407.

Barkan, E. 1992. *The Retreat of Scientific Racism.* Cambridge: Cambridge University Press.

Barlow, A. 2005. "Globalization, racism and the expansion of the American penal system." In *African Americans in the US Economy,* ed. C. Conrad, J. Whitehead, and P. Mason. Lanham: Rowman and Littlefield.

Barmaki, R. 2009. "Criminals/refugees in the age of the welfareless states: Zygmunt Bauman on ethnicity, asylum and the new 'criminal.'" *International Journal of Criminology and Sociological Theory* 2 (1): 251–66.

Barron, C. 2011. *Governing Girls: Rehabilitation in the Age of Risk*. Black Point, NS: Fernwood Publishing.

Barron, C., and D. Lacombe. 2005. "Moral panic and the nasty girl." *Canadian Review of Sociology and Anthropology. La Revue Canadienne de Sociologie et d'Anthropologie* 42 (1): 51–69. http://dx.doi.org/10.1111/j.1755-618X.2005.tb00790.x.

Baskin, D., I. Sommers, R. Tessler, and H. Steadman. 1989. "Role incongruence and gender variation in the provision of prison mental health services." *Journal of Health and Social Behavior* 30 (3): 305–14. http://dx.doi.org/10.2307/2136962.

Batacharya, S. 2006. "A fair trial: Race and the retrial of Kelly Ellard." *Canadian Women's Studies* 25 (1–2): 181–89.

BC Civil Liberties Association. 2012. *Police-Involved Deaths: The Need for Reform.* Vancouver: BC Civil Liberties Association.

BC Employment and Assistance Act, S.B.C. 2002, c 40.

BCCLA (British Columbia Civil Liberties Association). 2013. "RCMP officer on trial for assault on First Nations teenage girl." January 22. http://bccla.org/news/2013/01/rcmp-officer-on-trial-for-assault-on-first-nations-teenage-girl/ (Accessed on August 20, 2013).

Beagan, B., and Z. Kumas-Tan. 2009. "Approaches to diversity in family medicine." *Canadian Family Physician Medecin de Famille Canadien* 55 (8): 21–28.

Beckett, C., and M. Macey. 2001. "Race, gender and sexuality: The oppression of multiculturalism." *Women's Studies International Forum* 24 (3–4): 309–19. http://dx.doi.org/10.1016/S0277-5395(01)00185-6.

Beckett, K., and B. Western. 2001. "Governing social marginality." *Punishment & Society* 3(1): 43–59.

Bedeski, R. 1999. "Canada faces much larger tide of humanity." *Victoria Times-Colonist*, 7 August.

Bell, C. 2006. "Subject to exception: Security certificates, national security and Canada's role in the 'War on Terror.'" *Canadian Journal of Law and Society* 21 (1): 63–83. http://dx.doi.org/10.1353/jls.2006.0031.

Bell, S. 2012. "Immigration fraud crackdown drastically increases the number of Canadians having their citizenship revoked." *National Post*, 2 December.

Benedict, R. 1983. *Race and Racism*. London: Routledge and Kegan Paul.

Bennett, L., and A. Reed. 1999. "The new face of urban renewal: The near north redevelopment initiative and the Cabrini-Green neighbourhood." In *Without Justice for All*, ed. A. Reed. Boulder: Westview.

Ben-Porat, G. 2008. "Policing multicultural states: Lessons from the Canadian model." *Policing and Society* 18 (4): 411–25. http://dx.doi.org/10.1080/10439460802094686.

Beresford, P. 2002. "Thinking about 'mental health': Towards a social model." *Journal of Mental Health (Abingdon, UK)* 11 (6): 581–84. http://dx.doi.org/10.1080/09638230020023921.

Berger, B. 2006. "Our evolving judicature: Security certificates, detention review, and the federal court." *University of British Columbia Law Review.* 39 (1): 101–37.

Berger, P. 2001. "Science misapplied: Mandatory addiction screening and treatment for welfare recipients in Ontario." *Canadian Medial Association Journal* 165 (4): 443–44.

Bhabha, F. 2005. "The chill sets in: National security and the decline of equality rights in Canada." *University of New Brunswick Law Journal* 54: 191–217.

Bhui, K., M. Ascoli, and O. Nuamh. 2012. "The place of race and racism in cultural competence: What can we learn from the English experience about the narratives of evidence and argument?" *Transcultural Psychiatry* 49 (2): 185–205. http://dx.doi.org/10.1177/1363461512437589.

Bierne, P., and J. Messerschmidt. 1995. *Criminology*. 2nd ed. Fort Worth, TX: Harcourt Brace.

Bilge, S. 2006. "Behind the 'culture' lens: Judicial representations of violence against minority women." *Canadian Women's Studies* 25 (1/2): 173–80.

Bingham, E., and R. Sutton. 2012. *Cruel, Inhuman and Degrading? Canada's Treatment of Federally-Sentenced Women with Mental Health Issues*. Toronto, ON: International Human Rights Program, University of Toronto Faculty of Law; Saint-Lazare, PQ: Canadian Electronic Library, 2012.

Bjornstrom, E., R. Kaufman, R. Peterson, and M. Slater. 2010. "Race and ethnic representations of lawbreakers and victims in crime news: A national study of television coverage." *Social Problems* 57 (2): 269–93. http://dx.doi.org/10.1525/sp.2010.57.2.269.

Black, D. 1976. *The Behavior of Law*. New York: Academic Press.

Blackburn, R. 1998. "Criminality and the interpersonal circle in mentally disorder offenders." *Criminal Justice and Behavior* 25 (2): 155–76. http://dx.doi.org/10.1177/0093854898025002001.

Blanchfield, M. 2009. "Canada plans to share fingerprint database with U.K., Australia." *Canwest News Service*, 22 August.

Bloch, A., and L. Schuster. 2005. "At the extremes of exclusion: Deportation, detention and dispersal." *Ethnic and Racial Studies* 28 (3): 491–512. http://dx.doi.org/10.1080/0141987042000337858.

Block, S., and G. Galabuzi. 2011. *Canada's Colour Coded Labour Market: The Gap for Racialized Workers*. Ottawa: Canadian Centre for Policy Alternatives.

Boast, N., and P. Chesterman. 1995. "Black people and secure psychiatric facilities: Patterns of processing and the role of stereotyping." *British Journal of Criminology* 35 (2): 218–35.

Bobier, P. 1998. "Privacy at risk: Finger-scanning for ideology and profit." *Government Computer* (February): 1–5.

Bolaria, B., and P. Li. 1988. *Racial Oppression in Canada*. 2nd ed. Toronto: Garamond Press.

Bonilla-Silva, E. 2001. *White Supremacy and Racism in the Post-Civil Rights Era*. Boulder, CO: Lynne Rienner.

Bonnycastle, K.D. 2009. "Not the usual suspects." In *The CSI Effect: Television, Crime and Governance*, ed. M. Byers and M. Johnson. Lanham: Lexington Books.

Bonnycastle, K.D. 2012. *Stranger Rape: Rapists, Masculinity and Penal Governance*. Toronto: University of Toronto Press.

Bosworth, M. 2011. "Deportation, detention and foreign-national prisoners in England and Wales." *Citizenship Studies* 15 (5): 583–95. http://dx.doi.org/10.1080/13621025.2011.583789.

Bosworth, M., B. Bowling, and M. Lee. 2008. "Globalization, ethnicity and racism: An introduction." *Theoretical Criminology* 12 (3): 263–73.

Bowden, C., and S. Brennan. 2012. *Police-Reported Hate Crime in Canada 2010*. Ottawa: Statistics Canada.

Bradimore, A., and H. Bauder. 2011. Mystery Ships and Risky Boat People: Tamil Refugee Migration in the Newsprint Media. Metropolis BC, Working Paper Series 11–02.

Brannagan, C. 2011. "Police misconduct and public accountability: A commentary on recent trends in Canadian justice system." *Windsor Review of Legal and Social Issues* 30: 61–89.

Breitkreuz, R. 2005. "Engendering citizenship? A critical feminist analysis of Canadian welfare-to-work policies and the employment experiences of lone mothers." *Journal of Sociology and Social Welfare* 32 (2): 147–65.

Brennan, S. 2011. "Violent victimization of Aboriginal women in the Canadian provinces, 2009." *Juristat* (May): 1–20.

Brennan, S. 2012. "Police-reported crime statistics in Canada, 2011." *Juristat* (July): 1–39.

Brewer, R., and N. Heitzeg. 2008. "The racialization of crime and punishment." *American Behavioral Scientist* 51 (5): 625–44. http://dx.doi. org/10.1177/0002764207307745.

Brion, F. 2011. "Using gender to shape difference: The doctrine of cultural offence and cultural defence." In *Racial Criminalization of Migrants in the 21st Century*, ed. S. Palidda. Burlington, VT: Ashgate.

Britton, D. 2011. *The Gender of Crime*. Lanham: Rowman and Littlefield.

Broadbent, E. 2010. *The Rise and Fall of Economic and Social Rights: What Next?* Montreal: Congress of the Canadian Federation for the Humanities and Social Sciences (May 29).

Brock, D.R. 2009. *Making Work, Making Trouble: The Social Regulation of Sexual Labour*. 2nd ed. Toronto: University of Toronto Press.

Brockman, J. 2003. "Aspirations and appointments to the judiciary." *Canadian Journal of Women and the Law* 15 (1): 138–66.

Brodeur, J. 2003. "Violence and the police." In *International Handbook of Violence Research*, ed. W. Heitmeyer and J. Hagan. Norwell, MA: Kluwer Academic Publishers. http://dx.doi.org/10.1007/978-0-306-48039-3_11.

Brodie, J. 2008. "We are all equal now: Contemporary gender politics in Canada." *Feminist Theory* 9 (2): 145–64.

Brown, J. 2008. "Ottawa refuses to help Canadian in Sudan: Lawyer." *Toronto Star*, April 28.

Brown, M. 2004. *Their Own Voices: African Canadians in the Greater Toronto Area Share Their Experiences of Police Profiling*. Toronto: African Canadian Community Coalition on Racial Profiling.

Browne, S. 2005. "Getting carded: Border control and the politics of Canada's permanent resident card." *Citizenship Studies* 9 (4): 423–38. http://dx.doi. org/10.1080/1362102050021 1420.

Browne, S. 2010. "Digital epidermalization: Race, identity and biometrics." *Critical Sociology* 36 (1): 131–50. http://dx.doi.org/10.1177/0896920509347144.

Brzozowski, J., A. Taylor-Butts, and S. Johnson. 2006. *Victimization and Offending among the Aboriginal Population in Canada*. Ottawa: Canadian Centre for Justice Statistics.

Buffam, H.V.B. 2009. "'Bright lights and dark knights': Racial publics and the juridical mourning of gun violence in Toronto." *Law Text Culture* 13 (1): 55–80.

Building Bridges, Breaking Barriers Access Project. 2003. *Final Report*. Toronto: Centre for Addiction and Mental Health.

Burgess-Proctor, A. 2006. "Intersections of race, class, gender and crime: Future directions for feminist criminology." *Feminist Criminology* 1 (1): 27–47. http:// dx.doi.org/10.1177/1557085105282899.

Burman, J. 2010. "Suspects in the city: Browning the 'not-quite' Canadian citizen." *Cultural Studies* 24 (2): 200–13. http://dx.doi.org/10.1080/09502380903541647.

Busfield, J. 1996. *Men, Women and Madness: Understanding Gender and Mental Disorder*. New York: New York University Press.

Byers, M. 2009–10. "The stuff of legend: T/Selling the story of Reena Virk." *Canadian Ethnic Studies* 41–42 (3–1): 27–48.

Cainkar, L., and S. Maira. 2005. "Targeting Arab/Muslim/South Asian Americans: Criminalization and cultural citizenship." *Amerasia Journal* 31 (3): 1–27.

Cameron, A. 2006. "Stopping the violence: Canadian feminist debates on restorative justice and intimate violence." *Theoretical Criminology* 10 (1): 49–66. http://dx.doi.org/10.1177/1362480606059982.

Campbell, C. 2000. *Betrayal and Deceit: The Politics of Canadian Immigration.* West Vancouver: Jasmine Books.

Canada Border Services Agency (CBSA). 2007. *Internal Audit Report of IT Systems under Development — Phase 3.* http://cbsa-asfc.gc.ca/agency-agence/reports-rapports/ae-ve/2007/itrs-ticr-eng.html (Accessed on November 19, 2012).

Canada Border Services Agency (CBSA). 2010. *Detentions and Removals Program — Evaluation Study.* http://www.cbsa-asfc.gc.ca/agency-agence/reports-rapports/ae-ve/2010/dr-rd-eng.html#s02 (Accessed on February 1, 2011).

Canadian Bar Association (CBA). 2010. *Bill C-49, Preventing Human Smugglers from Abusing Canada's Immigration System Act.* Ottawa: Canadian Bar Association National Citizenship and Immigration Law Section.

Canadian Civil Liberties Association (CCLA). 2010. *Who Belongs? Rights, Benefits, Obligations and Immigration Status: A Discussion Paper.* Toronto: Canadian Civil Liberties Association.

Canadian Council for Refugees (CCR). 2005. *Closing the Front Door on Refugees: Report on the First Year of the Safe Third Country Agreement.* http://ccrweb.ca/S3C.htm (Accessed on November 21, 2012).

Canadian Council for Refugees (CCR). 2007. "Supplementary submission to Cabinet with respect to the designation of the U.S. as a safe third country for refugees." http://ccrweb.ca/S3C.htm (Accessed on November 21, 2012).

Canadian Council for Refugees (CCR). 2009a. *Detention and Best Interests of the Child: Report Summary.* Montreal: Canadian Council for Refugees. http://ccrweb.ca/files/detentionchildren.pdf (Accessed on March 11, 2013).

Canadian Council for Refugees (CCR). 2009b. "Supreme court denial of leave on safe third regretted." Media Release. http://ccrweb.ca/en/bulletin/09/02/05 (Accessed on November 21, 2012).

Canadian Islamic Congress. 2003. "Islamic congress finds most police departments have incomplete data on rising tide of hate-motivated crimes." http://www.canadianislamiccongress.com/cic2010/2003/03/10 (Accessed on January 29, 2014).

Canadian Press. 2012. "Kelly Ellard, 30, waives latest parole hearing for 1997 murder of Victoria teen Reena Virk." *Times Colonist*, 28 November.

Canadian Race Relations Foundation (CRRF). 2003. *Facing Hate in Canada.* http://www.crr.ca/divers-files/en/pub/faSh/ePubFaShFacHateCan.pdf (Accessed on December 4, 2013).

Canadian Resource Centre for Victims of Crime. 2005. *The Impact of Victimization.* www.crcvc.ca/docs/victimization.pdf (Accessed January 8, 2013).

Cao, L. 2011. "Visible minorities and confidence in the police." *Canadian Journal of Criminology and Criminal Justice* 53 (1): 1–26. http://dx.doi.org/10.3138/cjccj.53.1.1.

Caragata, L. 2003. "Neoconservative realities: The social and economic marginalization of Canadian women." *International Sociology* 18 (3): 559–80. http://dx.doi.org/10.1177/0268580903018003006.

Carlen, P., and J. Tombs. 2006. "Reconfigurations of penality: The ongoing case of the women's imprisonment and reintegration industries." *Theoretical Criminology* 10 (3): 337–60. http://dx.doi.org/10.1177/1362480606065910.

Carrington, P., ed. 2011. "Symposium on racial profiling and police culture." *Canadian Journal of Criminology and Criminal Justice* 53 (1): 63–131.

Castel, R. 1991. "From dangerousness to risk." In *The Foucault Effect: Studies in Governmentality*, ed. G. Burchell, C. Gordon, and P. Miller. Hemel Hempstead: Harvester Wheatsheaf.

CBC News. 2007a. "Tearful killer granted day parole in Virk murder." 21 June. http://www.cbc.ca/news/canada/british-columbia/tearful-killer-granted-day-parole-in-virk-murder-1.637671/ (Accessed August 11, 2013).

CBC News. 2007b. "Top court rules against security certificates." 23 February. http://www.cbc.ca/news/canada/top-court-rules-against-security-certificates-1.633453/ (Accessed on November 6, 2012).

CBC News. 2007c. "Government tables new security certificate legislation." 22 October. http://www.cbc.ca/news/canada/government-tables-new-security-certificate-legislation-1.631274/ (Accessed on November 24, 2013).

CBC News. 2009a. "The murder of Reena Virk and trials of Kelly Ellard." 12 June. http://www.cbc.ca/news/canada/the-murder-of-reena-virk-and-trials-of-kelly-ellard-1.792656/ (Accessed on November 24, 2013).

CBC News. 2009b. "BC to deny welfare to alleged criminals." 19 October. http://www.cbc.ca/news/canada/british-columbia/b-c-to-deny-welfare-to-alleged-criminals-1.850494/ (Accessed on November 24, 2013).

CBC News. 2009c. "Security certificates and secret evidence." 21 August. http://www.cbc.ca/news/canada/security-certificates-and-secret-evidence-1.777624/ (Accessed on November 24, 2013).

CBC News. 2011a. "Ottawa police file defence in Bonds civil suit." 31 January. http://www.cbc.ca/news/canada/ottawa/ottawa-police-file-defence-in-bonds-civil-suit-1.1103202. (Accessed on January 29, 2014).

CBC News. 2011b. "Ottawa police officer charged in Stacy Bonds case." 15 March. http://www.cbc.ca/news/canada/ottawa/story/2011/03/15/ottawa-stacey-bonds-officer-charged.html (Accessed on November 24, 2013).

CBC News. 2011c. "Stun guns: Facts about stun guns and their use in Canada." 21 April.

CBC News. 2012a. "Hundreds of women join RCMP harassment lawsuit." 30 July. http://www.cbc.ca/news/canada/british-columbia/hundreds-of-women-join-rcmp-harassment-lawsuit-1.1153438/ (Accessed on November 24, 2013).

CBC News. 2012b. "Vancouver police apologize for not catching Pickton sooner: Serial killer operated for years undetected." 18 December. http://www.cbc.ca/news/canada/british-columbia/vancouver-police-apologize-for-not-catching-pickton-sooner-1.1191106/ (Accessed on November 24, 2013).

CBC News. 2012c. EI program for high unemployment areas axed. 24 October. http://www.cbc.ca/news/canada/prince.edward.island/ei-program-for-high-unemployment-areas-axed-1.1216665 (Accessed on February 11, 2014).

CBC News. 2012d. "Supreme Court reviews first anti-terrorism act." 12 June. http://www.cbc.ca/news/canada/supreme-court-reviews-first-anti-terrorism-act-case-1.1256918/ (Accessed on November 24, 2013).

CBC News. 2013a. "RCMP accused of rape in report on BC aboriginal women." 13 February. http://www.cbc.ca/news/canada/british-columbia/rcmp-accused-of-rape-in-report-on-b-c-aboriginal-women-1.1305824/ (Accessed on November 24, 2013).

CBC News. 2013b. "RCMP has a bullying problem, watchdog says." 14 February. http://www.cbc.ca/news/canada/rcmp-has-a-bullying-problem-watchdog-says-1.1376168/ (Accessed on November 24, 2013).

CBC News. 2013c. "B.C. board backs moving child killer Schoenborn to Manitoba." 15 February. http://www.cbc.ca/news/canada/british-columbia/b-c-board-backs-moving-child-killer-schoenborn-to-manitoba-1.1345402 (Accessed on November 24, 2013).

Cermele, J., S. Daniels, and K.L. Anderson. 2001. "Defining normal: Constructions of race and gender in the DSM-IV casebook." *Feminism & Psychology* 11 (2): 229–47. http://dx.doi.org/10.1177/0959353501011002011.

Chaimowitz, G. 2012. "The criminalization of people with mental illness." *Canadian Journal of Psychiatry* 57 (2): 1–6.

Chakkalakal, T. 2000. "Reckless eyeballing: Being Reena in Canada." In *Rude: Contemporary Black Cultural Criticism*, ed. R. Walcott. Toronto: Insomniac Press.

Chambliss, W. 1995. "Crime control and ethnic minorities: Legitimizing racial oppression by creating moral panics." In *Ethnicity, Race and Crime*, ed. D. Hawkins. Albany: State University of New York Press.

Chan, W. 2004. "Undocumented migrants and Bill C-11: The criminalization of race." In *What Is a Crime? Defining Criminal Conduct in Contemporary Society*, ed. Law Commission of Canada. Vancouver: UBC Press.

Chan, W., D.E. Chunn, and R. Menzies, eds. 2005. *Women, Madness and the Law: A Feminist Reader*. London: Glasshouse Press.

Chan, W., and K. Mirchandani, eds. 2002. *Crimes of Colour: Racialization and the Justice System in Canada*. Toronto: University of Toronto Press.

Charter of Rights and Freedoms, *The Constitution Act, 1982*, being Schedule B to the Canada Act 1982 (UK) 1982, c.11.

Chartrand, P. 2005. "Aboriginal people and the criminal justice system in Saskatchewan: What next?" *Saskatchewan Law Review* 68: 253–92.

Cheema, M. 2009. "Missing subjects: Aboriginal deaths in custody, data problems, and racialized policing." *Appeal* 14: 84–100.

Chesney-Lind, M., and J. Pollock. 1995. "Women's prisons: Equality with a vengeance." In *Women, Law and Social Control*, ed. A. Merlo and J. Pollock. Boston: Allyn and Bacon.

Chigwada-Bailey, R. 2003. *Black Women's Experiences of Criminal Justice*. 2nd ed. Winchester: Waterside Press.

Choudhry, S. 2001. "Protecting equality in the face of terror: Ethnic and racial profiling and s. 15 of the Charter." In *The Security of Freedom: Essays on Canada's Anti-Terrorism Bill*, ed. R. Daniels, P. Macklem, and K. Roach. Toronto: University of Toronto Press.

Chow-White, P., and T. Duster. 2011. "Do health and forensic DNA databases increase racial disparities?" *PLoS Medicine* 8 (10), 1–3.

Chrisjohn, R., and S. Young. 2006. *The Circle Game: Shadows and Substance in the Indian Residential School Experience in Canada*. Penticton, BC: Theytus Books.

Chu, D., and J. Song. 2008. "Chinese immigrants' perceptions of the police in Toronto, Canada." *Policing* 31 (4): 610–30. http://dx.doi.org/10.1108/13639510810910599.

Chunn, D.E., and R. Menzies. 1990. "Gender, madness and crime: The reproduction of patriarchal and class relations in a psychiatric court clinic." *Journal of Human Justice* 1 (2): 33–54.

Chunn, D.E,. and R. Menzies. 1998. "Out of mind, out of law: The regulation of 'criminally insane' women inside British Columbia's public mental hospitals, 1888–1973." *Canadian Journal of Women and the Law* 10 (2): 306–37.

Chunn, D.E., and S.M. Gavigan. 2004. "Welfare law, welfare fraud, and the moral regulation of the 'never deserving' poor." *Social & Legal Studies* 13 (2): 219–43. http://dx.doi.org/10.1177/0964663904042552.

Chute, T. 2005. *Globalization, Security and Exclusion. CRS Working Paper No. 3.* Toronto: Centre for Refugee Studies, York University.

Citizens for Public Justice. 2012. *Poverty Trends Scorecard: Canada 2012.* www.cpj.ca (Accessed on December 4, 2012).

Citizenship and Immigration Canada (CIC). 2009. "News release: Government of Canada to prevent immigration fraud through international cooperation." 21 August. http://www.cic.gc.ca/english/department/media/releases/2009/2009-08-21.asp (Accessed on November 24, 2013).

Cohen, S. 1973. *Folk Devils and Moral Panics.* St. Albans: Paladin.

Cohen, S. 2002. *Folk Devils and Moral Panics: The Creation of the Mods and Rockers.* 3rd ed. New York: Routledge.

Cohen, T. 2012a. "Border agency deports record numbers." *Victoria Times-Colonist,* 10 November.

Cohen, T. 2012b. "Federal agencies seek extra $27M to fight bogus refugees, deport criminals." *Victoria Times-Colonist,* 9 November.

Coleman, T., and D. Cotton. 2010. *Police Interactions with Persons with a Mental Illness: Police Learning in the Environment of Contemporary Policing.* Calgary: Mental Health Commission of Canada.

Collins, S. 2005. "An understanding of poverty from those who are poor." *Action Research* 3 (1): 9–31.

Comack, E. 1996. *Women in Trouble: Connecting Women's Law Violations to Their Histories of Abuse.* Black Point, NS: Fernwood Publishing.

Comack, E. 2008. "Out there." In *Here: Masculinity, Violence and Prisoning.* Black Point, NS: Fernwood Publishing.

Comack, E. 2012. *Racialized Policing: Aboriginal People's Encounters with the Police.* Black Point, NS: Fernwood Publishing.

Comack, E., and S. Brickey. 2007. "Constituting the violence of criminalized women." *Canadian Journal of Criminology and Criminal Justice* 49 (1): 1–36. http://dx.doi.org/10.3138/5523-4873-1386-5453.

Commission of inquiry into the Actions of Canadian Officials in Relation to Maher Arar. 2006. Reporting of the Events Relating to Maher Arar: Analysis and Recommendations. Ottawa: Public Works.

Commission on Systemic Racism in the Ontario Criminal Justice System. 1995. *Final Report.* Toronto: Queen's Printer for Ontario.

Connell, R. 2009. *Gender in World Perspective.* 2nd ed. Cambridge: Polity Press.

Coontz, S. 1992. *The Way We Never Were: American Families and the Nostalgia Trap.* New York: Basic Books.

Correctional Investigator of Canada. 2012. *Spirit Matters: Aboriginal People and the Corrections and Conditional Release Act: Final Report.* http://www.oci-bec.gc.ca/index-eng.aspx (Accessed November 22, 2013).

Correctional Investigator of Canada. 2013. *Aboriginal Offenders—A Critical Situation. Backgrounder.* Ottawa. http://www.oci-bec.gc.ca/index-eng.aspx (Accessed November 22, 2013).

Cossins, A. 2003. "Saints, sluts and sexual assault: Rethinking the relationship between sex, race and gender." *Social & Legal Studies* 12 (1): 77–103.

Coulter, K. 2009. "Women, poverty policy and the production of neoliberal politics in Ontario, Canada." *Journal of Women, Politics & Policy* 30 (1): 23–45. http://dx.doi.org/10.1080/15544770802367788.

Covey, R. 2008–09. "Criminal madness: Cultural iconography and insanity." *Stanford Law Review* 61: 1375–427.

Covington, J. 1995. "Racial classification in criminology: The reproduction of racialized crime." *Sociological Forum* 10 (4): 547–68.

Craig, W., and Y. Harel. 2004. "Bullying, physical fighting and victimization." In *Young People's Health in Context. Health Behavior in School Aged Children (HBSC) Study: International Report from the 2001/2002 Survey (No. 4)*, ed. C. Currie, C. Roberts, A. Morgan, and R. Smith, 133–44. Copenhagen: World Health Organization.

Crawford, A. 2002. "Introduction: governance and security." In *Crime and Insecurity: The Governance of Safety in Europe*, ed. A. Crawford, 1–24. Portland, OR: Willan Publishing.

Crenshaw, K. 1989. "Demarginalizing the intersection of race and sex: A black feminist critique of antidiscrimination doctrine, feminist theory and antiracist politics." *University of Chicago Legal Forum*, 139–67.

Crenshaw, K. 1991. "Mapping the margins: Intersectionality, identity politics, and violence against women of colour." *Stanford Law Review* 43 (6): 1241–99. http://dx.doi.org/10.2307/1229039.

Crenshaw, K. 2011. "Twenty years of critical race theory: Looking back to move forward." *Connecticut Law Review* 43 (5): 1253–354.

Crépeau, F., and D. Nakache. 2006. "Controlling irregular migration in Canada: Reconciling security concerns with human protection. *IRPP (Institute for Research on Public Policy)*." *Choices (New York, NY)* 12 (1): 1–36.

Crew, B.K. 1991. "Sex differences in criminal sentencing: Chivalry or patriarchy?" *Justice Quarterly* 8 (1): 59–83. http://dx.doi.org/10.1080/07418829100090911.

Crookshanks, R. 2012. "Marginalization through a custom of deservingness: Sole-support mothers and welfare law in Canada." *Appeal: Review of Current Law and Legal Reform* 17: 97–113.

Culhane, D. 2003. "Their spirits live within us: Aboriginal women in Downtown Eastside Vancouver emerging into visibility." *American Indian Quarterly* 27 (3–4): 593–606. http://dx.doi.org/10.1353/aiq.2004.0073.

Cunningham, M., and M. Vigen. 2002. "Death row inmate characteristics, adjustment, and confinement: A critical review of the literature." *Behavioral Sciences & the Law* 20 (1–2): 191–210. http://dx.doi.org/10.1002/bsl.473.

Daly, K. 1989. "Rethinking judicial paternalism: Gender, work-family relations, and sentencing." *Gender & Society* 3 (1): 9–36. http://dx.doi.org/10.1177/089124389003001002.

Daly, K. 1993. "Class-race-gender: Sloganeering in search of meaning." *Social Justice (San Francisco, CA)* 20 (1/2): 56–71.

Daly, K. 1994. *Gender, Crime and Punishment.* New Haven, CT: Yale University Press.

Daly, K. 1997. "Different ways of conceptualizing sex/gender in feminist theory and their implications for criminology." *Theoretical Criminology* 1 (1): 25–51. http://dx.doi.org/10.1177/1362480697001001003.

Daly, K. 1998. "Women's pathways to felony court: Feminist theories of lawbreaking and problems of representation." In *Criminology at the Crossroads: Feminist Readings in Crime and Justice*, ed. K. Daly and L. Maher, 135–54. New York: Oxford University Press.

Daly, K., and L. Maher, eds. 1998. *Criminology at the Crossroads: Feminist Readings in Crime and Justice*. New York: Oxford University Press.

Daly, K., and M. Chesney-Lind. 1988. "Feminism and criminology." *Justice Quarterly* 5 (4): 497–538. http://dx.doi.org/10.1080/07418828800089871.

D'Arcy, S. 2007. "The 'Jamaican criminal' in Toronto, 1994: A critical ontology." *Canadian Journal of Communication* 32: 241–59.

Datesman, S.K., and F.R. Scarpitti, eds. 1980. *Women, Crime, and Justice*. New York: Oxford University Press.

Dauvergne, C. 2008. *Making People Illegal: What Globalization Means for Migration and Law*. New York: Cambridge University Press. http://dx.doi.org/10.1017/CBO9780511810473.

Dauvergne, M. 2012a. "Adult criminal court statistics in Canada, 2010/2011." *Juristat* (May): 1–27.

Dauvergne, M. 2012b. "Adult correctional statistics in Canada, 2010/2011." *Juristat* (Oct.): 1–14.

Dauvergne, M., and S. Brennan. 2011. *Police-Reported Hate Crime in Canada, 2009*. Ottawa: Juristat, Statistics Canada.

Dauvergne, M., K. Scrim, and S. Brennan. 2008. *Hate Crime in Canada, 2006*. Ottawa: Canadian Centre for Justice Statistics.

Davies, W.H. 2011. *Inquiry into the Death of Frank Paul. Final Report: Alone and Cold*. Victoria, BC: Ministry of the Attorney General, Criminal Justice Branch.

Davis, A. 2006. "Translating narratives of masculinity across borders: A Jamaican case study." *Caribbean Quarterly* 52 (2/3): 22–38.

Davis, A.Y. 1981. *Women, Race and Class*. New York: Random House.

Davis, D. 2007. "Narrating the mute: Racializing and racism in a neoliberal moment." *Souls* 9 (4): 346–60. http://dx.doi.org/10.1080/10999940701703810.

Dawson, M., M.J. Hubbert, and J. Poon. 2010. "Documenting resources for victims & survivors of violence in Canada—A Workshop Discussion Paper." Social and Legal Responses to Violence in Canada Research Unit, University of Guelph, June.

Decoste, R. 2012. "The wimpy numbers behind Kenney's 'great immigration crackdown'?" *Huffington Post*, December 3.

DeCoux Hampton, M., L. Chafetz, and M.C. White. 2010. "Exploring the impact of race on mental health service utilization among African Americans and whites with severe mental illness." *Journal of the American Psychiatric Nurses Association* 16 (2): 78–88. http://dx.doi.org/10.1177/1078390310362264.

De Genova, N. 2011. "Deportable labour and the spectacle of security." In *The Contested Politics of Mobility: Borderzones and Irregularity*, ed. V. Squire, 91–116. New York: Routledge.

Dej, E., and J.M. Kilty. 2012. "'Criminalization creep': A brief discussion of the criminalization of HIV/AIDS nondisclosure in Canada." *Canadian Journal of Law and Society* 27 (1): 55–66. http://dx.doi.org/10.3138/cjls.27.1.055.

de Lint, W. 1998. "Regulating autonomy: Police discretion as a problem for training." *Canadian Journal of Criminology* 40 (3): 277–304.

Denny, D., T. Ellis, and R. Barn. 2006. "Race, diversity and criminal justice in Canada: A view from the UK." *Internet Journal of Criminology*, 1–22.

http://www.internetjournalofcriminology.com/ijcarticles.html (Accessed on January 8, 2013).

Denov, M.S., and K.M. Campbell. 2005. "Criminal injustice: Understanding the causes, effects, and responses to wrongful conviction in Canada." *Journal of Contemporary Justice* 21 (3): 224–49. http://dx.doi.org/10.1177/1043986205278627.

Derosa, K. 2012. "Mandatory detention for refugee claimants has already proven to be a failure, critics say." *Victoria Times Colonist*, November 16.

Deutschmann, L. 2007. *Deviance and Social Control*. 4th ed. Toronto: Nelson Thomson Learning.

Dhamoon, R., and Y. Abu-Laban. 2009. "Dangerous (internal) foreigners and nation-building: The case of Canada." *International Political Science Review* 30 (2): 163–83.

Dick, C. 2011. "A tale of two cultures: Intimate femicide, cultural defences, and the law of provocation." *Canadian Journal of Women and the Law* 23 (2): 519–47. http://dx.doi.org/10.3138/cjwl.23.2.519.

Diduck, A. 1998. "Conceiving the bad mother: The focus should be on the child to be born." *University of British Columbia Law Review* 32: 199–225.

Disha, I., J. Cavendish, and R. King. 2011. "Historical events and spaces of hate: Hate crimes against Arabs and Muslims in post-9/11 America." *Social Problems* 58 (1): 21–46. http://dx.doi.org/10.1525/sp.2011.58.1.21.

Dixon, B., and D. Gadd. 2006. "Getting the message? 'New' labour and the criminalization of 'hate'." *Criminology & Criminal Justice* 6 (3): 309–28. http://dx.doi.org/10.1177/1748895806065532.

Do, C. 2012. "Aboriginal children's and youth's experiences of bullying and peer victimization in a Canadian context." Ottawa: Masters of Art Thesis, University of Ottawa.

Doe, J. 2003. *The Story of Jane Doe*. Toronto: Random House.

Donzelot, J. 1980. *The Policing of Families*. New York: Pantheon.

Douglas, J. 2011. "The criminalization of poverty: Montreal's policy of ticketing homeless youth for municipal and transportation by-law infractions." *Appeal* 16: 49–64.

Dowden, C., and S. Brennan. 2012. "Police-reported hate crime in Canada, 2010." *Juristat* (April): 1–20.

Dowler, K. 2004. "Dual realities? Criminality, victimization, and the presentation of race on local television news." *Journal of Criminal Justice* 27 (2): 79–99.

Doyle, A. 1998. "'Cops': Television policing as policing reality." In *Entertaining Crime: Television Reality Programs*, ed. M. Fishman and G. Cavender, 95–116. New York: Aldine de Gruyter.

Doyle, A. 2003. *Arresting Images: Crime and Policing in Front of the Television Camera*. Toronto: University of Toronto Press.

Doyle, A., and R.V. Ericson. 1996. "Breaking into prison: News sources and correctional institutions." *Canadian Journal of Criminology* 38 (2): 155–90.

Duffy, M., and R. Provost. 2009. "Constitutional canaries and the elusive quest to legitimize security detentions in Canada." *Case Western Reserve Journal of International Law* 40: 531–60.

Duster, T. 1997. "Pattern, purpose, and race in the drug war." In *Crack in America*, ed. C. Reinarman and H.G. Levine, 260–87. Berkeley: University of California Press.

Dylan, A., C. Regehr, and R. Alaggia. 2008. "And justice for all? Aboriginal victims of sexual violence." *Violence against Women* 14 (6): 678–96. http://dx.doi.org/10.1177/1077801208317291.

Eaton, M. 1986. *Justice for Women? Family Court and Social Control.* Milton Keynes, UK: Open University Press.

Edwards, A.R. 1989. "Sex/gender, sexism and criminal justice: Some theoretical considerations." *International Journal of the Sociology of Law* 17 (2): 165–84.

Ehrenreich, B., and D. English. 1978. *For Her Own Good: 150 Years of the Expert's Advice to Women.* New York: Anchor Press/DoubleDay.

Eid, P. 2011. *Racial Profiling and Systemic Discrimination of Racialized Youth.* Quebec: Commission des droits de la personne et des droits de la jeunesse.

Eisler, L., and B. Schissel. 2004. "Privation and vulnerability to victimization for Canadian youth: The contexts of gender, race and geography." *Youth Violence and Juvenile Justice* 2 (4): 359–73. http://dx.doi.org/10.1177/1541204004267784.

Ennis, B.J., and T.R. Litwack. 1974. "Psychiatry and the presumption of expertise: Flipping coins in the courtroom." *California Law Review* 62 (3, May): 693–752. http://dx.doi.org/10.2307/3479746.

Ericson, R.V. 1976. "Penal psychiatry in Canada: The method of our madness." *University of Toronto Law Journal* 26 (1): 17–27. http://dx.doi.org/10.2307/825453.

Ericson, R.V. 1981. *Making Crime: A Study of Detective Work.* Toronto: Butterworths.

Ericson, R.V. 1982. *Reproducing Order: A Study of Police Patrol Work.* Toronto: University of Toronto Press.

Ericson, R.V., and K.D. Haggerty. 1997. *Policing the Risk Society.* Toronto: University of Toronto Press.

Ericson, R.V., P. Baranek, and J.B.L. Chan. 1987. *Visualizing Deviance: A Study of News Organization.* Toronto: University of Toronto Press.

Ericson, R.V., P. Baranek, and J.B.L. Chan. 1989. *Negotiating Control: A Study of News Sources.* Toronto: University of Toronto Press.

Ericson, R.V., P. Baranek, and J.B.L. Chan. 1991. *Representing Order: Crime, Law and Justice in the News Media.* Toronto: University of Toronto Press.

Espin, O. 1998. *Women Crossing Boundaries.* New York: Routledge.

Farr, K.A. 2000. "Defeminizing and dehumanizing female murderers: Depictions of lesbians on death row." *Women & Criminal Justice* 11 (1): 49–66. http://dx.doi.org/10.1300/J012v11n01_03.

Fennell, P. 2002. "Radical risk management, mental health and criminal justice." In *Criminal Justice, Mental Health and the Politics of Risk,* ed. N. Gray, J. Laing, and L. Noaks, 69–88. London: Cavendish Publishing.

Fergusson, R., and J. Muncie. 2008. "Criminalising conduct." In *Security: Welfare, Crime and Society,* ed. A. Cochrane and D. Talbot, 94–126. Milton Keynes: Open University Press.

Fernando, S. 1988. *Race and Culture in Psychiatry.* London: Tavistock/Routledge.

Fernando, S. 2012. "Race and culture issues in mental health and some thoughts on ethnic identity." *Counselling Psychology Quarterly* 25 (2): 113–23. http://dx.doi.org/10.1080/09515070.2012.674299.

Finkel, A. 2002. "Welfare for whom? Class, gender and race in social policy." *Labour* 49: 247–61.

Finkelhor, D., R. Ormrod, H. Turner, and S. Hamby. 2005. "The victimization of children and youth: A comprehensive, national survey." *Child Maltreatment* 10 (1): 5–25. http://dx.doi.org/10.1177/1077559504271287.

Fishman, M. 1978. "Crime waves as ideology." *Social Problems* 25 (5): 531–43. http://dx.doi.org/10.2307/800102.

Fishman, M. 1980. *Manufacturing the News*. Austin: University of Texas Press.

Fishman, M., and G. Cavender, eds. 1998. *Entertaining Crime: Television Reality Programs*. New York: Aldine de Gruyter.

Fitzgerald, R.T., and P.J. Carrington. 2011. "Disproportionate minority contact in Canada: Police and visible minority youth." *Canadian Journal of Criminology and Criminal Justice* 53 (4): 449–86. http://dx.doi.org/10.3138/cjccj.53.4.449.

Fitzgibbon, D. 2004. *Pre-emptive Criminalisation: Risk Control and Alternative Futures*. London: NAPO.

Foulks, E. 2004. "Racial bias in diagnosis and medication of mentally ill minorities in prisons and communities." *Journal of the American Academy of Psychiatry and the Law* 32: 34–35.

Franklin, C.A., and N.E. Fearn. 2008. "Gender, race, and formal court decision-making outcomes: Chivalry/paternalism, conflict theory or gender conflict?" *Journal of Criminal Justice* 36 (3): 279–90. http://dx.doi.org/10.1016/j.jcrimjus.2008.04.009.

Fraser, N. 1992. "Rethinking the public sphere: a contribution to the critique of actually existing democracy." In *Habermas and the Public Sphere*, ed. C. Calhoun, 109–42. Cambridge, MA: MIT Press.

Fraser, N., and L. Gordon. 1994. "A genealogy of 'dependency': Tracing a keyword of the US welfare state." *Signs (Chicago, IL)* 19 (2): 309–36. http://dx.doi.org/10.1086/494886.

Gaetz, S. 2004. "Safe streets for whom? Homeless youth, social exclusion and criminal victimization." *Canadian Journal of Criminology and Criminal Justice* 46 (4): 423–56. http://dx.doi.org/10.3138/cjccj.46.4.423.

Gaetz, S. 2009. "Whose safety counts? street youth, social exclusion, and criminal victimization." In *Finding Home: Policy Options for Addressing Homelessness in Canada*, ed. D. Hulchanski, J. David, P. Campsie, S. Chau, S. Hwang, and E. Paradis, 1–23. Toronto: Cities Centre, University of Toronto.

Gans, J. 1995. *The War against the Poor: The Underclass and Anti-poverty Policy*. New York: Basic Books.

Garber, M., J. Matlock, and R.L. Walkowitz, eds. 1993. *Media Spectacles*. New York: Routledge.

Garland, D. 2001. *The Culture of Control: Crime and Social Order in Contemporary Society*. Chicago: University of Chicago Press.

Gavigan, S.A.M. 1983. "Women's crime and feminist critiques." *Canadian Criminology Forum*, 6 (1): 75–90.

Gavigan, S.A.M. 1988. "Law, gender and ideology." In *Legal Theory Meets Legal Practice*, ed. A. Bayefsky, 283–95. Edmonton: Academic Press.

Gavigan, S.M. 1993. "Paradise lost, paradox revisited: The implications of familial ideology for feminist, lesbian, and gay engagement to law." *Osgoode Hall Law Journal* 31: 589–624.

Gazso, A. 2012. "Moral codes of mothering and the introduction of welfare-to-work in Ontario." *Canadian Review of Sociology* 49 (1): 26–49.

Gazso, A., and I. Waldron. 2009. "Fleshing out the racial undertones of poverty for Canadian women and their families: Re-envisioning a critical integrative approach." *Atlantis* 34 (1): 132–41.

Gibney, M., and R. Hansen. 2003. *Deportation and the Liberal State: The Forcible Return of Asylum Seekers and Unlawful Migrants in Canada, Germany and the United Kingdom*. UNHCR: New Issues in Refugee Research, Working Paper No. 77.

Gilens, M. 1996. "'Race coding' and white opposition to welfare." *The American Political Science Review* 90 (3): 593–604.

Gill, A. 2004. "Voicing the silent fear: South Asian women's experiences of domestic violence." *Howard Journal* 43 (5, Dec.): 465–83. http://dx.doi.org/10.1111/j.1468-2311.2004.00343.x.

Gilliom, J. 2005. "Resisting surveillance." *Social Text* 83,23 (2): 71–83.

Gilman, M. 2008. "Welfare, privacy and feminism." *University of Baltimore Law Forum* 39 (1): 25–49.

Glenn, E. 2002. *Unequal Freedom: How Race and Gender Shaped American Citizenship and Labor.* Cambridge, MA: Harvard University Press.

Global Detention Project. 2012. "Immigration detention in Canada." Geneva: Global Detention Project. http://www.globaldetentionproject.org/countries/americas/canada/introduction.html (Accessed on November 20, 2012).

Glover, K.S. 2007. "Police discourse on racial profiling." *Journal of Contemporary Criminal Justice* 23 (3): 239–47. http://dx.doi.org/10.1177/1043986207306866.

Godfredson, J.W., S.D. Thomas, J.R. Ogloff, and S. Luebbers. 2011. "Police perceptions of their encounters with individuals experiencing mental illness: A Victorian survey." *Australian and New Zealand Journal of Criminology* 44 (2): 180–95. http://dx.doi.org/10.1177/0004865811405138.

Godfrey, R. 2005. *Under the Bridge.* Toronto: HarperCollins.

Godfrey, T. 2012. "Proposed deportation law under fire." *Toronto Sun*, October 1.

Goel, R. 2000. "No women at the center: The use of the Canadian sentencing circle in domestic violence cases." *Wisconsin Women's Law Journal* 15: 293–334.

Goffman, E. 1962. *Asylums: Essays on the Social Situation of Mental Patients and Other Inmates.* Chicago: Aldine Publishing.

Goldberg, D. 1997. *Racial Subjects: Writing on Race in America.* New York: Routledge.

Goldberg, D. 2002. *The Racial State.* Malden, MA: Blackwell.

Goldsmith, A. 2008. "The governance of terror: Precautionary logic and counterterrorist law reform after September 11." *Law & Policy* 30 (2): 141–67. http://dx.doi.org/10.1111/j.1467-9930.2008.00272.x.

Goodey, J. 2003. "Migration, crime and victimhood." *Punishment and Society* 5 (4): 415–31. http://dx.doi.org/10.1177/14624745030054003.

Goodey, J. 2004. *Victims and Victimology: Research, Policy and Practice.* London: Pearson Education UK.

Gordon, T. 2005. "The political economy of law and order policies: Policing, class struggle and neoliberal restructuring." *Studies in Political Economy* 75: 53–77.

Gosine, A. 2007. "Youth make nations: Three Toronto stories." *TOPIA: Canadian Journal of Cultural Studies* 17 (Spring): 51–66.

Gould, S. 1996. *The Mismeasure of Man.* New York: Norton.

Gova, A., and R. Kurd. 2008. *The Impact of Racial Profiling.* Working Paper No. 08-14. Vancouver: Metropolis BC.

Grabe, J.E., K.D. Trager, M. Lear, and J. Rauch. 2006. "Gender in crime news: A case study test of the chivalry hypothesis." *Mass Communication & Society* 9 (2): 137–63. http://dx.doi.org/10.1207/s15327825mcs0902_2.

Greenberg, G.A., and R.A. Rosenheck. 2008. "Homelessness in the state and federal prison population." *Criminal Behaviour and Mental Health* 18 (2): 88–103. http://dx.doi.org/10.1002/cbm.685.

Gregg, J., and S. Saha. 2006. "Losing culture on the way to competence: The use and misuse of culture in medical education." *Academic Medicine* 81 (6): 542–47. http://dx.doi.org/10.1097/01.ACM.0000225218.15207.30.

Grenier, M. 1992. "The centrality of conflict in Native-Indian coverage by the Montreal Gazette." In *Critical Studies of Canadian Mass Media*, ed. M. Grenier, 16. Markham, ON: Butterworths.

Gurney, M. 2012. "The Vincent Li interview: A look into the diseased mind of a repentant killer." *National Post*, May 12. fullcomment.nationalpost.com/2012/05/22/the-vincent-li-interview-a-look-into-the-diseased-mind-of-a-repentant-killer/ (Accessed March 4, 2013).

Gustafson, K. 2009. "The criminalization of poverty." *Journal of Criminal Law and Criminology* 99 (3): 643–716.

Ha-Redeye, O., and D. Simard. 2010. *Media Narratives in Times of Turmoil: Depictions of Minorities in Canada Post 9/11*. Annual Meeting of the World Institute for Research and Publication-Law.

Hall, S. 1980. "Race, articulation and societies structured in dominance." In *Sociological Theories: Race and Colonialism*. Paris: UNESCO.

Hall, S., C. Critcher, T. Jefferson, J. Clarke, and B. Roberts. 1978. *Policing the Crisis*. London: MacMillan.

Haney, L. 2004. "Introduction: Gender, welfare and states of punishment." *Social Politics* 11 (3): 333–62.

Hannah-Moffat, K. 2005. "Criminogenic need and the transformative risk subject: Hybridizations of risk/need in penality." *Punishment and Society* 7 (1): 29–51. http://dx.doi.org/10.1177/1462474505048132.

Hannah-Moffat, K., and M. Shaw, eds. 2000. *An Ideal Prison? Critical Essays on Women's Imprisonment in Canada*. Black Point, NS: Fernwood Publishing.

Hannah-Moffat, K., and P. Maurutto. 2010. "Re-contextualizing pre-sentence reports." *Punishment and Society* 12 (3): 262–86. http://dx.doi.org/10.1177/1462474510369442.

Hanniman, W. 2008. "Canadian Muslims, Islamophobia and national security." *International Journal of Law, Crime and Justice* 36 (4): 271–85. http://dx.doi.org/10.1016/j.ijlcj.2008.08.003.

Harcourt, B.E. 2011. "Reducing mass incarceration: Lessons from the deinstitutionalization of mental hospitals in the 1960s." *Ohio State Journal of Criminal Law* 9 (1): 53–88.

Harell, A., S. Soroka, and A. Mahon. 2008. "Is welfare a dirty word? Canadian public opinion on social assistance policies." *Policy Options* 29 (September): 53–56.

Hartry, A. 2012. "Gendering crimmigration: The intersection of gender, immigration and the criminal justice system." *Berkeley Journal of Gender, Law & Justice* 27 (1): 1–27.

Hate Crimes Community Working Group. 2006. *Addressing Hate Crime in Ontario—Final Report*. Toronto. http://www.attorneygeneral.jus.gov.on.ca/english/about/pubs/hatecrimes/ (Accessed on December 13, 2012).

Heidensohn, F. 1985. *Women and Crime*. Basingstoke, UK: Macmillan.

Helly, D. 2004. "Are Muslims discriminated against in Canada since September 2001?" *Canadian Ethnic Studies* 36 (1): 24–47.

Henman, P., and G. Marston. 2008. "The social division of welfare surveillance." *Journal of Social Policy* 37 (2): 187–205.

Henricks, N.J., C.W. Ortiz, N. Sugie, and J. Miller. 2007. "Beyond the numbers: Hate crimes and cultural trauma within Arab American immigrant

communities." *International Review of Victimology* 14 (1): 95–113. http://dx.doi.
org/10.1177/026975800701400106.

Henry, F., and C. Tator. 2002. *Discourses of Domination.* Toronto: University of
Toronto Press.

Henry, F., and C. Tator. 2006. *Racial Profiling in Canada.* Toronto: University of
Toronto Press.

Henry, F., P. Hastings, and B. Freer. 1996. "Perceptions of race and crime in
Ontario: Empirical evidence from Toronto and the Durham region." *Canadian
Journal of Criminology* 38 (4): 469–76.

Herd, D., A. Mitchell, and E. Lightman. 2005. "Rituals of degradation: Administration
as policy in the Ontario Works programme." *Social Policy and Administration*
39 (1): 65–79. http://dx.doi.org/10.1111/j.1467-9515.2005.00425.x.

Hermer, J., and J. Mosher. 2002. *Disorderly People: Law and the Politics of Exclusion in
Ontario.* Black Point, NS: Fernwood Publishing.

Herrnstein, R., and C. Murray. 1994. *The Bell Curve: Intelligence and Class Structure
in American Life.* New York: Free Press.

Hesson, T. 2012. "Jose Antonio Vargas challenges NYT and AP to drop 'illegal
immigrant.'" *ABC News,* September 21. http://abcnews.go.com (Accessed on
October 15, 2012).

Hickling, F. 2002. "The political misuse of psychiatry: An African-Caribbean
perspective." *Journal of the American Academy of Psychiatry and the Law* 30:
112–19.

Hickman, T.A. 1989. *Royal Commission on the Donald Marshall, Jr., Prosecution: Digest
of Findings and Recommendations.* Halifax, N.S.

Hicks, J. 2004. "Ethnicity, race and forensic psychiatry: Are we color-blind?"
Journal of the American Academy of Psychiatry and the Law 32: 21–33.

Hier, S., and B.S. Bolaria. 2007. *Race and Racism in 21st Century Canada.*
Toronto: University of Toronto Press.

Hill Collins, P. 1990. *Black Feminist Thought: Knowledge, Consciousness, and the Politics
of Empowerment.* London: HarperCollins Academic.

Hill Collins, P. 2000. *Black Feminist Thought: Knowledge, Consciousness, and the Politics
of Empowerment.* 2nd ed. New York: Routledge.

Hill Collins, P. 2004. *Black Sexual Politics: African Americans, Gender and the New
Racism.* New York: Routledge. http://dx.doi.org/10.4324/9780203309506.

Hodgson, J. 2001. "Police violence in Canada and the USA: Analysis and
management." *Policing: International Journal of Police Strategies & Management*
24 (4): 520–49.

Hodson, J. 2010. "Coleman defends welfare fraud suits." *MetroNews Vancouver,* May 26.
http://metronews.ca/news/vancouver/45277/coleman-defends-welfare-fraud-
suits/ (Accessed on November 16, 2012).

Hogeveen, B. 2005. "'If we are tough on crime, if we punish crime, then people
get the message': Constructing and governing the punishable young offender in
Canada during the late 1990s." *Punishment & Society* 7 (1): 73–89.

Holmes, R. 2010. "The BCCLA: Working to end racial profiling." In *Racial
Profiling: A Special BCCLA Report on Racial Profiling in Canada,* ed. BC Civil
Liberties Association, 3. Vancouver: BC Civil Liberties Association.

Hudson, B. 2006. "Beyond white man's justice: Race, gender and justice
in late modernity." *Theoretical Criminology* 10 (1): 29–47. http://dx.doi.
org/10.1177/1362480606059981.

Huff, C.R., and M. Killias, eds. 2008. *Wrongful Conviction: International Perspectives on Miscarriages of Justice*. Philadelphia: Temple University Press.

Huffington Post. 2012. "Canada: A nation of foreign terrorists according to Bill C-43." October 23. http://www.huffingtonpost.ca/irwin-cotler/billc-43_b_2005209.html (Accessed November 5, 2012).

Huffington Post. 2013. "Integrated prom in Wilcox County in Georgia deemed a success." April 29. http://www.huffingtonpost.com/2013/04/29/integrated-prom-wilcox-county-georgia_n_3178005.html (accessed November 11, 2013).

Hugill, D. 2010. *Missing Women, Missing News: Covering Crisis in Vancouver's Downtown Eastside*. Black Point, NS: Fernwood Publishing.

Human Rights First. 2008. *2008 Hate Crime Survey*. New York. http:// www.humanrightsfirst.org.

Human Rights Watch. 2013. *Those Who Take Us Away: Abusive Policing and Failures in Protection of Indigenous Women and Girls in Northern British Columbia, Canada*. New York. http://www.hrw.org/reports/2013/02/13/those-who-take-us-away-0 (Accessed August 9, 2013).

Hyatt, S. 2011. "What was neoliberalism and what comes next? The transformation of citizenship in the law-and-order state." In *Policy Worlds*, ed. C. Shore, S. Wright, and D. Però. New York: Berghahn Books.

Hylton, J. 2002. "The justice system and Canada's Aboriginal peoples: The persistence of racial discrimination." In *Crimes of Colour*, ed. W. Chan and K. Mirchandani, 139–56. Toronto: University of Toronto Press.

Hyman, I. 2009. *Racism as a Determinant of Immigrant Health*. Ottawa: Strategic Initiatives and Innovations Directorate, Public Health Agency of Canada.

Ibrahim, M. 2005. "The securitization of migration: A racial discourse." *International Migration (Geneva, Switzerland)* 43 (5): 163–87. http://dx.doi.org/10.1111/j.1468-2435.2005.00345.x.

Ignaski, P. 2001. "Hate crimes hurt more." *American Behavioral Scientist* 45 (4): 627–38.

Immigration and Refugee Protection Act, S.C. 2001, c 27.

International Civil Liberties Monitoring Group (ICLMG). 2003. *In the Shadow of the Law: A Report by the International Civil Liberties Monitoring Group (ICLMG) in Response to Justice Canada's 1st Annual Report on the Application of the Anti-Terrorism Act (Bill C-36)*. http://iclmg.ca/en (Accessed on November 22, 2013).

Ivanova, I. 2009. *BC's Growing Gap: Family Income Inequality 1976–2006*. Vancouver: Canadian Centre for Policy Alternatives.

Jackson, M., S. Normandeau, F. Guay, E. Harper, D. Damant, and M. Rinfret-Raynor, eds. 2007. "Erased realities: The violence of racism in the lives of immigrant and refugee girls of colour." In *Preventing Violence Against Girls: Should Programs Be Gender-Specific? Conference Proceedings*, ed. S. Normandeau, F. Guay, E. Harper, D. Damant, and M. Rinfret-Raynor. Montreal, October 25, 2002.

Jhappan, R. 1996. "Post-modern race and gender essentialism or a post-mortem of scholarship." *Studies in Political Economy* 51: 15–58.

Jiwani, Y. 1999. "Erasing race: The story of Reena Virk." *Canadian Women's Studies* 19 (3): 178–84.

Jiwani, Y. 2005. "Walking a tightrope: The many faces of violence in the lives of racialized immigrant girls and young women." *Violence against Women* 11 (7): 846–75. http://dx.doi.org/10.1177/1077801205276273.

Jiwani, Y. 2006. *Discourses of Denial: Mediations of Race, Gender, and Violence.* Vancouver: UBC Press.

Jiwani, Y. 2011. "Mediations of race and crime: Racializing crime, criminalizing race." In *Diversity, Crime and Justice in Canada*, ed. B. Perry, 39–56. Don Mills, ON: Oxford University Press.

Jiwani, Y., and M.L. Young. 2006. "Missing and murdered women: Reproducing marginality in news discourse." *Canadian Journal of Communication* 31 (4): 895–917.

John Howard Society of Alberta. 2006. *An Examination of Citizen Involvement in Complaints Regarding Police.* Edmonton.

Johnson, G. 2012. "'Millennium bomber,' a convicted terrorist with Canadian ties, gets 37 years for plot to blow up L.A. airport." *Canadian Press*, October 24. http://cnews.canoe.ca/CNEWS/Crime/2012/10/24/20305836.html (Accessed November 16, 2012).

Johnson, L., and D. Roediger. 1997. "'Hertz, don't it?' Becoming colorless and staying black in the crossover." In *Birth of a Nation'hood*, ed. T. Morrison and C.B. Lacour, 197–239. New York: Pantheon.

Jones, R., and Y. Luo. 1999. "The culture of poverty and African-American culture." *Sociological Perspectives* 42 (3): 439–58. http://dx.doi.org/10.2307/1389697.

Kanstroom, D. 2005. "Immigration law as social control." In *Civil Penalties, Social Consequences*, ed. C. Mele and T. Miller, 161–84. New York: Routledge.

Keating, F., and D. Robertson. 2004. "Fear, black people and mental illness: A vicious circle?" *Health & Social Care in the Community* 12 (5): 439–47. http://dx.doi.org/10.1111/j.1365-2524.2004.00506.x.

Keenan, K.T., and J. Brockman. 2010. *Mr. Big: Exposing Undercover Investigations in Canada.* Black Point, NS: Fernwood Publishing.

Keith, M. 1993. "From punishment to discipline? Racism, racialization and the policing of social control." In *Racism, the City and the State*, ed. M. Cross and M. Keith, 193–209. Washington, DC: IOM.

Kendall, J. 2001. "Circles of Disadvantage: Aboriginal Poverty and Underdevelopment in Canada." *American Review of Canadian Studies* 31 (1): 43–59.

Kendall, K. 1993. *Program Evaluation of Therapeutic Services at the Prison for Women.* Ottawa: Correctional Service of Canada.

Kent, J. 2011. "Border bargains and the 'new' sovereignty: Canada–US border policies from 2001–2005 in perspective." *Geopolitics* 16 (4): 792–818.

Kilty, J. 2010. "Gendering violence, remorse, and the role of restorative justice: Deconstructing public perceptions of Kelly Ellard and Warren Glowatski." *Contemporary Justice Review* 13 (2): 155–72.

Kilty, J.M. 2012. "'It's like they don't want you to get better': Psy control of women in the carceral context." *Feminism & Psychology* 22 (2): 162–82. http://dx.doi.org/10.1177/0959353512439188.

Kilty, J.M., and S. Frigon. 2006. "Karla Homolka—From a woman *in danger* to a *dangerous* woman: Chronicling the shifts." *Women & Criminal Justice* 17 (4): 37–61. http://dx.doi.org/10.1300/J012v17n04_03.

King, W.R., and T.M. Dunn. 2004. "Dumping: Police-initiated transjurisdictional transport of troublesome persons." *Police Quarterly* 7 (3): 339–58. http://dx.doi.org/10.1177/1098611102250586.

Kitzinger, C., and R. Perkins. 1993. *Changing Our Minds—Lesbian Feminism and Psychology.* London: Onlywoman Press.

Klaszus, J. 2007. "The hidden world of hate crime: Aboriginals fear being re-victimized by police and justice system." *Fast Forward Weekly*, Calgary, December 27. http://www.ffwdweekly.com/article/news-views/news/hidden-world-hate-crime/ (Accessed February 1, 2013).

Klein, S., and A. Long. 2003. *A Bad Time to be Poor*. Vancouver: Canadian Centre for Policy Alternatives and the Social Planning and Research Council of BC.

Klein, S., and J. Pulkingham. 2008. *Living on Welfare in BC: Experiences of Longer-Term 'Expected to Work' Recipients*. Vancouver: Canadian Centre for Policy Alternatives and Raise the Rates.

Klein, S., L. Copas, and A. Montani. 2012. *BC's Welfare Recipients Need Immediate Relief*. Vancouver: Canadian Centre for Policy Alternatives.

Kline, M. 1993. "Complicating the ideology of motherhood: Child welfare law and First Nation women." *Queen's Law Journal* 18: 306–42.

Kline, M. 1994. "The colour of law: Ideological representations of First Nations in legal discourse." *Social & Legal Studies* 3 (4): 451–76. http://dx.doi.org/10.1177/096466399400300401.

Knowles, C. 1996. "Racism and psychiatry." *Transcultural Psychiatric Research Review* 33 (3): 297–318. http://dx.doi.org/10.1177/136346159603300303.

Koostachin, J. 2012. *Criminalization of Indigenous People Part 1 — A Foreign System: Incarceration of Indigenous Women*. New Socialist Webzine, September 1. http://www.newsocialist.org/index.php/642-criminalization-of-indigenous-people-part-i-a-foreign-system-incarceration-of-indigenous-women (Accessed on October 23, 2012).

Koring, P. 2009. "Abdelrazik sues Ottawa for $27-million." *Globe and Mail*, September 24. http://m.theglobeandmail.com/news/politics/abdelrazik-sues-ottawa-for-27-million/article4287125/?service=mobile (Accessed on November 13, 2012).

Koring, P. 2011. "Canadian Abousfian Abdelrazik taken off United Nations terror list." *Globe and Mail*, November 30. http://www.theglobeandmail.com/news/world/canadian-abousfian-abdelrazik-taken-off-united-nations-terror-list/article4179856/ (Accessed on November 13, 2012).

Krieger, N. 2006. "If 'race' is the answer, what is the question?—on 'race', racism and health: a social epidemiologist's perspective." A web forum organized by the Social Science Research Council. http://raceandgenomics.ssrc.org/Krieger/ (Accessed on February 15, 2013).

Kruger, E., M. Mulder, and B. Korenic. 2004. "Canada after 11 September: Security measures and 'preferred' immigrants." *Mediterranean Quarterly* 15 (4): 72–87. http://dx.doi.org/10.1215/10474552-15-4-72.

Kumar, M. 2007. "Imagining the terrorist: Racialization of Asian identities since 9/11." *Kasarinlan: Philippine Journal of Third World Studies* 22 (2): 4–21.

Kurzban, I. 2008. "Democracy and immigration." In *Keeping Out the Other: A Critical Introduction to Immigration Enforcement Today*, ed. D.C. Brotherton and P. Kretsedemas, 63–75. New York: Columbia University Press.

Laing, R.D. 1965. *The Divided Self: An Existential Study in Sanity and Madness*. Baltimore: Penguin Books.

Lamberti, J., R. Weisman, S. Schwarzkopf, N. Price, R. Ashton, and J. Trompeter. 2001. "The mentally ill in jails and prisons: Towards an integrated model of prevention." *Psychiatric Quarterly* 72 (1): 63–77. http://dx.doi.org/10.1023/A:1004862104102.

LaPrairie, C. 1997. "Reconstructing theory: Explaining aboriginal over-representation in the criminal justice system in Canada." *Australian and New Zealand Journal of Criminology* 30 (1): 39–54. http://dx.doi. org/10.1177/0004865897030000104.

LaPrairie, C. 2002. "Aboriginal over-representation in the criminal justice system: A tale of nine cities." *Canadian Journal of Criminology* 44: 181–208.

Lawson, E. 2013. "Disenfranchised grief and social inequality: Bereaved African Canadians and oppositional narratives about the violent deaths of family and family members." *Ethnic and Racial Studies* (Published online 24 May 2013) http://dx.doi.org/10.1080/01419870.2013.800569.

Lazar, A., and M. Lazar. 2004. "The discourse of the new world order: 'Outcasting' the double face of threat." *Discourse & Society* 15 (2): 223–42. http://dx.doi.org/10.1177/0957926504041018.

LeFrancois, B.A., R. Menzies, and G. Reaume, eds. 2013. *Mad Matters: A Critical Reader in Canadian Mad Studies.* Toronto: Canadian Scholars' Press.

Legomsky, S. 2007. "The new path of immigration law: Asymmetric incorporation of criminal justice norms." *Washington & Lee Law Review* 64: 469–528.

Levin, D. 2012. "Beach essentials in china: Flip-flops, a towel and a ski mask." *New York Times*, August 3. http://www.nytimes.com/2012/08/04/world/asia/in-china-sun-protection-can-include-a-mask.html?_r=0 (Accessed on November 10, 2012).

Levine-Rasky, C. 2012. "Who are you calling bogus?: Saying no to Roma refugees." *Canadian Dimension* 46 (5). http://canadiandimension.com/articles/4959/ (Accessed on November 11, 2012).

Li, G. 2008. "Private security and public policing." *Juristat* 28 (10): 1–14.

Li, P. 1999. *Race and Ethnic Relations in Canada.* 2nd ed. Don Mills, ON: Oxford University Press.

Li, P. 2007. "Contradictions of racial discourse." In *Interrogating Race and Racism*, ed. V. Agnew, 37–54. Toronto: University of Toronto Press.

Lightman, E., D. Herd, and A. Mitchell. 2008. "Precarious lives: Work, health and hunger among current and former welfare recipients in Toronto." *Journal of Policy Practice* 7 (4): 242–59. http://dx.doi.org/10.1080/15588740802258508.

Lindell, R. 2012. "Tighter timelines for refugee claims come with a $34 million price tag." *Global News*, September 11. http://globalnews.ca/news/285399/tighter-timelines-for-refugee-claims-come-with-a-34-million-price-tag/ (Accessed October 18, 2012).

Lingard, L., S. Tallett, and J. Rosenfield. 2002. "Culture and physician-patient communication: A qualitative exploration of residents' experiences and attitudes." *Annals of Royal Society of Physicians and Surgeons Canada* 35 (6): 331–40.

Lipsitz, G. 1997. "The greatest story ever sold: Marketing and the O.J. Simpson trial." In *Birth of a Nation'hood*, ed. T. Morrison and C.B. Lacour, 3–29. New York: Pantheon Books.

Little, M. 1998. *No Car, No Radio, No Liquor Permit: The Moral Regulation of Single Mothers in Ontario, 1920–1997.* Toronto: Oxford University Press.

Lombroso, C. 1876. *Criminal Man.* Milan: Hoepli.

Lombroso, C., and W. Ferrero. 1895. *The Female Offender.* London: T.F. Unwin. http://dx.doi.org/10.1037/14150-000.

Loring, M., and B. Powell. 1988. "Gender, race and DSM-III: A study of the objectivity of psychiatric diagnostic behavior." *Journal of Health and Social Behavior* 29 (1): 1–22. http://dx.doi.org/10.2307/2137177.

Lowman, J. 2000. "Violence and the outlaw status of (street) prostitution in Canada." *Violence against Women* 6 (9): 987–1011. http://dx.doi.org/10.1177/10778010022182245.

Lowry, M. 2002. "Creating human insecurity: The national security focus in Canada's immigration system." *Refuge: Canada's Periodical on Refugees* 21 (1): 28–39.

Lyon, D. 2008. "Biometrics, identification and surveillance." *Bioethics* 22 (9): 499–508.

MacAlister, D. 2012. *Police Involved Deaths: The Need for Reform.* Vancouver: BC Civil Liberties Association.

MacIntosh, C. 2012. "Insecure refugees: The narrowing of asylum-seeker rights to freedom of movement and claims determination post 9/11 in Canada." *Review of Constitutional Studies* 16: 181–209.

Macklin, A. 2005. "Disappearing refugees: Reflections on the Canada–UA safe third country agreement." *Columbia Human Rights Law Review* 36: 365–426.

Madden, A. 2002. "Risk management in the real world." In *Criminal Justice, Mental Health and the Politics of Risk*, ed. N. Gray, J. Laing, and L. Noaks, 15–26. London: Cavendish Publishing.

Magnet, S. 2007. "Are biometrics race-neutral?" June 5. http://www.anonequity.org/weblog/archives/2007/06/are_biometrics_raceneutral.php (Accessed November 19, 2012).

Magnet, S. 2011. *When Biometrics Fail: Gender, Race and the Technology of Identity.* Durham: Duke University Press.

Maki, K. 2011. "Neoliberal deviants and surveillance: Welfare recipients under the watchful eye of Ontario Works." *Surveillance & Society* 9 (1): 47–63.

Makin, K. 2012. "Canadians finally getting it: Crime is on the decline." *Globe and Mail,* January 25. http://www.theglobeandmail.com/news/national/canadians-finally-getting-it-crime-is-on-the-decline/article542609/ (Accessed on October 18, 2012).

Makuch, S., N. Craik, and S. Leisk. 2004. *Canadian Municipal and Planning Law.* 2nd ed. Toronto: Thomson Carswell.

Mallea, P. 2010. *The Fear Factor: Stephen Harper's 'Tough on Crime' Agenda.* Ottawa: Canadian Centre for Policy Alternatives.

Mallea, P. 2012. "The disastrous consequences of the omnibus crime bill." March 6. http://rabble.ca/blogs/bloggers/mgregus/2012/03/disastrous-consequences-omnibus-crime-bill (Accessed on October 30, 2012).

Mason, D. 2000. *Race and Ethnicity in Modern Britain.* Oxford: Oxford University Press.

Massoglia, M. 2008. "Incarceration, health and racial disparities." *Law and Society Review* 42 (2): 275–306.

McCall, L. 2009. "The complexity of intersectionality." In *Intersectionality and Beyond: Law, Power and the Politics of Location*, ed. E. Grabham, et al., 49–76. London: Routledge.

McDonald, S., and K. Scrim. 2011. "Canadians' awareness of victim issues: A benchmarking study." *Victims of Crime Research Digest* 4: 4–8.

McKiernan, M. 2012. "Bill enabling deportation of foreign criminals too tough, lawyers say." *Canadian Lawyer Magazine,* October 3. http://www.canadianlawyermag.com/legalfeeds/1082/Bill-enabling-deportation-of-foreign-criminals-too-tough-lawyers-say.html (Accessed November 23, 2012).

McLaren, J. 2002. "The state, child snatching and the law: The seizure and indoctrination of Sons of Freedom children in British Columbia." In

Regulating Lives: Historical Essays on the State, Society, the Individual, and the Law, ed. J. McLaren, R. Menzis, and D.E. Chunn, 259–93. Vancouver: UBC Press.

McLaren, J.P.S. 1986. "Chasing the social evil: Moral fervour and the evolution of Canada's prostitution laws, 1867–1917." *Canadian Journal of Law and Society* 1: 125–65.

McLaren, J.P.S. 1988. "Maternal feminism in action: Emily Murphy, police magistrate." *Windsor Yearbook of Access to Justice* 8: 234–51.

McLaren, J.P.S. 2005. "The despicable crime of nudity: Law, the state and civil protest among Canada's Doukhobors, 1899–1935." *Advocate (Boston, MA)* 63 (March): 211–20.

McMullan, J. 2005. *News, Truth and Crime: The Westray Disaster and its Aftermath.* Black Point, NS: Fernwood Publishing.

McMurtry, R., and A. Curling. 2008. *The Review of the Roots of Youth Violence: Executive Summary.* Toronto: Queen's Printer for Ontario.

McNiel, D., R. Binder, and J. Robinson. 2005. "Incarceration associated with homelessness, mental disorder, and co-occurring substance abuse." *Psychiatric Services (Washington, DC)* 56 (7): 840–46. http://dx.doi.org/10.1176/appi. ps.56.7.840.

Melossi, D. 2003. "'In a peaceful life': Migration and the crime of modernity in Europe/Italy." *Punishment and Society* 5 (4): 371–97. http://dx.doi. org/10.1177/14624745030054001.

Meloy, M., and S. Miller. 2010. *The Victimization of Women: Law, Policies and Politics.* New York: Oxford University Press.

Mendelson, T., L. Kubzansky, G. Datta, and S. Buka. 2008. "Relation of female gender and low socioeconomic status to internalizing symptoms among adolescents: A case of double jeopardy?" *Social Science & Medicine* 66 (6): 1284–96. http://dx.doi.org/10.1016/j.socscimed.2007.11.033.

Menendian, S. 2012. "The new politics of race." December 7. http://www.race-talk. org/the-new-politics-of-race/ (Accessed December 7, 2012).

Menzies, R. 1987. "Psychiatrists in blue: Police apprehension of mental disorder and dangerousness." *Criminology* 25 (3): 429–54. http://dx.doi. org/10.1111/j.1745-9125.1987.tb00805.x.

Menzies, R. 1989. *Survival of the Sanest: Order and Disorder in a Pre-Trial Psychiatric Clinic.* Toronto: University of Toronto Press.

Menzies, R., and D.E. Chunn. 2012 (forthcoming). "Mapping the intersections of psycho-legal power: A tale of murder, madness, and motherhood from British Columbia history." *Australasian Canadian Studies* 30 (1–2).

Metro News. 2013. "'Not guilty' verdict in Sgt. Steven Desjourdy sexual assault trial." Ottawa. 3 April.

Miles, R. 1989. *Racism.* London: Routledge.

Miles, R. 2000. "Apropos the idea of 'race' … again." In *Theories of Race and Racism: A Reader*, 2nd ed., ed. L. Black and J. Solomos, 180–98. New York: Routledge.

Millar, P., and A. Owusu-Bempah. 2011. "Whitewashing criminal justice in Canada: Preventing research through data suppression." *Canadian Journal of Law and Society* 26 (3): 653–61. http://dx.doi.org/10.3138/cjls.26.3.653.

Miller, J. 2005. "African immigrant damnation syndrome: The case of Charles Ssenyonga." *Sexuality Research & Social Policy* 2 (2): 31–50. http://dx.doi. org/10.1525/srsp.2005.2.2.31.

Miller, J., and A. Garran. 2007. "The web of institutional racism." *Smith College Studies in Social Work* 77 (1): 33–67. http://dx.doi.org/10.1300/J497v77n01_03.

Mirchandani, K., and W. Chan. 2007. *Criminalizing Race, Criminalizing Poverty.* Black Point, NS: Fernwood Publishing.

Monahan, J. 2007. "Clinical and actuarial predictions of violence. II Scientific status." In *Modern Scientific Evidence: The Law and Science of Expert Testimony,* ed. D. Faigman, D. Kaye, M. Saks, J. Sanders, and E. Cheng, 300–18. St. Paul, MN: West Publishing Company.

Morrison, T., and C.B. Lacour, eds. 1997. *Birth of a Nation'hood: Gaze, Script, and Spectacle in the O.J. Simpson Case.* New York: Pantheon Books.

Morrow, M., and J. Weisser. 2012. "Towards a social justice framework of mental health recovery." *Studies in Social Justice* 6 (1): 27–43.

Mosher, C. 1996. "Minorities and misdemeanours: The treatment of black public order offenders in Ontario's criminal justice system—1892–1930." *Canadian Journal of Criminology* 38: 413–38.

Mosher, C.J. 1998. *Discrimination and Denial: Systemic Racism in Ontario's Legal and Criminal Justice Systems, 1892–1961.* Toronto: University of Toronto Press.

Mosher, J. 2000. "Managing the disentitlement of women: Glorified markets, the idealized family, and the undeserving other." In *Restructuring Caring Labour: Discourse, State Practice, and Everyday Life,* ed. S. Neysmith. New York: Oxford University Press.

Mosher, J., and J. Hermer. 2005. *Welfare Fraud: The Constitution of Social Assistance as a Crime.* Ottawa: Paper prepared for the Law Commission of Canada.

Moulds, E. 1980. "Chivalry and paternalism: Disparities of treatment in the criminal justice system." In *Women, Crime and Justice,* ed. S.K. Datesman and F.R. Scarpitti, 277–99. New York: Oxford University Press.

Munch, C. 2012. *Victim Services in Canada 2009/2010.* Ottawa: Statistics Canada.

Muncie, J., E. McLaughlin, and M. Langan, eds. 1996. *Criminological Perspectives: A Reader.* London: Sage.

Muncie, J. 2003. "Youth, risk and victimization." In *Victimisation: Theory, Research and Policy,* ed. P. Davies, P. Francis, and V. Jupp, 46–60. Basingstoke: Palgrave.

Murakawa, N. 2005. "Electing to punish: Congress, race and the American criminal justice state." PhD Dissertation, Yale University.

Murdocca, C. 2004. "The racial profile: Governing race through knowledge production." *Canadian Journal of Law and Society* 18: 153–67.

Murphy, C. 2012. "Canadian police and policing policy, post 9/11." In *Canadian Criminal Justice Policy: Contemporary Perspectives,* ed. K. Ismaili, J. Sprott, and K. Varma, 5–29. Don Mills, ON: Oxford University Press.

Myers, T. 2006. *Caught: Montreal's Modern Girls and the Law, 1869–1945.* Toronto: University of Toronto Press.

Naffine, N. 1987. *Female Crime: The Construction of Women in Criminology.* Sydney: Allen & Unwin.

Naffine, N. 1996. *Feminism and Criminology.* Philadelphia: Temple University Press.

Naidoo, J. 1992. "The mental health of visible ethnic minorities in Canada." *Psychology and Developing Societies* 4 (2): 165–86. http://dx.doi. org/10.1177/097133369200400205.

National Council of Welfare. 2009. *Welfare Incomes 2009.* Ottawa: National Council of Welfare.

National Council of Welfare. 2010. *Poverty Profile 2007: Depth of Poverty*. Ottawa: National Council of Welfare.

National Council of Welfare. 2012. *Poverty Profile*. Special Edition. Ottawa: National Council of Welfare.

National Film Board of Canada. 1990. *After the Montreal Massacre*. Videorecording. Toronto: CBC.

Native Women's Association of Canada. 2010. *Sisters in Spirit*. Ottawa: Native Women's Association of Canada.

Naumetz, T. 2011. "Mass detention of 300 Tamil migrants cost $18-million says Canada Border Services Agency." *The Hill Times*, February 14. http://www.hilltimes.com/news/2011/02/14/mass-detention-of-300-tamil-migrants-cost-%2418-million-says-canada-border-services-agency/25475 (Accessed November 20, 2012).

Neighbors, H., J. Jackson, L. Campbell, and D. Williams. 1989. "The influence of racial factors on psychiatric diagnosis: A review and suggestions for research." *Community Mental Health Journal* 25 (4): 301–11. http://dx.doi.org/10.1007/BF00755677.

Neighbors, H., S. Trierweiler, B. Ford, and J. Muroff. 2003. "Racial differences in DSM diagnosis using a semi-structured instrument: The importance of clinical judgment in the diagnosis of African Americans." *Journal of Health and Social Behavior* 44 (3): 237–56. http://dx.doi.org/10.2307/1519777.

Nelson, J. 2011. "Panthers or thieves: Racialized knowledge and the regulation of Africville." *Journal of Canadian Studies. Revue d'Etudes Canadiennes* 45 (1): 121–42.

Neubeck, K., and N. Cazenave. 2002. "Welfare racism and its consequences." In *Work, Welfare and Politics*, ed. F. Fox-Piven, J. Acker, M. Hallock, and S. Morgan, 19–34. Portland: University of Oregon Press.

Ng, C. 1997. "The stigma of mental illness in Asian cultures." *Australian and New Zealand Journal of Psychiatry* 31 (3): 382–90. http://dx.doi.org/10.3109/00048679709073848.

Nightingale, M. 1991. "Judicial attitudes and differential treatment: Native women in sexual assault cases." *Ottawa Law Review* 23 (1): 71–98.

No One Is Illegal (NOII). 2012. "Axe the Refugee Exclusion Act!" March 5. http://toronto.nooneisillegal.org/node/670 (Accessed on May 25, 2012).

Noh, S., M. Beiser, V. Kaspar, F. Hou, and J. Rummens. 1999. "Perceived racial discrimination, depression and coping: A study of Southeast Asian refugees in Canada." *Journal of Health and Social Behavior* 40 (3): 193–207. http://dx.doi.org/10.2307/2676348.

Nyers, P. 2011. "Forms of irregular citizenship." In *The Contested Politics of Mobility: Borderzones and Irregularity*, ed. V. Squire. New York: Routledge.

Odartey-Wellington, F. 2009. "Racial profiling and moral panic: Operation threat and the Al-Qaeda sleeper cell that never was." *Global Media Journal* 2 (2): 25–40.

Offen, L. 1986. "The female offender and psychiatric referral: The medicalization of female deviance?" *Medicine and Law* 5 (4): 339–48.

O'Grady, B., S. Gaetz, and K. Buccieri. 2011. *Can I See Your ID? The Policing of Youth Homelessness in Toronto. The Homeless Hub Report #5*. Toronto: Justice for Children, and Youth and Homeless Hub Press.

Ogrodnik, L. 2010. *Child and Youth Victims of Police-Reported Violent Crime, 2008.* Ottawa: Canadian Centre for Justice Statistics.

Okin, S.M. 1989. *Justice, Gender, and the Family*. New York: Basic Books.

Omi, M., and H. Winant. 1994. *Racial Formation in the United States from the 1960s to the 1990s*. 2nd ed. New York: Routledge.

Ontario Federation of Community Mental Health and Addictions Programs. 2009. *Embracing Cultural Competence in the Mental Health and Addiction System*. Position Paper. Toronto.

Ontario Human Rights Commission. 1995. *Final Report on Systemic Racism in Ontario's Criminal Justice System*. Toronto: Queen's Printer for Ontario.

Ontario Human Rights Commission. 2003. *Paying the Price: The Human Cost of Racial Profiling*. Toronto: Ontario Human Rights Commission.

Ontario Human Rights Commission. 2012. *Minds That Matter: Report on the Consultation on Human Rights, Mental Health and Addictions*. Toronto: Ontario Human Rights Commission.

Oppal, W.T. 2012. *Forsaken: The Report of the Missing Women Commission of Inquiry. Executive Summary*. Vancouver, BC.

Oriola, T., N. Neverson, and C. Adeyanju. 2012. "'They should have just taken a gun and shot my son': Taser deployment and the downtrodden in Canada." *Social Identities* 18 (1): 65–83. http://dx.doi.org/10.1080/13504630.2012.629514.

Osberg, L. 2012. *Instability Implications of Increasing Inequality: What Can Be Learned from North America?* Ottawa: Canadian Centre for Policy Alternatives.

Ostertag, S., and W. Armaline. 2011. "Image isn't everything: Contemporary system racism and anti-racism in the age of Obama." *Humanity & Society* 35 (3): 261–89. http://dx.doi.org/10.1177/0160597611103500304.

Painter, N. 2010. *The History of White People*. New York: W.W. Norton.

Palidda, S. 2011. *Racial Criminalization of Migrants in the 21st Century*. Burlington, VT: Ashgate.

Patel, T., and D. Tyrer. 2011. *Race, Crime and Resistance*. London: Sage Publications.

Patychuk, D. 2011. *Health Equity and Racialized Groups: A Literature Review*. Toronto: Health Nexus/Health Equity Council.

Peake, L., and B. Ray. 2001. "Racializing the Canadian landscape: Whiteness, uneven geographies and social justice." *The Canadian Geographer* 45 (1): 180–86. http://dx.doi.org/10.1111/j.1541-0064.2001.tb01183.x.

Pearson, P. 1997. *When She Was Bad: Violent Women and the Myth of Innocence*. Toronto: Random House.

Peay, J. 2011. *Mental Health and Crime*. New York: Routledge.

Pedicelli, G. 1998. *When Police Kill: Police Use of Force in Montreal and Toronto*. Montreal: Vehicule Press.

Penfold, S., and G. Walker. 1984. *Women and the Psychiatric Paradox*. Milton Keynes: Open University Press.

People's Commission on Immigration and Security Measures. 2007. *Final Report*. Montreal, February.

Perreault, S. 2008a. *Immigrants and Victimization 2004*. Ottawa: Canadian Centre for Justice Statistics.

Perreault, S. 2008b. *Visible Minorities and Victimization 2004*. Ottawa: Canadian Centre for Justice Statistics.

Perreault, S. 2012. "Homicide in Canada, 2011." *Juristat* (Dec.): 1–36.

Perreault, S., and S. Brennan. 2010. "Criminal victimization in Canada, 2009." *Juristat* (Summer).

Perry, B., and S. Alvi. 2012. "'We are all vulnerable': The *in terrorem* effects of hate crimes." *International Review of Victimology* 18 (1): 57–71. http://dx.doi.org/10.1177/0269758011422475.

Perry, B., ed. 2003. *Hate and Bias Crime: A Reader*. New York: Routledge.

Persson, A., and C. Newman. 2008. "Making monsters: Heterosexuality, crime and race in recent Western media coverage of HIV." *Sociology of Health & Illness* 30 (4): 632–46. http://dx.doi.org/10.1111/j.1467-9566.2008.01082.x.

Peter, T. 2006. "Mad, bad, or victim? Making sense of mother-daughter sexual abuse." *Feminist Criminology* 1 (4): 283–302. http://dx.doi.org/10.1177/1557085106292779.

Pilgrim, D. 2007. "The survival of psychiatric diagnosis." *Social Science & Medicine* 65 (3): 536–47. http://dx.doi.org/10.1016/j.socscimed.2007.03.054.

Pinals, D., I. Packer, W. Fisher, and K. Roy-Bunjnowski. 2004. "Relationship between race and ethnicity and forensic clinical triage dispositions." *Psychiatric Services (Washington, DC)* 55 (8): 873–78. http://dx.doi.org/10.1176/appi.ps.55.8.873.

Piven, F., and R. Cloward. 1987. "The contemporary relief debate." In *The Mean Season: The Attack on the Welfare State*, ed. F. Block, R. Cloward, B. Ehrenreich, and F. Piven, 45–108. New York: Pantheon Books.

Pivot Legal Society. 2002. *To Serve and Protect: A Report on Policing in Vancouver's Downtown Eastside*. Vancouver: Pivot Legal Society.

Pollack, S. 2005. "Taming the shrew: Regulating prisoners through women-centered mental health programming." *Critical Criminology* 13 (1): 71–87. http://dx.doi.org/10.1007/s10612-004-6168-5.

Pollack, S. 2008. "Locked in, locked out: Imprisoning women in the shrinking and punitive welfare state." Waterloo, ON: Faculty of Social Work, Wilfrid Laurier University.

Pollack, S., V. Green, and A. Allspach. 2005. *Women Charged with Domestic Violence in Toronto: The Unintended Consequences of Mandatory Charge Policies*. Toronto: Woman Abuse Council of Toronto.

Pollak, O. 1961. *The Criminality of Women*. New York: Barnes.

Postman, N. 1985. *Amusing Ourselves to Death: Public Discourse in the Age of Show Business*. New York: Penguin Books.

Power, E. 2005. "The unfreedom of being other: Canadian lone mothers' experiences of poverty and 'life on the cheque.'" *Sociology* 39 (4): 643–60.

Poynting, S., and B. Perry. 2007. "Climates of hate: Media and state inspired victimization of Muslims in Canada and Australia since 9/11." *Current Issues in Criminal Justice* 19: 151–71.

Poynting, S., and V. Mason. 2006. "Tolerance, freedom, justice and peace?: Britain, Australia and anti-Muslim racism since 11 September 2001." *Journal of Intercultural Studies (Melbourne, Vic.)* 27 (4): 365–91. http://dx.doi.org/10.1080/07256860600934973.

Pratt, A. 2010. "Between a hunch and a hard place: Make suspicion reasonable at the Canadian border." *Social & Legal Studies* 19 (4): 461–80. http://dx.doi.org/10.1177/0964663910378434.

Pratt, A., and M. Valverde. 2002. "From deserving victims to 'masters of confusion': redefining refugees in the 1990s." *Canadian Journal of Sociology* 27 (2): 135–61.

Price, T., B. David, and D. Otis. 2004. "The use of restraint and seclusion in different racial groups in an inpatient forensic setting." *Journal of the American Academy of Psychiatry and the Law* 32: 163–68.

Prins, H. 2005. "Mental disorder and violent crime: A problematic relationship." *Journal of Community and Criminal Justice* 52 (4): 333–57.

Privy Council Office (PCO). 2004. *Securing an Open Society: Canada's National Security Policy.* Ottawa: National Library of Canada.

Provine, D., and R. Doty. 2011. "The criminalization of immigrants as a racial project." *Journal of Contemporary Criminal Justice* 27 (3): 261–77.

Pruegger, V. 2009. *Alberta Hate/Bias Crime Report.* Calgary: Alberta Hate Crimes Committee.

Pruegger, V., D. Cook, and S. Richter-Salomons. 2009. *Inequality in Calgary: The Racialization of Poverty.* The City of Calgary Community and Neighbourhood Services: Social Research Unit.

Public Safety and Emergency Preparedness Canada. 2004. *Securing an Open Society: Canada's National Security Policy.* May. http://www.pco-bcp.gc.ca/index. asp?lang=eng&page=information&sub=publications&doc=aarchives/natsec-secnat/natsec-secnat-eng.htm (Accessed on November 18, 2013).

Public Safety Canada. 2008. *Smart Border Declaration and Action Plan.* March 5. http://actionplan.gc.ca/en/page/bbg-tpf/canada-us-border-cooperation (Accessed on November 19, 2012).

Public Safety Canada. 2012. *Security Certificates.* February 15. http://www. publicsafety.gc.ca/cnt/ntnl-scrt/cntr-trrrsm/scrt-crtfcts-eng.aspx (Accessed on November 12, 2012).

Quadagno, J. 1994. *The Color of Welfare: How Racism Undermined the War on Poverty.* New York: Oxford University Press.

Quadagno, J. 2000. "Another face of inequality: Racial and ethnic exclusion in the welfare state." *Social Politics* 7 (2): 229–37. http://dx.doi.org/10.1093/sp/7.2.229.

Rafter, N., and F. Heidensohn, eds. 1995. *International Feminist Perspectives in Criminology: Engendering a Discipline.* Philadelphia: Open University Press.

Rajiva, M., and S. Batacharya, eds. 2010. *Critical Perspectives on a Canadian Murder.* Toronto: Canadian Scholars' Press.

Randall, M. 2010. "Sexual assault law, credibility, and 'ideal victims': Consent, resistance, and victim blaming." *Canadian Journal of Women and the Law* 22 (2): 397–433. http://dx.doi.org/10.3138/cjwl.22.2.397.

Rattansi, A. 2007. *Racism: A Very Short Introduction.* New York: Oxford University Press.

Ray, L., and D. Smith. 2001. "Racist offenders and the politics of 'hate crime.'" *Law and Critique* 12: 203–221.

Razack, S. 1998a. *Looking White People in the Eye: Gender, Race and Culture in Courtrooms and Classrooms.* Toronto: University of Toronto Press.

Razack, S. 1998b. "*R.D.S. v. Her Majesty the Queen*: A case about home." *Constitutional Forum* 9 (3): 59–65.

Razack, S. 2000. "Gendered racial violence and spatialized justice: The murder of Pamela George." *Canadian Journal of Law and Society* 15 (2): 91–130.

Razack, S. 2005. "Geopolitics, culture clash and gender after September 11." *Social Justice (San Francisco, CA)* 32 (4): 11–31.

Razack, S. 2007. "The camp: A place where law has declared that the rule of law does not operate." *Public* 36: 109–23.

Razack, S. 2012. "Memorializing colonial power: The death of Frank Paul." *Law & Social Inquiry* 37 (4): 908–32. http://dx.doi.org/10.1111/j.1747-4469. 2012.01291.x.

Regehr, C., R. Alaggia, L. Lambert, and M. Saini. 2008. "Victims of sexual violence in the Canadian criminal courts." *Victims & Offenders* 3 (1): 99–113. http://dx.doi. org/10.1080/15564880701783699.

Reid, C., and A. Tom. 2006. "Poor women's discourses of legitimacy, poverty and health." *Gender & Society* 20 (3): 402–21. http://dx.doi. org/10.1177/0891243206286939.

Reiman, J. 2007. *The Rich Get Richer, and the Poor Get Prison.* 8th ed. Boston: Pearson.

Reiner, R. 1992. "Policing a postmodern society." *Modern Law Review* 55 (6): 761–81.

Rennison, C.M. 2009. "A new look at the gender gap in offending." *Women & Criminal Justice* 19 (3): 171–90. http://dx.doi.org/10.1080/08974450903001461.

Representative for Children and Youth. 2013. *Who Protected Him? How B.C.'s Child Welfare System Failed One of Its Most Vulnerable Children.* February 2013.

Richie, B. 1996. *Compelled to Crime: The Gender Entrapment of Black Battered Women.* New York: Routledge.

Richie, B. 2000. "A Black feminist reflection on the antiviolence movement." *Signs (Chicago, IL)* 25 (4): 1133–37. http://dx.doi.org/10.1086/495533.

Richmond, A. 2002. "Globalization: Implication for immigrants and refugees." *Ethnic and Racial Studies* 25 (5): 707–27. http://dx.doi.org/10.1080/01419870220 00000231.

Roach, K. 1996. "Systemic racism and criminal justice policy." *Windsor Yearbook of Access to Justice* 15: 236–49.

Roach, K. 2005. "Canada's response to terrorism." In *Global Anti-Terrorism Law and Policy*, ed. V. Ramraj, M. Hor, and K. Roach. New York: Cambridge University Press.

Roberts, B. 1988. *Whence They Came: Deportation from Canada, 1900–1935.* Ottawa: University of Ottawa Press.

Roberts, D. 1993. "Motherhood and crime." *Iowa Law Review* 79: 95–141.

Roberts, J. n.d. *Disproportionate Harm: Hate Crime in Canada: An Analysis of Recent Statistics.* Ottawa: Department of Justice, WD1995-11e.

Roberts, J.V. 2007. "Public confidence in criminal justice in Canada: A comparative and contextual analysis." *Canadian Journal of Criminology and Criminal Justice* 49 (2): 153–84.

Robson, R. 1998. "Convictions: Lesbians and criminal justice." In *Sappho Goes to Law School*, ed. R. Robson, 29–42. New York: Columbia University Press.

Robson, R. 2004. "Lesbianism and the death penalty: A 'hard core' case." *Women's Studies Quarterly* 32 (3/4): 181–91.

Rock, P. 1988. "On the birth of organizations." *LSE Quarterly* 2 (2): 123–53.

Rogers, R. 2000. "The uncritical acceptance of risk assessment in forensic practice." *Law and Human Behavior* 24 (5): 595–605. http://dx.doi. org/10.1023/A:1005575113507.

Rollock, D., and E. Gordon. 2000. "Racism and mental health into the 21st century: Perspectives and parameters." *American Journal of Orthopsychiatry* 70 (1): 5–13. http://dx.doi.org/10.1037/h0087703.

Romero, M. 2008. "Crossing the immigration and race border: A critical race theory approach to immigration studies." *Contemporary Justice Review* 11 (1): 23–37. http://dx.doi.org/10.1080/10282580701850371.

Rose, W. 2002. "Crimes of color: Risk, profiling, and the contemporary racialization of social control." *International Journal of Politics Culture and Society* 16 (2): 179–205. http://dx.doi.org/10.1023/A:1020572912884.

Rosenberg, S. 2003. "Neither forgotten nor fully remembered: Tracing an ambivalent public memory on the 10th anniversary of the Montreal Massacre." *Feminist Theory* 4 (1): 5–27.

Rosenhan, D.L. 1973. "On being sane in insane places." *Science* 179 (4070): 250–58. http://dx.doi.org/10.1126/science.179.4070.250.

Rossiter, M., and K. Rossiter. 2009. "Diamonds in the rough: Bridging gaps in supports for at-risk immigrant and refugee youth." *International Migration and Integration* 10 (4): 409–29. http://dx.doi.org/10.1007/s12134-009-0110-3.

Rudin, J. 1995. *Aboriginal Peoples and the Justice System*. Ottawa: Report of the Royal Commission on Aboriginal Peoples.

Rudner, M. 2004. "Challenge and response: Canada's intelligence community and the war on terrorism." *Canadian Foreign Policy* 11 (2): 17–39. http://dx.doi.org/10.1080/11926422.2004.9673364.

Russo, R. 2008. "Security, securitization and human capital: The new wave of Canadian immigration laws." *World Academy of Science, Engineering and Technology* 44: 738–47.

Rustin, M. 1991. "Psychoanalysis, racism and anti-racism." In *The Good Society and the Inner World*, ed. M. Rustin. London: Verso.

Rygiel, K. 2011. "Governing borderzones of mobility through e-borders." In *The Contested Politics of Mobility: Borderzones and Irregularity*, ed. V. Squire. New York: Routledge.

Said, E. 1979. *Orientalism*. Toronto: Random House of Canada.

Salaita, S. 2005. "Ethnic identity and imperative patriotism: Arab Americans before and after 9/11." *College Literature* 32 (2): 147–68. http://dx.doi.org/10.1353/lit.2005.0033.

Sangster, J. 2001. *Regulating Girls and Women: Sexuality, Family, and the Law in Ontario, 1920–1960*. Toronto: Oxford University Press.

Satzewich, V. 2000. "Whiteness limited: Racialization and the social construction of 'peripheral Europeans.'" *Social History* 66: 271–90.

Satzewich, V. 2010. *Race and Ethnicity in Canada: A Critical Introduction*. Don Mills,ON: Oxford University Press.

Savarese, J. 2010. "'Doing no violence to the sentence imposed': Racialized sex worker complainants, racialized offenders, and the feminization of the *homo sacer* in two sexual assault cases." *Canadian Journal of Women and the Law* 22 (2): 365–95. http://dx.doi.org/10.3138/cjwl.22.2.365.

Sayad, A. 2004. *The Suffering of the Immigrant*. Cambridge: Polity Press.

Schissel, B. 1997. *Blaming Children: Youth Crime, Moral Panics, and the Politics of Hate*. Black Point, NS: Fernwood Publishing.

Schissel, B. 2006. *Still Blaming Children: Youth Conduct and the Politics of Child Hating*. Black Point, NS: Fernwood Publishing.

Schizophrenia Society of Ontario. 2010. *Double Jeopardy: Deportation of the Criminalized Mentally Ill.* Toronto: Schizophrenia Society of Ontario.

Schultz, A., D. Williams, B. Israel, A. Becker, E. Parker, S. James, and J. Jackson. 2000. "Unfair treatment, neighborhood effects, and mental health in the Detroit metropolitan area." *Journal of Health and Social Behavior* 41 (3): 314–32. http://dx.doi.org/10.2307/2676323.

Scoffield, H. 2012. "UN criticizes canada on crime bill and youth." *Huffington Post*, October 9. http://www.huffingtonpost.ca/2012/10/09/un-canada-crime-bill_n_1951935.html (Accessed on November 21, 2012).

Scrim, K. 2010. "Aboriginal victimization in Canada: A summary of the literature." In *Victims of Crime: Research Digest No. 3*, ed. S. McDonald. Ottawa: Department of Justice.

Scull, A.T. 1977. *Decarceration: Community Treatment and the Deviant: A Radical View*. Englewood Cliffs, NJ: Prentice-Hall.

Seccombe, K., D. James, and K. Walters. 1998. "'They think you ain't much of nothing': The social construction of the welfare mother." *Journal of Marriage and the Family* 60 (4): 849–65. http://dx.doi.org/10.2307/353629.

Semati, M. 2010. "Islamophobia, culture and race in the age of empire." *Cultural Studies* 24 (2): 256–75.

Sheehy, E. 2005. "Causation, common sense, and the common law: Replaying unexamined assumptions with what we know about male violence against women or from *Jane Doe to Bonnie Mooney*." *Canadian Journal of Women and the Law* 17 (1): 87–116. http://dx.doi.org/10.1353/jwl.2006.0018.

Shephard, M., and S. Verma. 2003. "They only arrested the 'Muhammads.'" *Toronto Star*, January 12. http://www.ocap.ca/node/626 (Accessed November 13, 2012).

Showalter, E. 1985. *The Female Malady: Women, Madness and English Culture, 1830–1980*. New York: Pantheon Books.

Showler, P. 2009. "The bogus refugee myth." *Ottawa Citizen*, August 12. http://www2.canada.com/ottawacitizen/news/opinion/story.html?id=275910f3-db33-4e65-822f-c78f1bc307e1 (Accessed November 27, 2012).

Showler, P. 2012. "Faster refugee processing system puts more pressure on legal aid support." September 14. http://maytree.com/blog/2012/09/refugee-system-pressure-on-legal-aid-support/ (Accessed November 27, 2012).

Sidel, R. 2000. "The enemy within: The demonization of poor women." *Journal of Sociology and Social Welfare* 27 (1): 73–84.

Siltanen, J. 2002. "Paradise Paved? Reflections on the Fate of Social Citizenship in Canada." *Citizenship Studies* 6 (4): 395–414. http://dx.doi.org/10.1080/13621020 22000041240.

Simon, J. 2007. *Governing through Crime*. New York: Oxford University Press.

Skinner, D. 2006. "Racialized futures: Biologism and the changing politics of identity." *Social Studies of Science* 36 (3): 459–88. http://dx.doi.org/10.1177/0306312706054859.

Smart, C. 1976. *Women, Crime and Criminology: A Feminist Critique*. Boston: Routledge & Kegan Paul.

Smart, C. 1989. *Feminism and the Power of Law*. London: Routledge. http://dx.doi.org/10.4324/9780203206164.

Smart, C. 1995. *Law, Crime and Sexuality*. Thousand Oaks, CA: Sage Publications.

Smith, A. 2006. "Heteropatriarchy and the three pillars of white supremacy." In *Color of Violence: The Incite! Anthology*, ed. A. Smith, B. Richie, and J. Sudbury. Cambridge, MA: South End Press.

Smith, D. 2008. "Criminology, contemporary society and race issues." In *Race and Criminal Justice*, ed. B. Singh. London: Sage Publications.

Smolash, W. 2009. "Mark of Cain(ada): Racialized security discourse in Canada's national newspapers." *University of Toronto Quarterly* 78 (2): 745–63. http://dx.doi.org/10.3138/utq.78.2.745.

Snider, L. 1994. "Feminism, punishment and the potential of empowerment." *Canadian Journal of Law and Society* 9 (1): 74–104.

Sokoloff, N. 2008. "Expanding the intersectional paradigm to better understand domestic violence in immigrant communities." *Critical Criminology* 16 (4): 229–55. http://dx.doi.org/10.1007/s10612-008-9059-3.

Solomos, J., and L. Black. 1996. *Racism and Society*. London: MacMillan.

Sossin, L. 2004. "Boldly going where no law has gone before: Call centres, intake scripts, database fields, and discretionary justice in social assistance." *Osgoode Hall Law Journal* 42: 363–414.

Spencer-Wood, S., and C. Matthews. 2011. "Impoverishment, Criminalization and the Culture of Poverty." *Historical Archaeology* 45 (93): 1–10.

Spivak, G. 2004. "Terror: A speech after 9/11." *Boundary* 31 (2): 81–103. http://dx.doi.org/10.1215/01903659-31-2-81.

Sportsnet.ca. 2013. "Quebec soccer federation explains turban ban." June 3. http://www.sportsnet.ca/soccer/quebec-soccer-federation-explains-turban-ban/ (Accessed November 11, 2013).

Stanbridge, K., and S. Kenney. 2009. "Emotions and the campaign for victims' rights in Canada." *Canadian Journal of Criminology and Criminal Justice* 51 (4): 473–509. http://dx.doi.org/10.3138/cjccj.51.4.473.

Steadman, H. 1972. "The psychiatrist as a conservative agent of social control." *Social Problems* 20 (2): 263–71. http://dx.doi.org/10.2307/799619.

Steel, Z., D. Silove, R. Brooks, S. Momartin, B. Alzuhari, and I. Susljik. 2006. "Impact of immigration detention and temporary protection on the mental health of refugees." *British Journal of Psychiatry* 188 (1): 58–64. http://dx.doi.org/10.1192/bjp.bp.104.007864.

Stenning, P. 2003. "Policing the cultural kaleidoscope: Recent Canadian experience." *Police and Society* 7: 13–47.

Stockton, R. 1994. "Ethnic archetypes and the Arab image." In *The Development of Arab-American Identity*, ed. E. McCarus. Ann Arbor: University of Michigan Press.

Stuart, H. 2003. "Violence and mental illness: An overview." *World Psychiatry; Official Journal of the World Psychiatric Association (WPA)* 2 (2): 121–24.

Stumpf, J.P. 2006. "The crimmigration crisis: immigrants, crime, & sovereign power." August 27. bepress Legal Series.Working Paper 1635. http://law.bepress.com/expresso/eps/1635.

Surette, R. 2010. *Media, Crime, and Criminal Justice: Images, Realities, and Policies.* 4th ed. Belmont, CA: Thomson/Wadsworth.

Swift, K., and M. Callahan. 2009. *At Risk: Social Justice in Child Welfare and Other Human Services*. Toronto: University of Toronto Press.

Symons, G. 2002. "Police constructions of race and gender in street gangs." In *Crimes of Colour: Racialization and the Criminal Justice System in Canada*, ed. W. Chan and K. Mirchandani. Toronto, ON: University of Toronto Press.

Szasz, T. 1970. *The Manufacture of Madness: A Comparative Study of the Inquisition and the Mental Health Movement*. New York: Harper & Row.

Tang, K. 2000. "Cultural stereotypes and the justice system: The Canadian case of *R. v. Ewanchuk*." *International Journal of Offender Therapy and Comparative Criminology* 44 (6): 681–91. http://dx.doi.org/10.1177/0306624X00446005.

Tang, S., and A. Browne. 2008. "'Race' matters: racialization and egalitarian discourses involving Aboriginal people in the Canadian health care context." *Ethnicity & Health* 13 (2): 109–27. http://dx.doi.org/10.1080/13557850701830307.

Tanovich, D. 2002. "Using the Charter to stop racial profiling: The development of an equality-based conception of arbitrary detention." *Osgoode Hall Law Journal* 40 (2): 145–87.

Tanovich, D. 2003–04. "E-Racing racial profiling." *Alberta Law Review* 41: 905–33.

Tanovich, D. 2008. "The charter of whiteness: Twenty-five years of maintaining racial injustice in the Canadian criminal justice system." *Supreme Court Law Review* 40: 655–86.

Tanovich, D. 2011. "Bonds: Gendered and racialized violence, strip searches, sexual assault and abuse of prosecutorial power." *Criminal Reports* 79 (6th): 132–50.

Terrill, W., and M. Reisig. 2003. "Neighborhood context and police use of force." *Journal of Research in Crime and Delinquency* 40: 291–321. http://dx.doi.org/10.1177/0022427803253800.

Tesfahuney, M. 1998. "Mobility, racism and geopolitics." *Political Geography* 17 (5): 499–515. http://dx.doi.org/10.1016/S0962-6298(97)00022-X.

Thobani, S. 2002. "Closing the nation's doors to immigrant women: The restructuring of Canadian immigration policy." *Atlantis* 24 (2): 16–26.

Thomas, J., D. Stubbe, and G. Pearson. 1999. "Race, juvenile justice, and mental health: New dimensions in measuring pervasive bias." *Journal of Criminal Law & Criminology* 89 (2): 615–70. http://dx.doi.org/10.2307/1144139.

Thompson, M. 2010. *Mad or Bad? Race, Class, Gender, and Mental Disorder in the Criminal Justice System.* El Paso, TX: LFB Scholarly Publishing.

Thornhill, E. 2008. "So seldom for us, so often against us: Blacks and the law in Canada." *Journal of Black Studies* 38 (3): 321–37. http://dx.doi.org/10.1177/0021934707308258.

Tifft, L., S. Maruna, and E. Elliott. 2006. "The state of criminology in the 21st century: A penpal rountable." *Contemporary Justice Review* 9 (4): 387–400. http://dx.doi.org/10.1080/10282580601014326.

Toronto Police Services. 2002. *Overview: 2001 Hate Bias Crime Statistical Report.* Toronto: Toronto Police Services.

Toronto Star. 2012. "Undermining the rule of law: The case of Omar Khadr." October 10. http://www.thestar.com/opinion/editorialopinion/2012/10/10/undermining_the_rule_of_law_the_case_of_omar_khadr.html (Accessed on November 9, 2012).

Toronto Star. 2012b. "Editorial: Conservatives' bill to deport 'foreign' criminals goes too far." November 17. http://www.thestar.com/opinion/editorials/2012/11/17/conservatives_bill_to_deport_foreign_criminals_goes_too_far.html (Accessed on November 22, 2012).

Totten, M. 2009. "Aboriginal youth and violent gang involvement in Canada: Quality prevention strategies." *IPC Review* 3: 135–56.

Upadhya, A. 2011. "Indo-Caribbean Canadian mental health service recipients: Processes of power and constructions of identity." *Open Access Dissertations and Theses.* Paper 4981.

Ussher, J. 1991. *Women's Madness: Misogyny or Mental Illness.* Hemel Hempstead: Harvester Wheatsheaf.

Ussher, J. 2011. *The Madness of Women: Myth and Experience*. New York: Routledge.

van Liempt, I., and S. Sersli. 2012. "State responses and migrant experiences with human smuggling: A reality check." *Antipode* 45 (4): 1029–46. doi: 10.1111/j.1467-8330.2012.01027.x.

Victoria Times Colonist. 2011. "Editorial: Assistance rates shame our province." August 30. http://firstcallbc.wordpress.com/2011/09/02/income-assistance-rates-shame-our-province/ (Accessed on December 2, 2012).

Villegas, P. 2012. "Assembling a visa requirement against the Mexican 'wave': Migrant illegalization, policy and affective 'crises' in Canada." *Ethnic and Racial Studies* 1–20.

Vinkers, D., S.C. de Vries, A.W.B. van Baars, and C.L. Mulder. 2010. "Ethnicity and dangerousness criteria for court ordered admission to a psychiatric hospital." *Social Psychiatry and Epidemiology* 45 (2): 221–24. http://dx.doi.org/10.1007/s00127-009-0058-9.

VIPIRG (Vancover Island Public Interest Research Group). 2011. Policing, Criminal Justice and Poverty in Victoria: Background Paper and Project Proposal. Victoria: VIPIRG.

VIPIRG (Vancover Island Public Interest Research Group). 2012. Out of Sight: Policing Poverty in Victoria. Victoria: VIPIRG.

Vitoroulis, I., and B. Schneider. 2009. "Bullying and victimization of immigrant youth: A literature review." Working Paper, Ontario Metropolis Centre.

Wacquant, L. 1997. "For an analytic of racial domination." *Political Power and Social Theory* 11: 221–34.

Wacquant, L. 2001. "Deadly symbiosis: When ghetto and prison meet and mesh." *Punishment and Society* 3 (1): 95–134. http://dx.doi.org/10.1177/14624740122228276.

Wacquant, L. 2005a. "'Enemies of the wholesome part of the nation': Postcolonial migrants in the prisons of Europe." *Sociologie* 1 (1): 31–51.

Wacquant, L. 2005b. "Race as civic felony." *International Social Science Journal* 57 (183): 127–42. http://dx.doi.org/10.1111/j.0020-8701.2005.00536.x.

Wacquant, L. 2009. *Punishing the Poor. The Neoliberal Government of Social Insecurity*. Durham: Duke University Press.

Walia, H. 2012. "Omar Khadr: Race, empire and unexceptional detention." http://www.guantanamobaymuseum.org/?url=waliatext (Accessed on August 31, 2012).

Walker, B. 2010. *Race on Trial: Black Defendants in Ontario's Criminal Courts, 1858–1958*. Toronto: University of Toronto Press.

Walklate, S. 2007. *Imagining the Victim of Crime*. Maidenhead, UK: Open University Press.

Wallace, B., S. Klein, and M. Reitsma-Street. 2006. *Denied Assistance: Closing the Front Door on Welfare in BC*. Vancouver: Canadian Centre for Policy Alternatives and Vancouver Island Public Interest Research Group.

Walters, W. 2011. "Rezoning the global: Technological zones, technological work and the (un)making of biometric borders." In *The Contested Politics of Mobility: Borderzones and Irregularity*, ed. V. Squire. New York: Routledge.

Warde, B. 2012. "Black male disproportionality in the criminal justice systems of the USA, Canada, and England: A comparative analysis of incarceration." *Journal of African-American Studies* 17 (4): 461–79. http://dx.doi.org/10.1007/s12111-012-9235-0.

Wark, W. 2004. "Terrorism: It's time to grow up." *The Globe and Mail*, April 1.

Watson, S. 2009. *The Securitization of Humanitarian Migration: Digging Moats and Sinking Boats*. New York: Routledge.

Weaver, R., N. Habibov, and L. Fan. 2011. "Analyzing the poverty reduction effectiveness of the Canadian provinces: Do political parties matter?" *Journal of Sociology and Social Welfare* 38 (1): 99–118.

Weber, L. 2001. *Understanding Race, Class, Gender and Sexuality: A Conceptual Framework*. Boston: McGraw-Hill.

Webster, C. 2008. "Thinking about the over-representation of certain groups in the Canadian criminal justice system: A conceptual framework." Department of Criminology, University of Ottawa.

Welch, M., and L. Schuster. 2005a. "Detention of asylum seekers in the US, UK, France, Germany and Italy: A critical view of the globalizing culture of control." *Criminal Justice* 5: 331–55.

Welch, M., and L. Schuster. 2005b. "Detention of asylum seekers in the UK and the USA: Deciphering noisy and quiet constructions." *Punishment and Society* 7 (4): 397–417. http://dx.doi.org/10.1177/1462474505057117.

Welsh, S., J. Carr, B. MacQuarrie, and A. Huntley. 2006. "'I'm not thinking of it as sexual harassment': Understanding harassment across race and citizenship." *Gender & Society* 20 (1): 87–107. http://dx.doi.org/10.1177/0891243205282785.

Wemmers, J. 2012. "Victims' rights are human rights: The importance of recognizing victims as persons." *Temida*, June: 71–84.

Whitaker, R. 2011–12. "The post-9/11 national security regime in Canada: Strengthening security, diminishing accountability." *Review of Constitutional Studies* 16 (2): 139–58.

White, M.D., and J. Ready. 2007. "The taser as a less lethal force alternative: Findings on use and effectiveness in a large metropolitan police agency." *Police Quarterly* 10 (2): 170–91. http://dx.doi.org/10.1177/1098611106288915.

Wieviorka, M. 2002. "The development of racism in Europe." In *A Companion to Racial and Ethnic Studies*, ed. D. Goldberg and J. Solomos. Oxford: Blackwell.

Williams, C. 2008. "Surveying the battlefield: Reflections on the reproductive dynamics of racism." *International Journal of Criminology and Sociological Theory* 1 (1): 62–79.

Williams, D.R., and R. Williams-Morris. 2000. "Racism and mental health: The African American experience." *Ethnicity & Health* 5 (3/4): 243–68. http://dx.doi.org/10.1080/713667453.

Williams, T. 2001. "Racism in justice: The report of the Commission on Systemic Racism in the Ontario criminal justice system." In *[Ab]using Power: The Canadian Experience*, ed. S.C. Boyd, D.E. Chunn, and R. Menzies. Black Point, NS: Fernwood Publishing.

Williams, T. 2009. "Intersectionality analysis in the sentencing of Aboriginal women in Canada. What difference does it make?" In *Intersectionality and Beyond: Law, Power and the Politics of Location*, ed. E. Grabham, et al. London: Routledge.

Wise, T.J. 2009. *Between Barack and a Hard Place: Racism and White Denial in the Age of Obama*. San Francisco: City Lights.

Wise, T.J. 2010. *Colorblind: The Rise of Post-Racial Politics and the Retreat from Racial Equity*. San Francisco: City Lights.

Wong, Y., and A. Tsang. 2004. "When Asian immigrant women speak: From mental health to strategies of being." *American Journal of Orthopsychiatry* 74 (4): 456–66. http://dx.doi.org/10.1037/0002-9432.74.4.456.

Wood, R. 2010. "The reality behind the 'knife crime' debate." *Race & Class* 52 (2): 97–103.

World Health Organization. 2005. *WHO Resource Book on Mental Health, Human Rights and Legislation*. Geneva: Department of Noncommunicable Diseases and Mental Health.

Wortley, S. 1996. "Justice for all? Race and perceptions of bias in the Ontario criminal justice system: A Toronto survey." *Canadian Journal of Criminology* 38: 439–67.

Wortley, S. 2006. *Police Use of Force in Ontario: An Examination of Data from the Special Investigations Unit*. Final Report. Toronto.

Wortley, S., and A. Owusu-Bempah. 2009. "Unequal before the law: Immigrant and racial minority perceptions of the Canadian criminal justice system." *Journal of International Migration and Integration* 10 (4): 447–73. http://dx.doi.org/10.1007/s12134-009-0108-x.

Wortley, S., and A. Owusu-Bempah. 2011. "The usual suspects: Police stop and search practices in Canada." *Policing and Society* 21 (4): 395–407. http://dx.doi.org/10.1080/10439463.2011.610198.

Wortley, S., and A. Owusu-Bempah. 2012. "Race, ethnicity, crime and criminal justice in Canada." In *Race, Ethnicity, Crime and Criminal Justice in the Americas*, ed. A. Kalunta-Crumpton. New York: Palgrave MacMillan.

Wortley, S., and J. Tanner. 2003. "Data, denials, and confusion: The racial profiling debate in Toronto." *Canadian Journal of Criminology and Criminal Justice* 45 (3): 367–90. http://dx.doi.org/10.3138/cjccj.45.3.367.

Wright, Mr. Justice D.H. 2004. *Final Report of the Commission of Inquiry into Matters Relating to Neil Stonechild*. Regina: Ministry of Justice, Queen's Printer.

Yang, L. 2007. "Application of mental illness stigma theory to Chinese societies: Synthesis and new directions." *Singapore Medical Journal* 48 (11): 977–85.

Yeo, M. 1991. "Murdered by misogyny: Lin Gibson's response to the Montreal Massacre." *Canadian Women's Studies* 12 (1): 8–11.

Yoshihama, M. 1999. "Domestic violence against women of Japanese descent in Los Angeles: Two methods of estimating prevalence." *Violence against Women* 5 (8): 869–97. http://dx.doi.org/10.1177/10778019922181536.

Zeman, K., and A. Bressan. 2008. *Factors Associated with Youth Delinquency and Victimization in Toronto, 2006*. Ottawa: Canadian Centre for Justice Statistics.

Zerbisias, A. 1994. "Let's not bury our city with Vivi." *Toronto Star*, April 8, p. A21.

Zine, J. 2004. "Anti-Islamophobia education as transformative pedagogy: Reflections from the educational front lines." *American Journal of Islamic Social Sciences* 2 (13): 110–19.

LEGAL CASES CITED

Canada (A.G.) v. Mossop [1993] 1 S.C.R. 554.
R. v. Curley, Nagmalik, and Issigaitok [1984] N.W.T.R. 281 (N.W.T. C.A.).
R. v. Keegstra [1990] 3 S.C.R. 397.
R. v. Miloszewski [1999] B.C.J. No 2710 Surrey Provincial Court Registry No. 96687–03-D2.
R. v. Swain [1991] 1 S.C.R. 933.
R.D.S. v. R. [1997] 3 S.C.R. 484.
R. v. Gladue [1999] S.C.J. No. 19 (QL).

INDEX